ZOETROPES AND THE POLITICS OF HUMANHOOD

NEW DIRECTIONS IN RHETORIC AND MATERIALITY
Barbara A. Biesecker, Wendy S. Hesford, and Christa Teston, Series Editors

ZOETROPES AND THE POLITICS OF HUMANHOOD

ALLISON L. ROWLAND

THE OHIO STATE UNIVERSITY PRESS

COLUMBUS

Library of Congress Cataloging-in-Publication Data
Names: Rowland, Allison L., author.
Title: Zoetropes and the politics of humanhood / Allison L. Rowland.
Other titles: New directions in rhetoric and materiality.
Description: Columbus : The Ohio State University Press, [2020] | Series: New directions
    in rhetoric and materiality | Includes bibliographical references and index. | Summary:
    "A rhetorical analysis that builds on necropolitical theory to critique the discursive
    practices of inclusion into humanhood. Looks at how language such as rhetorical figures
    and tropes produce and contest the shifting boundaries of the human"—Provided by
    publisher.
Identifiers: LCCN 2019049525 | ISBN 9780814214305 (cloth) | ISBN 0814214304 (cloth) |
    ISBN 9780814277850 (ebook) | ISBN 0814277853 (ebook)
Subjects: LCSH: Human beings—Philosophy. | Rhetoric. | Biopolitics. | Persuasion
    (Rhetoric)
Classification: LCC P301.5.P47 R69 2020 | DDC 808—dc23
LC record available at https://lccn.loc.gov/2019049525

Cover design by Thao Thai
Cover image by Sarah Knobel
Text design by Juliet Williams
Type set in Adobe Minion Pro

CONTENTS

ACKNOWLEDGMENTS

TO WRITE a sentence is to wrestle an alligator, to borrow Annie Dillard's famous observation. I have always loved this kinetic, tail-flipping metaphor, but it overlooks the significant intellectual labor that must precede any consensual sentence-level wrestling. For all this wrangling, writing a book can be more trudge than leap. Pete Simonson rooted for both the trudging and the leaping in sustained ways early in my career. Jerry Hauser convened an accountability group whose collective brain power propelled early drafts of this book. Rich treasures from my time at the University of Colorado at Boulder remain fellow students whose friendship and intellectual support persist well beyond graduate school: Mary Butler, Ace Eckstein, Chris Ingraham, and Jen Malkowski.

I benefit from generous mentorship and generative conversations among scholars of rhetoric, including E. Cram, Kelly Happe, Jenell Johnson, Jamie Landau, and John Lynch. Emily Winderman belongs on this list, and was generous enough to read an early chapter. Nate Stormer was a formative early reader and valued mentor. Lisa Keränen introduced me to the rhetoric of health and medicine in a graduate course. The Association for the Rhetoric of Science, Technology, and Medicine forms a scholarly community from which I greatly benefit. I thank Andrew Hansen for his genial camaraderie. In addition to nourishing connections with these scholars, the Rhetoric Society of America has also supplied incredible learning opportunities for me in the past ten years. I am especially indebted to the Biennial RSA Summer Institutes, where I have taken transformative workshops led by Twyla Gibson and Stuart Murray and Isaac West and Jeff Bennett.

I thank colleagues at St. Lawrence University. In the Performance & Communication Arts Department, Jess Prody and Jen Thomas support me with friendship. Kirk Fuoss and Randy Hill, thank you for chatting me up at that fateful NCA job fair. (Go to job fairs, job-seekers!) Angie Sweigart-Gallagher, Dan Gallagher, and Juraj Kittler enrich the good soup. Erik Johnson generously provided feedback on a drafted chapter. Liz Regosin, Penny Vlagopoulos, and Amy Hauber provide a sense of belonging here in Canton, New York. Same for Sarah Knobel, the artist whose viscerally compelling image graces the cover of this book. The tens of colleagues who have joined us for the annual Oral Communication Institute help me envision what collegiality ought to be. St. Lawrence University supported this work with a pretenure sabbatical.

To Denny and Rocky, my living-with family, I offer much gratitude. I thank Katy Desmond for thousands of fruit-bearing conversations. Andrew Maples, Brook Thompson, Kacie Warner—thank you for sympoietically making-together with me. I wrested a bond with Jorge Castillo and Amir Jaima from the crucible of a marginally successful team-taught first year course on masculinities. To the friends and family in this paragraph: thank you for your political commitments and your habits of mind, for they murmur in these pages.

Many caring hands, from both biological and chosen families, pitched in for child care during book writing: grandparents Christine and Dennis Morreale and Mary Ellen and Jonathan Rowland, as well as aunt Anna Morreale. As I write this our son is not yet two years old, but already tens and tens of people have cared for him, including care providers at Canton Day Care Center, Miss Bri's Puddlejumpers, and a number of St. Lawrence students. This labor stands on the back of that labor.

Tara Cyphers, my editor at The Ohio State University Press, has held a firm guiding hand. For their vision and infrastructural support, I thank the editors of the New Directions in Rhetoric and Materiality series: Barbara A. Biesecker, Wendy S. Hesford, and Christa Teston.

An early version of chapter 3 appears in "Zoetropes: Turning Fetuses into Humans at the National Memorial for the Unborn," *Rhetoric Society Quarterly* 47, no. 1 (2017). Brief excerpts from the introduction and conclusion were informed by my essay "Life-Saving Weapons: The Biolegitimacy of Drone Warfare," *Rhetoric & Public Affairs* 19, no. 4 (2016).

PREFACE

I OPEN this book with two admittedly obscure rhetorical devices: *catacosmesis* and *somatopeia*. I want to do more than remove these two oldies from rhetoric's cabinet of curiosities for a brief dusting. Instead, I float these devices as bellwethers, for they augur the kind of thinking that can happen at the interstices of rhetorical theory and necropolitics, the two scholarly terrains that this book traverses. This book is about public discourse transvaluing living existents. Catacosmesis and somatopeia are rhetorical devices that participate in the promotion and demotion of existents. While the terms themselves may be arcane, catacosmesis and somatopeia name fairly commonplace rhetorical strategies.

Catacosmesis orders terms by value or dignity. Essentially the rhetorical schema of ranking, the most important term in a series comes first, and the rest are arranged in descending order of significance. Across rhetorical handbooks, the most frequently cited example of catacosmesis is "sun and moon," which came first from Henry Peacham's 1577 *Garden of Eloquence*. While Peacham supplied examples only of paired phrases, series of three or more can be catacosmetic as well. Consider, for example, the implicit ranking in the well-worn tricola "animal, vegetable, mineral" and "men, women, and children." Whether language users intend to support particular hierarchies or not, catacosmetic rankings abound in all sorts of rhetorical productions.

These examples of catacosmesis bespeak its most notable feature for the purposes of this book—its relation to culturally contingent hierarchies. To be intelligible, and therefore to be effective as a rhetorical strategy, catacosmesis necessarily relies on a tacit understanding of the world as conforming to some hierarchical ranking. Peacham's pairs reveal his predictable sixteenth-century British commitments to particular arrangements. Consider the range of hierarchies evident in the other examples he provides: theological ("God and man"), gendered ("man and woman"), and biological ("life and death"). The rhetorical persuasiveness of catacosmesis relies on its capacity to refer to a naturally ordered world. Peacham knew this, and for him the schema reflected a ranking in which the "worthiest word is set first" because the "order is natural," thereby lending an "elegance" and "propriety" to the words.[1] The etymology of catacosmesis, derived from the Greek *kata kosmos,* further supports its reliance on an alleged natural hierarchy. While *kata* meant "according to" or "toward," *kosmos* meant a universe particularly ordered. Jann Puhvel described *kosmos* as "a notion of ordering, arraying, arranging, and structuring discrete units or parts into a whole which is 'proper' in either practical, moral, or esthetic ways."[2] In both its conceptual and etymological foundations, catacosmesis puts the world in proper order.

For its coherence, catacosmesis is indebted to the Great Chain of Being, the ranked model of hierarchy seeded by the ancient Greeks and fully formed in the Middle Ages. The rhetorical resources inherited from the Great Chain of Being will weave their way through this book (and appear prominently in the first chapter). Like so many other rhetorical devices that rely on the edifying completion of a pattern, catacosmesis is compelling to the extent that it is satisfying, and it is satisfying to the extent that it alludes to resonant hierarchical arrangements for a given public at a given time.[3] At times, catacosmesis is didactic, even authoritative. It can whisper "Here is what is important; here is what we should care about, in this order." Catacosmesis smuggles hierarchy and, in its more insidious forms, bolsters empire.

Turning to the other device at hand, somatopeia[4] denotes the figure of speech in which an imaginary, deceased, or distant other is represented as

---

1. Peacham, *Garden of Eloquence.* Of course, not all terms that arrive in pairs or series are catacosmetic. The rhetorical scheme of *auxesis,* or climax, arranges terms in ascending rather than descending order.

2. Puhvel, "The Origins of Greek *Kosmos,*" 154.

3. I am in Jeanne Fahnestock's debt here. Even though Fahnestock devotes an entire chapter to the effects of series in *Rhetorical Figures in Science,* she does not name catacosmesis.

4. A note on spelling: *prosopopeia* has evolved as an acceptable and less bloated spelling of *prosopopoeia.* For the sake of orthographic parity between the two terms, I take the same liberty with *somatopeia,* dropping the silent *o.*

having a body. For example, Genesis 4:7 advises, "But if you do not do what is right, sin is crouching at your door." Here sin is somatopeically rendered as having a body; for sin to be described as crouching, it must have a body with which to crouch. To crouch is to stoop or bend low, with arms close to the body. A crouch carries connotations of hiding, self-defense, or sneaking around. In this instance, sin is not merely em-bodied but em-bodied with particular morphological features arranged in culturally specific, expressive ways. By fracturing em-body with a hyphen, I intend to emphasize its distinction from vernacular definitions of embody that mean to represent or symbolize. Somatopeia manifests bodies.

Like many rhetorical handbooks throughout the ages, Jeanne Fahnestock's authoritative *Rhetorical Style* relegates somatopeia to a list of cognates for personification, a move that strips the rich meaning imbued in *somato poein,* to "make body" or to "do body." *Somato poein* shares etymological roots with the more commonly known trope of prosopopeia (*prosopon poein*), to "make face." If prosopopeia renders an absent or distant other as having a face, somatopeia renders an absent or distant other as having a body. Prosopopeia is often compared to ventriloquy. If prosopopeia ventriloquizes existents into speaking, then somatopeia makes existents crouch and gesture, mime and dance.

To be prosopopeically rendered as having a face humanizes an existent and is frequently found in sequence with rendering an existent as having a voice (the trope of apostrophe), implicating the existent into regimes of communication. A vein of scholars (including Paul de Man, Paul Ricoeur, Cynthia Chase, and Diane Davis) have discussed these animating rhetorical effects of prosopopeia (and I address these features at length in the chapter on fetal life). The rhetorical-material consequences of being rendered as having a body via somatopeia, however, have not been documented. I posit that just as prosopopeia implicates existents into regimes of communication (through the rendering of face/voice), somatopeia implicates existents into regimes of biopolitical regulation (through the rendering of body, or specifically, a body available for control and management). To be somatopeically embodied is a prerequisite for biopolitical control; only em-bodied existents can be subject to biopolitical and necropolitical management. Despite somatopeia's membership among the more archaic figures of speech, the meaning manifest in its etymology bears significance for contemporary biopolitical control.

A foundational tenet of this book asserts that tropes—moments where language "turns" from the literal—constitute existents into existents intelligible to biopolitical regimes. Even though it is technically a schema rather than a trope, catacosmesis demonstrates a nascent hierarchy in language use. Within the scope of my project, I forefront the etymological roots of somatopeia to capture the body-forging that occurs in the crucible of empire. This book is about the rhetorical devices like catacosmesis, somatopeia, and many others that transvalue existents. I call them zoetropes, part of the broader genre of zoerhetorics. Zoerhetorics and the Great Chain of Being participate in the processes of transvaluation that predict much of our lives in this moment of empire, everything from drone warfare to what's in our guts, from reproductive politics to breaking a sweat at the gym.

Hierarchy's Thresholds

IN AN ADVANCED undergraduate rhetorical theory class, I supplied a group of students with a series of ten index cards. One word was printed on each card: metal, tree, man, God, rock, child, fish, ape, plant, and woman. There were no directions other than this one sentence: Put the cards in their proper order. After some grumbling when I refused to clarify the assignment, the students arranged the cards in this sequence: God, man, woman, child, ape, fish, tree, plant, metal, rock. In other words, lo and behold, the students faithfully recreated the order of the Great Chain of Being, or the ranked "natural" order of the world that we have inherited from the Middle Ages.[1] In this hierarchy, God and man trump all and other animals, and other living existents are evaluated based on how similar they are to humans. Inanimate or nonliving things like rocks get assigned to the end of the line.

I relate my experience teaching this activity for three reasons. First, university students, like anyone else, have absorbed and therefore can reproduce the dominant hierarchy of their particular cultural milieu. Second—and herein lies the teachable moment—this activity makes them squirm! They wiggle in discomfort. They immediately challenge the hierarchy that they have recreated, especially along lines of gender or age. They say things like "We can't

---

1. I am indebted to Professor Jenell Johnson at the University of Wisconsin, Madison, for inspiring this pedagogical activity.

rank humans because all humans are equal." Finally, this classroom activity underscores a fundamental claim of necropolitical theory: *to exist is to exist in hierarchy.* Why should we pay attention to hierarchy—or, more specifically, to the dominant hierarchy of contemporary Western culture? There is more at stake than just a classroom lesson. Across the globe, bodies are nourished or malnourished, appreciated or attenuated, succored or scored, martyred or murdered, based on their position in a given sociopolitical hierarchy. Put another way, hierarchies drive distributions of livability.

At its best, this classroom activity gives students an opportunity to grapple with hard questions about the persistent arrangements of the world that we inhabit. How do we come to know the hierarchy? Why do we readily accept some elements of the hierarchy more than others? How do we personally invest in the hierarchy? The shortest (if vague and noncommittal) answer to these questions is "rhetoric." This book is an attempt to provide a better answer by putting rhetorical theory into conversation with necropolitics, a field of critical studies that foregrounds death as the primary mode of political management.

This book names the rhetorical patterns that promote and demote the status of living beings as a necropolitical means of parsing populations: *zoerhetorics.* Zoerhetorics are discursive and material practices that transvalue lives across a particular public. Zoerhetorics can be direct or subtle; they can come from dominant or marginalized groups; they can circulate within publics or counterpublics; they can be inclusive or exclusive; and they can modulate or maintain attributions of status in a given public. Zoerhetorical norms will vary according to the cultural norms of different public contexts. Most importantly, zoerhetorical valuations are inseparable from material conditions of living. When Donald Trump's supporters chant "Build that wall!" they are being zoerhetorical, insofar as a racial hierarchy of belonging fuels affective investments in American-identified border control. The "Black Lives Matter" movement is also zoerhetorical. In fact, it has a direct zoerhetorical assertion of value built right into its name.

The *zoe-* prefix (pronounced zoh-eh; rhymes with "no way") of zoerhetorics derives from an important book in biopolitical theory: Giorgio Agamben's *Homo Sacer.* According to Agamben's etymology, *zoe* (ζωή) is the ancient Greek word for life that encompasses the spectrum of all existents, including humans, animals, and plants.[2] It is the etymon for contemporary words like *zoo* and *protozoa.* For my purposes here, I take the prefix *zoe-* not for its

---

2. Agamben, *Homo Sacer.*

(dubious) etymological accuracy,[3] nor to reproduce Agamben's ontology of bare life, but rather for *zoe*'s capacities to both index biopolitical theory and encompass all modes of being alive.[4] If biopolitics is the branch of critical theory that makes sense of the way that "life itself" is regulated, zoerhetorics name the discursive formations by which various existents become intelligible to regimes of living.[5]

WHAT IS A ZOERHETORIC?

Let's walk through an extended example of a *zoerhetoric*. The CIA, under President Barack Obama's leadership, accidentally killed Pakistani children in drone strikes intended to target al Qaeda leaders. (This happened to over one hundred children between 2004 and 2018.[6]) After a few years of mounting public outcry, the White House issued a press release claiming that the number of civilian deaths as a result of US drone strikes was in the "single digits." There was no mention of children.[7] After this press release, senior officials like Republican senator Saxby Chambliss referred to the innocent people killed in these drone strikes as "collateral damage,"[8] a common military euphemism to describe the unintentional killing, injury, or damage to people or property.

The term *collateral damage* bears a rhetorical effect; it *does* something. In this case, members of an American-identified public are invited to think of the deaths (damage) of Pakistani people as secondary (collateral) to the primary goals of the mission. Note that no one explicitly stated, "It is okay if Pakistani people die in this American mission because American lives are more important than Pakistani lives." And yet implicitly the term *collateral damage* suggests a hierarchy of living existents for the particular public within which

---

3. See Dubreuil and Eagle, "Leaving Politics," for a critique of Agamben's etymological claims about *bios* and *zoe*.

4. Agamben, *Homo Sacer*, 187.

5. I am aware that the prefix *zoo-* is more grammatically faithful to the Greek than *zoe-*. What's more, *zoo-* has already proved a productive partner for coining neologisms in social theory. I am thinking of examples like Debra Hawhee's *zoostylistics* (*Rhetoric in Tooth and Claw*) or Diane Davis's *autozoography* ("Autozoography"), both of which were heralded by Jacques Derrida's *zoopoetics* (*The Animal That Therefore I Am*). However, for the concepts of zoerhetorics and zoetropes advanced in this book, I stick with the prefix *zoe-* for the conceptual resonance with the Victorian-era optical toy. Zoetropes (both the rhetorical and optical devices) produce life in the moment that they turn.

6. Serle and Purkiss, "Drone Wars: The Full Data."

7. United States Senate Intelligence Committee, "Open Hearing on the Nomination of John O. Brennan."

8. As quoted in Rosen, "Obama Aides Defend Claim of Low Civilian Drone Casualties."

it was circulated. Zoerhetorics like collateral damage discursively include and exclude certain living beings from what we might call the good life. Zoerhetorics like collateral damage happen all around us, all the time, and they matter because they affect the livability of lives.

If the reductive and exclusionary zoerhetoric of *collateral damage* described Pakistani children just once in the American-identified public sphere, it would not be particularly remarkable or persuasive. Instead, the incontrovertible damage occurs when a message of differential life value is reiterated many times, in multiple material-discursive formations, across multiple publics, sustained by multiple institutions, mixing and percolating with other demoting zoerhetorics regarding a particular group. In her recent tome *Infertility*, Robin Jensen uses percolation as a means of describing how layers of rhetoric accrue and interact like sediment. When the same zoerhetorical topoi percolate and resurface again and again for particular groups, we see lasting consequences for livability, or what Judith Butler calls livable life.[9]

Contextualized within the violence of racial assemblages, which animate and condition mainstream American-identified understandings of people from Pakistan and people of color more generally,[10] it is not outlandish to assert that many members of the nationalist-identified American public really believe that Pakistani people are worth less than American people. In the case at hand, the use of *collateral damage* reactivates and appropriates an existing hierarchy for the purpose of justifying American military force. As a newer face of the seemingly endless (and ends-less, according to Jeremy Engels and William Saas) war on terror, drones have become the new normal. When the value of a particular group of people is effectively subordinated across a particular public, zoerhetorical transvaluation has occurred.

A rhetoric like *collateral damage* is just one of the manifold ways in which existents can be rhetorically transvalued and hierarchies jostled or maintained. While Obama-era White House rhetoric packaged drones as ethical, sanitized interventions, it was at the expense of understanding drones as deadly weapons in an asymmetric war.[11] While this book does not address war or military zoerhetorics specifically (although I do that elsewhere, for war and military rhetorics are necessarily zoerhetorically rich), I used the example of collateral damage because it is a common phrase that illuminates a number of important features of zoerhetorics. Zoerhetorics can operate subtly; they circulate in already racialized (and gendered and sexualized) discursive formations;

9. Butler, *Frames of War.*
10. On racial assemblages, see Weheliye, *Habeas Viscus.*
11. Rowland, "Life-Saving Weapons."

they resurface existing hierarchies; and they function grounded in particular publics.

Zoetropes and the Politics of Humanhood takes the term *zoetrope* as a special kind of zoerhetoric. Zoetropes are zoerhetorical tropes; that is, they are rhetorical devices or figures that result in zoerhetorical transvaluation. Zoetropological theory approaches tropes as moments when discursive practices swerve from literal meaning and have a material effect. In perhaps the most influential early treatment of the subject of tropes, the *Rhetorica ad Herennium* defined tropes as language use that "departs from the ordinary meaning of the words."[12] In classical Greek *tropos* meant "turn," an etymology that Donna Haraway stretched to mean "swerve" or "trip."[13] Similarly, Jane Sutton and Mari Lee Mifsud compare the turn of *strophe* to the kinetic turn in dance.[14] Language users rely on the departures, swerves, or deviations of tropes as "part of our original evolutionary equipment."[15]

Christian Lundberg offers a useful four-pillared taxonomy of tropes as they appear in rhetorical theory. The first frame conceives of tropes as adornments to otherwise literal language. The second identifies the use of tropes as a set of discourses ("the trope of x," such as "the trope of war," in Lundberg's example). These first two can be set aside, for the next two trope types resonate more for my purposes. Lundberg's third frame, best illustrated by Kenneth Burke's famous work "Four Master Tropes," names tropes as epistemological, as modes of knowing or finding truth. Lundberg's fourth frame and his contribution to the discussion conceives of tropes as a generative matrix: "This approach views the notion of trope as generative, rather than simply ornamental, and understands all signification as tropological, rather than understanding the trope as a specialized form of discourse or mode of knowing."[16] Although I do not route my argument through the work of Jacques Lacan like Lundberg does, our conclusions dovetail around the generative nature of tropes. Contrary to a dominant strand of the rhetorical tradition, tropes produce effects beyond those of mere adornment or beautification as the so-called flowers of rhetoric. As a fundamental condition of language "inexpungeable from discourse," figuration makes existents and their worlds.[17]

Zoetropes share a name and a conceptual resonance with the Victorian-era visual toy (see figure 1). Zoetropological theory explores the animating powers

---

12. [Cicero], *Rhetorica ad Herennium*, 333.

13. Haraway, *The Companion Species Manifesto*, 20.

14. Sutton and Mifsud, "Figuring Rhetoric."

15. Lanham, *Handlist of Rhetorical Terms*, 80.

16. Lundberg, "Enjoying God's Death," 389.

17. White, *Tropics of Discourse*, 2. See also Rowland, "Zoetropes."

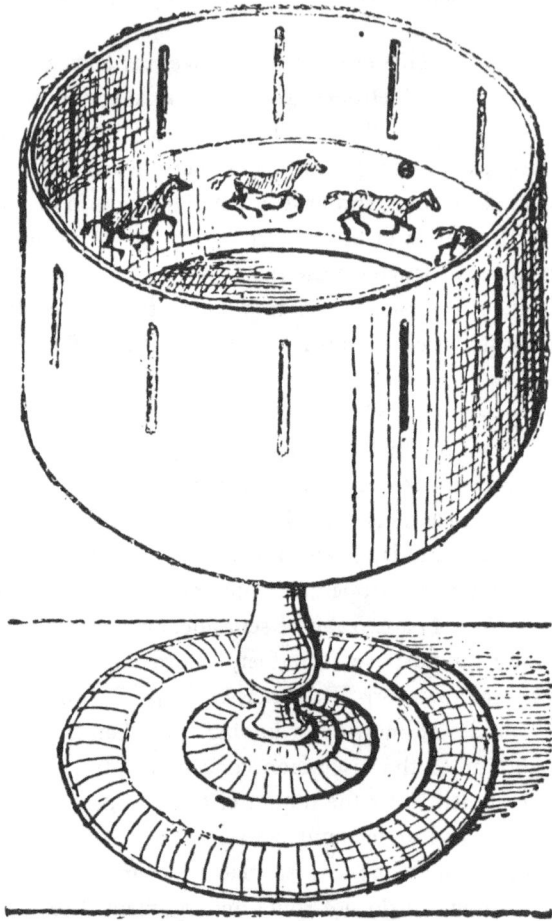

FIGURE 1. Victorian-era zoetrope. This toy was also called
the "Wheel of Life." Creative Commons license.

of figuration from the position of tropes as constitutive. Just as the optically
illusive zoetrope device creates animated "life" in the movement of its turning, life is also created in the turning movement of zoetropological rhetorics.
What we experience as alive or liveliness is an effect of tropes. Nathan Stormer
calls this the "invocation" power of tropes.[18] Although Stormer refers specifically to *apostrophe,* the trope of breaking address, other tropes can raise and
conjure beings. Referencing Nietzsche's mobile "army of tropes" marshaled

18. Stormer, "Looking in Wonder," 663.

in the service of anthropomorphic personification, Paul de Man hints at the life-giving qualities of tropes for animals and objects.[19] Diane Davis, drawing from Emmanuel Levinas and de Man, reverses the commonsense wisdom that speakers produce tropes. Instead, tropes produce speakers and, I would add, other existents. In Cynthia Chase's words, an existent's intelligibility is a "tropological product."[20]

This book takes Diane Davis's troped speakers and extends them into the territory of necropolitics and empire studies. In Davis's words, the mere-ornamentation theory of tropes retains the "comforting fiction of the knowing and speaking subject."[21] Relegating tropes to superfluous decor supports the collective fantasy of transcendent humanhood. With this central insight in mind, I assert that Davis's important work misses a necropolitical sensibility. Even as Davis locates rhetoric within a shared corporeal vulnerability—a vulnerability that she acknowledges as unevenly experienced—she does not address the conditions of empire that distribute livability and suffering. My contribution leavens the constitutive power of tropes with the fundamental tenets of necropolitical theory. The primary work of necropolitics is to parse existents into groups meant for life, subhumanity, and death (a catacosmetic list, by the way).[22] Tropes and necropolitics, then, are logically enchained: in order to be alive, an existent must be troped into the world; once an existent is intelligible as living in the world, she is parsed into necropolitical hierarchy. Let me collapse that: if alive, troped; if troped, parsed. Tropes conjure existents and order worlds.

As one of the myriad vitality-conjuring tropes, somatopeia means the *tropological attribution of a body intelligible to necropolitical ranking.* Somatopeic embodiment is an effect that emerges in and through publics. Biopolitics and necropolitics parse and regulate life. Once an existent has been rhetorically quickened through figuration, that existent is immediately subject to bio-necro regulation. Put another way, an existent troped becomes an existent intelligible to the ongoing processes of hierarchical valuation obligated by empire. Necropolitics *requires* that living existents differ by value; without such ranked valuations, empire would have no means by which to sustain its systemic exploitations or the foundational fictions of deservingness that sustain them.

---

19. De Man, *The Resistance to Theory,* 241.

20. Chase, *Decomposing Figures,* 4.

21. Davis, *Inessential Solidarity,* 38.

22. Here I adapt Weheliye's similarly catacosmetic list of "full humans, not-quite-humans, and nonhumans," in *Habeas Viscus,* 81.

This process of ongoing hierarchy-driven valuation marks a difference from important work on the rhetorical constitution of a group of existents like Maurice Charland's constitutive rhetoric.[23] Charland described an important process by which the Quebecois were hailed into a collective political identity.[24] At the same time, his constitutive rhetoric neither addressed the system of hierarchy that dominant groups impose on other groups nor contextualized the Quebecois within a broader field of empire. In a recent supplement to constitutive rhetoric, Michael Paul Vicaro proposed a deconstitutive rhetoric, an effect of speech texts that, without the subject's investment or consent, strips the subject of "rights-bearing subject of law" status.[25] Sweeping together both constitutive and deconstitutive rhetoric, zoerhetorical theory accounts for both group-driven transvaluations and outsider-imposed transvaluations, *and watches for broader relational patterns of exploitation in both.* To form or to be robbed of political identity is an effect of zoerhetorical transvaluation trussed to hierarchy. Even as they shape-shift among and between different cultures and historical moments, the fundamentally exploitative nature of hierarchies prevails. In other words, the existents near the ladder's pinnacle *require* the depressed valuations of existents on the bottom, just as the few bricks near the top of a pyramid require the foundational support of the many bricks that rest underneath.

In this book I focus on zoetropes in the contemporary US as they traverse the biopolitical and necropolitical fault lines of race, gender, and sexuality. A compelling archive of critical scholarship addresses these biopolitical hierarchies. Scholars such as Mel Chen, Jasbir Puar, and Alexander Weheliye, just to name a few, have produced influential scholarship on race, gender, and sexuality as it intersects with necropolitics. As the regulation of life and death, respectively, biopolitics and necropolitics tend to focus on the discourses and practices of exclusion for a particular group. As tools to think with, they help theorists attune to the ways in which groups are dehumanized, marginalized, or otherwise othered. Similarly, in my home discipline of rhetoric, critical scholars explore the rhetorical means by which exclusions occur. These scholars link marginalizing discursive formations to patterns of disenfranchisement, violence, or neglect with a focus on gender, race, and/or sexuality.

The core foci of this book are the material-discursive practices of valuation that result in inclusion in or exclusion from *humanhood*. Humanhood names the shifting constellation of circulating status markers whose aggregate

---

23. See Hariman, "Status, Marginality, and Rhetorical Theory," for a treatment of nascent status attributions in arguments about rhetoric itself.

24. Charland, "Constitutive Rhetoric."

25. Vicaro, "Deconstitutive Rhetoric," 337.

emergent effect is the attribution of *human* for a particular group of existents in a particular public. When formed with other words, the suffix *hood* means "a state or condition of being." Humanhood, then, is the state or condition of being attributed the status of human.

Humanhood resonates with what Walter Mignolo called *humanitas* and then later the model/human. According to the Western colonial logic seeded in Christian theology and rooted in the Renaissance, the (implicitly white and male) *humanitas* believes himself to be the superior expression of the human species. The model human developed the criteria for classifying other human existents, while enjoying the benefits of describing these racial classifications as rational.[26] Mignolo reminds us that humanhood's origin story is Eurocentric:

> The question is not "what is human and humanity" but rather who defined themselves as humans in their praxis of living and applied their self-definition to distinguish and classify and rank lesser humans. . . . The invention of the model/human was fundamental in building, managing, and controlling the [colonial matrix of power] by silencing all other self-identification of the species.[27]

While Mignolo writes in the context of the European colonization of Latin America, his arguments about the invention of humanhood as a ranking system resonate in contemporary contexts as well. Mignolo, in turn, is indebted to Sylvia Wynter's historical models (or, in her terms, genres) of *Man*.[28] Both scholars concur that Man's whiteness remains a defining feature. *Humanitas,* model human, Man, humanhood—all these terms attempt to capture the way that colonial encounters incentivized one group to impose a self-serving ranking system on another group under the guise of neutral rationality.

Therefore, humanhood in this book refers neither reductively to biological species nor ahistorically to a stable ontological category. Counterintuitively, not all humans (by biological species) experience zoerhetorical transvaluation resulting in attributions of humanhood. Simone de Beauvoir's famous claim about women can be instructively appropriated here: one is not born, *but rather becomes,* a human. Note that this is similar to what Judith Butler means when, in *Precarious Life,* she refers to various entities as being pulled under "the sign of the Human."[29] Of the other against whom (or against which) the

---

26. Mignolo, *The Darker Side of Western Modernity,* 83.
27. Mignolo and Walsh, *On Decoloniality: Concepts, Analytics, Praxis,* 153.
28. McKittrick, *Sylvia Wynter: On Being Human as Praxis.*
29. Butler, *Precarious Life,* 49.

human is made, Butler writes, "It is the inhuman, the beyond the human, the less than human, the border that secures the human in its ostensible reality."[30] This book dwells at the edges of these ever-flexing borders that secure the human.

As a status marker, humanhood dons the knapsack of privilege in its most well-stocked form. But the key political project of this book is *not* to open the doors and expand the tent of humanhood to shelter more existents from the battering storms of vulnerable corporeality, even as I recognize that social movements have effectively used this strategy to make some lives more livable (and others less livable). Pulling more existents into the tent does little to critique the way that the tent itself is founded on a relation of exteriority predicated on that long list of markers of belonging: race, gender, sexuality, ability, and more. Instead, the project of this book is to explore the material-discursive practices that sustain the violent fiction of humanhood, especially as they arrive in tropological form.

Many scholars and other stakeholders use the term *personhood* to denote the ethical obligations and agentic qualities of existents attributed humanhood. For this project, however, *humanhood* serves more adequately because *personhood* often denotes a legal status, available for both human and nonhuman existents, that I do not specifically address here.[31] Corporations, chimpanzees, dolphins, and elephants have in various times and places been granted legal *personhood,* but this status does not necessarily or always result in the status attributions of *humanhood.* Noting that they are often treated as synonyms, Jenell Johnson argues, "Just as members of *Homo sapiens* have been argued in and out of humanhood, they have also been argued in and out of personhood."[32] Humanhood is certainly bound with the legal recognition implied in the term *personhood,* but personhood's legal ramifications make it less useful for this project.

Humanhood and other status attributions are mutable and differ across publics. Consider again the example of the Pakistani children accidentally killed in US drone strikes. In their own communities, and among those concerned with global human rights, these children were and are considered human; in other words, they are attributed the full status of humanhood. They warrant, in Butler's language, grievability. However, among a US American nationalist- or patriot-identified public, that is, among the folks effectively persuaded by the "collateral damage" claim from US officials, the dead Pakistani children have been precluded from the full status of humanhood.

---

30. Butler, *Undoing Gender,* 218.
31. Mitchell, "Humans, Nonhumans, and Personhood."
32. Johnson, "Disability, Animals, and the Rhetorical Boundaries of Personhood," 374.

Herein lies a crucial lesson for zoerhetorical theory. A group of existents can be considered fully human among the members of one public and subhuman among the members of another public. I call this phenomenon *zoerhetorical sweep,* or the range of attributions of status for a given existent across multiple publics. For some existents, such as human fetuses or nonhuman mammals, the zoerhetorical sweep ranges widely, from very low (i.e., inconsequential organism) to very high (i.e., rights-bearing citizen) depending on the public being addressed.

Like the other biopolitical axes of gender, race, and sexuality, scholars tend to focus on humanhood's exclusionary moments rather than reading the inclusions and exclusions together, as two sides of the same coin. It is revealing that we have the familiar word *dehumanization* but not necessarily a precisely symmetrical word for the opposite process. To dehumanize is to "deprive of human character or attributes,"[33] and *dehumanize* bears a clear connotation of demotion or lowering. But what about the process of *making* an entity human? We may point to the word *humanize,* but it does not carry the same recognizability as *dehumanize,* nor does it necessarily carry a proportional transvaluation effect. To *humanize* means "to make human; to portray or endow with human characteristics, qualities, or attributes; to represent in human form; to adapt to human use."[34] The lack of semantic balance between the two words is telling; vernacular use attunes us to moments of dehumanization more than to the less visible moments of humanization.

One of the major problems with theories of dehumanization—a problem that this project intends to correct—is that they assume that what it means to be "human" is stable and essential across history and cultures. David Livingstone Smith, for example, seems to suggest throughout his 2012 book on dehumanization that all humans are just, well, obviously human.[35] Even though Livingstone Smith himself observes that who gets to "count" as human is culturally specific and contested, the only process he considers is dehumanization (rather than humanization). Like much of the scholarship on dehumanization, Livingstone Smith's work takes for granted the power-saturated ways in which we come to assume the mantle of humanhood, with its attendant entitlements and capacities, in the first place.

Attending only to dehumanization misses the broader context of hierarchy-driven distributions of livability. The philosopher Kate Manne's recent work on dehumanization troubles Livingstone Smith's approach from this angle. The classic humanist view, held by Livingstone Smith and many

---

33. *Oxford English Dictionary,* s.v. "dehumanize."
34. *Oxford English Dictionary,* s.v. "humanize."
35. Livingstone Smith, *Less Than Human.*

others, supposes that degrading and violent behavior between humans results from an inability to "recognize some shared or common humanity."[36] Rooting her argument in the context of misogyny, Manne reverses this formula. It is not the dehumanization of women that marks them as threatening, thereby enabling hostility and violence against them; rather, it is precisely their humanity that marks them as threatening. Instead of being perceived as not-quite-human, women are perceived as all-too-human against the backdrop of a hierarchy where their humanity is a trespassing, a disruption of a presupposed natural order. Manne's conclusory thoughts on the subject are a resounding endorsement of the importance of attending to hierarchy rather than just dehumanization:

> The mistreatment of historically subordinated groups often needs no special psychological story, such as dehumanization, to account for it. It can rather be explained in terms of current and historical social structures, hierarchical relations, norms and expectations, together with the fact that they are widely internalized and difficult to eradicate.[37]

Expectations about the natural order of the world structure not only misogynistic violence and aggression toward women, as Manne explores, but also violence and aggression toward other historically subordinated groups. In the language of zoerhetorical theory, struggles over attributions of humanhood are ongoing, and an existent who threatens the perceived natural order is the most at risk for zoerhetorical discipline. Zoerhetorical demotion bookends violence, at once both heralding violence by providing its precondition and then later offering a post hoc rationalization for it.

ORGANIZING THE BOOK

The first chapter reckons with the Great Chain of Being as it slinks and arcs its way across millennia. An explanation of contemporary zoerhetorical transvaluations must account for the ongoing and persistent presence of the Great Chain. The two scholarly terrains of this book—necropolitics and rhetorical theory—are pressed into service to make sense of the Great Chain. The defection from biopolitics to necropolitics underscores how the Great Chain provides the discursive resources of hierarchical differentiation today. The

---

36. Manne, *Down Girl*, 134.
37. Manne, *Down Girl*, 157.

rhetorical tradition has a distinct disciplinary complicity with the Great Chain of Being that must be acknowledged. Tropological resources for everyday language use are rooted in the Great Chain's features of plenitude, linearity, and gradation.

While the three case studies of this book may seem topically disparate at face value, they are united by the threshold of humanhood and its affiliated privileges, be they virtue, belonging, citizenship, vitality, or national identity. Remember, the sole ambition and perpetual outcome of necropolitics is to parse bodies into groups suitable for death, subhumanity, or the good life of humanhood. Humanhood animates the focal objects of each case study. Proceeding by order of magnitude, I begin with the very small, microbial, multispecies interests at the borders of what makes us human; then move to the fetus, perhaps the most zoerhetorically contested living entity in the contemporary moment; and end with the virtuous, vital biocitizen exercising her privilege. Chosen for their topical breadth, these case studies demonstrate the utility of zoerhetorical theory across a range of contemporary discursive practices. In particular, these case studies challenge the all-too-easy assumption that a zoerhetorical raising of all existents is ethical, safe, or fair. Because necropolitical power plays out over *bodies,* these case studies attend closely to bodies somatopeically made at the edges of humanhood.

A word on methodology: at first glance, it would appear that only textual analysis could support claims about tropes. However, the expansion of tropes from decorative to generative requires a corollary expansion of rhetorical methodologies. The *material effects* of zoetropes comprise the focal objects driving this inquiry. The central question animating each case study was, *how are existents transvalued here, and to what effect?* Textual analysis alone could only partially answer this question. Prior to training in rhetorical studies, I was trained as a qualitative researcher. Supplementing textual analysis with field methods made self-evident sense to me before the landmark pieces enjoining text and field made their respective cases.[38] At the unborn memorial and the athletic club, participant observation and interviews informed a rhetorical experience in dynamic relation with discursive artifacts at each site. In similar fashion, participating in the American Gut Project (by collecting my own feces and mailing the sample to the lab) provided an indispensable complement to public discourse about gut microbes. Affective or sensual experiences in the field informed the analysis and nosed their way into the prose. I acknowledge these experiences as my own partial perspective, influ-

---

38. Middleton, Senda-Cook, and Endres, "Articulating Rhetorical Field Methods"; McKinnon, Asen, Chávez, and Howard, *Text + Field.*

enced by my actions, expectations, and identities.[39] While theory-building is the organizing goal of this book, I do not consider methodological concerns as excluded from that purpose.[40]

The second chapter (and first case study) begins with some literal navel-gazing, if you will, by attending to the three pounds of microbiota that live inside the human belly. The American Gut Project is a citizen-science experiment that crowdsources samples of human fecal matter in an attempt to map the national microbiome. Participants pay about $100, mail in their fecal sample, and receive a document detailing the microbial makeup of their innards (as well as the satisfaction of participating in one of the largest citizen-science initiatives in the world). The microbes living in our guts spur all sorts of claims from popularizers of science, such as that we are "10 percent human" and therefore better conceived of as "superorganisms."

As research emerges on the frontier of our brilliant and varied gut microbiomes, the way this research is promoted by the American Gut Project and circulated in other popular science publics is circumscribed by a commitment to the master metaphor of war. In the process of rhetorically folding gut microbes into our human selves, we stake a claim about what kind of humanhood counts. As they emerged in the US in 2013–18, popular science discourses of the human microbiome engage in a racialized project of nation-building, linking gut microbes to people of color metonymically, visually, and somatopeically. In our current moment of microbiomania, we are entreated to conceive of the human body as a mini-empire—with all the relations of hierarchy, resource extraction, and racialization concomitant with empire.

The third chapter asks after norms of inclusion for one of the most publicly contested living existents in the contemporary US: the fetus. Multifarious sets of political, medical, legal, and vernacular rhetorics address the fetus's flourishing as well as its termination. When pro-life communities want to stop or discourage abortion, they appeal to the humanhood of the fetus. We have all seen bumper stickers or billboards that declare, for instance, "It's a child, not a choice." Pro-life fetal rhetorics like these are examples of *zoerhetorical inclusion*. Pro-life rhetorics say, *the fetus is one of us. The fetus belongs among us.* Discursive practices regarding fetal life can tell us something about how we are all invited (or not invited) into the elite club of humanhood—unborn and born alike.

---

39. Jamie Landau's advancement of *feeling rhetorical criticism* provides a useful guide for the social and often unconscious nature of affect. "Feeling Rhetorical Critics," in *Text + Field*.

40. Taking a cue from Lisa Melonçon and J. Blake Scott in *Methodologies for the Rhetoric of Health & Medicine*, an expansive approach to methodology includes an ongoing theory-building within its purview.

These claims are grounded in an exploration of how zoerhetorics operate at the National Memorial for the Unborn (NMU) in Chattanooga, Tennessee. The NMU is the largest memorial for unborn life in the US, and the way that the site and its participants discursively and materially frame the unborn demonstrates the process by which the fetus "turns" into a human. What I call zoetropes (rhetorical devices that transvalue an entity; that is, zoerhetorics that are also tropes) operate at the NMU to promote the fetal existent into a full-fledged human child. As a pro-choice feminist, I contextualize memorials to the unborn as part of the broader pro-life movement and chart their threats to reproductive rights. At the same time, I argue that the zoerhetorical "birth" of the fetal entity is similar to the process by which we *all* become human. Discourses of inclusion—including naming (*antonomasia*), en-voicing (*apostrophe*), en-facing (*prosopopeia*), and em-bodying (*somatopeia*)—operate zoetropologically.

Humanhood itself has its own zoerhetorical sweep. Even for existents attributed humanhood, a range of status attributions ranks them. For this reason, we must attune to bodies where privilege accumulates and to the existents that enjoy consistent ascendant zoerhetorical promotion. The fourth chapter explores zoerhetorics of populations nourished toward life and vitality as they exercise in athletic clubs in Boulder, Colorado. In this chapter, I introduce the figure of the "vital biocitizen" and critique the ways in which bodies targeted for vitality accrue and store privilege. Through rhetorical practices of training and whiteness, vital biocitizens justify this accumulation of privilege and therefore their high-status positions on the zoerhetorical hierarchy. The everyday mundanity of this case study serves as an important counter to the other case studies.

Finally, in my conclusory observations, I make a series of comparisons across these cases in order to locate propositions of zoerhetorical theory. Each of these case studies offers a zoerhetorical reading of a group of existents with unique status vis-à-vis humanity, belonging, and citizenship: the microbial life in human guts, the fetal life in human uteruses, and the vitality-performing human biocitizen. Taken together, these case studies sample the range of zoerhetorics in the contemporary US. While zoerhetorics may very well lurk around the edges of all language, these case studies punctuate moments where inclusion means ascendant attributions of humanhood. The book's conclusion offers a series of topoi (topical resources) and horoi (boundary markers) for zoerhetorics.

In sum, public discourse is rife with both zoerhetorics and zoetropes, but we (and by "we" I mean we both as everyday language users and as scholars) are not always very good at recognizing zoerhetorics as hierarchical, patterned, or governed by larger global forces like necropolitics. *Zoetropes and the Politics of Humanhood* attunes us to the rhetorical patterns that promote or demote particular existents as they circulate in particular publics. Necropolitical theory helps us bear in mind that the work of empire constantly parses populations into worthy lives, subhuman lives, and lives sentenced to death. This book draws attention to the discourses and practices of valuation that result in inclusion or exclusion from humanhood, a particularly salient zoerhetorical threshold.

This mini-glossary serves as a resource for the rest of the book:

> *humanhood*: The shifting constellation of status markers (these can be communicated through norms, practices, or discursive formations) whose aggregate emergent effect is the attribution of "humanness" for a group across a particular public. Humanhood is the highest threshold of the zoerhetorical hierarchy and works in tandem with gender, race, and sexuality to demarcate groups. Counterintuitively, not all existents who are human by species experience zoerhetorical transvaluation into humanhood. Humanhood is not to be confused with the legal notion of personhood, although existents that experience social attributions of humanhood may also experience the protections afforded by legal personhood.
>
> *maintenance zoerhetoric*: Public discourse or practice that stabilizes or fixes the status of existents to reflect the order preferred by a particular public. Note that a maintenance zoerhetoric in one public can be a destabilizing rhetoric in another public. For example, when *Time* magazine named the "silencebreakers" of the #metoo movement the 2017 people of the year, it was a maintenance zoerhetoric for a feminist-identified public but a destabilizing zoerhetoric for the dominant US American-identified public. If the zoerhetorical hierarchy is a muscle, maintenance zoerhetorics tone the muscle whereas destabilizing zoerhetorics tweak it.
>
> *somatopeia*: The tropological attribution of a body intelligible for necropolitical gradation. All existents that are intelligible as existents experience somatopeic em-bodiment.
>
> *zoerhetorics*: Consequential and public discourses or practices that transvalue the status of a group of existents across a particular public or publics, especially along the biopolitical fault lines of species, race, gender, sexuality, and ability. In the example above, I explained how referring to children killed in US drone strikes as "collateral damage" is a zoerhetoric. Zoerhetorical transvaluation is ongoing for all existents.

zoerhetorical literacy: An existent's learned capacity to attune to the potential transvaluations in a given artifact, event, or practice. A primary goal of this book is to raise zoerhetorical literacy.

zoerhetorical hierarchy: A ranked arrangement of existents who, proportional to their contested position on the hierarchy for a given public, experience partisan distributions of livability (adapted from linguist Mel Y. Chen's concept of "animacy hierarchy"[41]). The work of necropolitical regimes involves parsing existents into groups nourished toward vital life, groups suspended in subhumanity, or groups targeted for death. Zoerhetorical hierarchies are historically and culturally contingent, but in the West, they generally follow the model offered by the Great Chain of Being.

zoerhetorical sweep: The fluctuating range of value attributions for a group of existents across a given public or multiple publics. The title of Melanie Joy's 2011 book *Why We Love Dogs, Eat Pigs, and Wear Cows* demonstrates the zoerhetorical sweep of nonhuman mammals in a humorous rendering. There is a wide zoerhetorical sweep even among existents attributed humanhood.

zoetrope: Shortened form of zoerhetorical trope; a figure of speech, rhetorical device, or schema that transvalues the status of a group of existents. I identify in the third chapter, for example, how the rhetorical devices of apostrophe, prosopopeia, and somatopeia transvalue human fetal life.

---

41. Chen, *Animacies*.

CHAPTER 1

Zoerhetorical Theory

ZOERHETORICAL PATTERNS move like beads on a string. One bead stands for a group of existents. The zoerhetorical hierarchy is pliant, in the sense that beads can shift back and forth along the necklace's string. While each bead can move independently, sometimes beads link together and form a coalition that moves as a unit. (Later, I explain how this is an example of metonymic sliding together.) Sometimes, a bead that has been traditionally associated with its neighbors breaks away and aligns with a new group. When this happens, other beads slide over to accommodate it. Despite the constant fluidity of the shifting beads, the order in which they are arranged very rarely changes. The chain rarely snaps. Vitality is the supple thread that links living beings together, but with this vitality comes a constant demand for hierarchical differentiation. This book identifies and describes the patterns by which these beads move in response to the necropolitical demands of ranking and sorting.

These beads on a string describe the Great Chain of Being, perhaps the most all-encompassing and historically consistent demonstration of catacosmesis, or ranked arrangement, in Western culture. The Great Chain of Being categorizes all kinds of things—living or not—in fixed hierarchical relation with one another. Carolyn Miller describes the Chain: "God at the top of the chain and successive levels of angels, humans in their various ranks, wild and domestic animals, plants, minerals and metals, and the underworld at the very bottom."[1] In various texts, the Great Chain is visually rendered as a ladder, pyramid, or tree.

In this chapter, I explore the compelling affinity between necropolitics and rhetoric through the figure of the Great Chain of Being. In addition to its startling persistence in contemporary life, the Great Chain is noteworthy for the way it underwrites a number of schemas (like catacosmesis), tropes (like prosopopeia), and other common rhetorical resources (like god terms). Ordinary language, or at least English, relies on the Great Chain to a surprising extent. While this is not a work of historical scholarship, some historical excavation will be necessary to emphasize the Chain's persistence in contemporary Western life. Necropolitical theory, as a rejoinder and corrective to biopolitical theory's emphasis on life, provides a framework for understanding how contemporary regimes of living parse existents into groups targeted for vitality, subhumanity, or death. Rhetorical theory helps us make sense of the publicly circulating discursive formations and practices that create, sustain, and legitimate necropolitical distributions of livability. This first chapter lays out key assumptions of zoerhetorical theory, including the crucial concepts of *zoe*, empire, hierarchy, and the residual power of the Great Chain of Being.

BIOPOLITICAL THEORY IN NECROPOLITICAL WORLDS

Biopolitics names a lively branch of critical theory that makes sense of the way that life itself is regulated. Michel Foucault debuted the term *biopolitics* in a series of lectures in France in the seventies, using it to refer to the changes in the late eighteenth and early nineteenth centuries in which biological life became an object of political discipline and governance. Biopolitics studies the multiple strategies by which life itself is regulated and optimized, and it is considered the primary apparatus of governmentality that emerged at the end of the eighteenth century. (Governmentality refers to the way that governments create citizens that are best suited to fulfill their policies.) To be clear, biopower refers not to a state's power to control and discipline its subjects but rather explores, in Jeff Nealon's words, the "enabling link between the individual's life and the life of the socius: the only thing that we as biopolitical subjects have in common, one might say, is that we're all individuals, charged with the task of creating and maintaining our lives."[2] All discourses and practices regarding the managing of life, including but not limited to distribution

---

1. As quoted in Walsh, "The Great Chain of Being," 9.
2. Nealon, *Plant Theory*, 3.

of risk, public health, life insurance, mortality, disease, and environment, are rendered intelligible through biopolitical logic. Although biopolitics as a general strategy of power is Western European in origin, its colonial reach means that biopower proliferates globally.[3] As a set of competing theories, the explanatory power of biopolitics is evident given the thousands of scholarly works that reference biopolitics published in the last twenty-five years.

The *zoe-* prefix of zoerhetorics derives from, but is not particularly faithful to, an important book in biopolitical theory: Giorgio Agamben's *Homo Sacer: Sovereign Power and Bare Life.* According to Agamben's contested etymology, *zoe* (ζωή) is an ancient Greek word for "life" that encompasses the spectrum of all living existents, including humans, animals, and plants.[4] Agamben compared *zoe,* mere biological existence, with *bios,* active political life. Using this *zoe/bios* distinction as a reference, Agamben offered his theory of bare life, a figure whose *bios* was so degraded as to be stripped of political significance. According to Agamben, the exclusion of bare life from the polis—think of figures like the detainee, the landless refugee, the plantation slave—is the ban upon which Western society is founded. In other words, excluding people from full political participation is exactly that which creates the political system in the first place. A certain unassailable logic girds Agamben's central observation: in order to have an inside there must be an outside.

I borrow the prefix *zoe-* from Agamben's oeuvre partially because of his centrality to biopolitical theory, but I use *zoe* in a markedly different way, influenced more by Rosi Braidotti than by her fellow countryman, Agamben. Like Agamben, Braidotti believes that the power relations around *zoe/bios* are the "defining feature of our historicity."[5] Yet Braidotti is more aroused by *zoe* than by *bios.* She elaborates:

Life is half animal: *zoe* and half discursive: *bios. Zoe,* of course, is the poor half of a qualitative distinction that foregrounds *bios* defined as intelligent life. Centuries of Christian indoctrination have a left deep mark here: *bios* is divinely ordained and holy, whereas *zoe* is quite gritty. . . . *Zoe* is mindlessly material and the idea of life carrying on independently of agency and even regardless of rational control, is the dubious privilege attributed to the non-humans.[6]

3. Povinelli, *Geontologies.*
4. Agamben, *Homo Sacer.*
5. Braidotti, *Transpositions,* 135.
6. Braidotti, "The Ethics of Becoming Imperceptible," 138.

Importantly, Braidotti identifies a hierarchy between *bios* and *zoe*. Smuggled into Agamben's preference for *bios,* Braidotti contends, is the rational sovereign individual of Western culture as the highest expression of humanhood, a preference formed by the influence of the Great Chain of Being. For this book, I take the prefix *zoe-* neither for its disputable etymology,[7] nor to reproduce Agamben's categorical ontology of bare life, but rather for its capacities to index biopolitics and encompass all modes of gritty liveliness. If, as Braidotti insists, "*zoe* has a monstrously strong capacity . . . for upsetting established categorical distinctions of thought,"[8] then I wish to leverage some of that monster strength to rattle the Great Chain.

Indeed, a veritable zoo of existents—not just those attributed the *bios* of humanhood—are subject to transvaluations along the linear gradations of the dominant sociopolitical hierarchy of the contemporary US. These existents include humans, animals, plants, and microbial life such as human embryos or bacteria. By the way, I use the term *existents* throughout the book, borrowing from Elizabeth Povinelli. With this term, Povinelli emphasized the "biontological enclosure of existence (to characterize all existents as endowed with the qualities associated with Life)."[9] Of course, biopolitics has tended to focus on the human. As Povinelli explains, "Western ontologies are covert biontologies—Western metaphysics [measures] all forms of existence (*bios, zoe*) by the qualities of one form of existence."[10] This one form of existence, of course, refers to humans. The hierarchy depends on the rhetorical maintenance of this system—of Man as that with whom all other living entities are compared and found wanting in varying degrees.

From biopolitics we also inherit an emphatic attention to life itself; or, in Paolo Virno's words, "life breaks through the center of the public scene."[11] Zoerhetorics modulate the value of lives along biopolitically intelligible regimes of living in particular publics. Integral to the operation of zoerhetorics are the status-laden thresholds of belonging, such as animality, humanity, and citizenship, which are in turn striated by biopolitically entrenched lines of difference: species, gender, race, and sexuality.

But there's a problem with this biopolitical emphasis on life. Not all existents experience the biopolitical optimization of lives, yet the preponderance of scholarly work on biopolitics addresses these vitality-advancing processes. What Foucault called thanatopolitics and Achille Mbembe called necropol-

---

7. Dubreuil and Eagle, "Leaving Politics."
8. Braidotti, *Transpositions,* 142.
9. Povinelli, *Geontologies,* 5.
10. Povinelli, *Geontologies,* 5.
11. Virno, *A Grammar of the Multitude,* 81.

itics describe the way in which regimes of power target populations for life and death.[12] When he described *homo sacer* and positioned the concentration camp as the paradigm of modernity, Agamben articulated something like a necropolitics (although he doesn't use the word—he uses the Foucauldian *thanatopolitics*). He wrote that the fundamental activity of sovereign power is the production of bare life. The necropolitical production of death is just as important as the biopolitical production of life.

The most influential contribution to necropolitical theory is Achille Mbembe's 2003 flagship essay that coined the term. Mbembe replaced *thanatopolitics* with *necropolitics* to describe the power that targets those deemed unworthy of life.[13] Mbembe wondered why scholars endlessly discuss the optimization of life, when complicit and always present with biopolitical regimes are populations targeted for death, living in what he called "deathworlds." Whereas Foucault thought that some sort of rupture had to occur before biopolitics became lethal, Mbembe maintained that the vitality-building and vitality-diffusing functions of biopower were continuous with each other, as two sides of the same coin. He asked, "Is the notion of biopower sufficient to account for the contemporary ways in which the political, under the guise of war, or of resistance, or the fight against terror, makes the murder of the enemy its primary and absolute objective?"[14] His answer was no.

For Mbembe, modern examples of deathworlds, where subjects are targeted for death rather than nourished toward life, include South Africa under apartheid and the Israeli occupation of Palestine. The following events have been described as operations of necropolitical power by scholars extending Mbembe's project: racial slavery in the Atlantic world (Sexton); the treatment of HIV-infected South Africans under apartheid (Decoteau); Palestinians in Israeli-occupied Palestine (Puar); the mass incarceration of black men in the US (Dillon); and drone strikes in Pakistan (Allinson). According to Claire Decoteau, necropolitics circulate when it becomes clear "whose life is worth living and who must die for the sake of the nation."[15] A system of ranking always accompanies necropolitical exclusion.

This is not to say that we should fully jettison biopolitics. Instead, Jasbir Puar pioneered holding taut what she called the "bio-necro tension." In mak-

---

12. In this book, I choose to use Mbembe's necropolitics rather than Foucault's thanatopolitics for two reasons. First, the emphasis on *necros* (physical death) over *thanatos* (spiritual death; death personified) drums home Mbembe's attempt to make physical death and suffering more visible. The second reason is the simple mathematics of scholarly citation; *necropolitics* is used far more often than *thanatopolitics*.

13. Mbembe, "Necropolitics," 12.

14. Mbembe, "Necropolitics," 12.

15. Decoteau, *Ancestors and Antiretrovirals*, 22.

ing sense of the complex bio-necro relationship, Puar elaborated, "The latter makes its presence known at the limits and through the excess of the former; the former masks the multiplicity of its relationships to death and killing in order to enable the proliferation of the latter."[16] When I use the terms *biopolitics* and *necropolitics,* I intend to keep in tension Puar's "bio-necro collaboration." This collaboration "conceptually acknowledges biopower's direct activity in death, while remaining bound to the optimization of life, and necropolitics' nonchalance toward death even as it seeks out killing as a primary aim."[17] The bio-necro collaboration demands attunement to the deathly imperative in every life-building project. In this book, I use the terms *biopolitics* and *necropolitics* to delineate an emphasis on life or death, respectively, but I do so with an awareness that they haunt each other. For both Mbembe and Puar, biopolitics fails to engage the racial assemblages that supply the chaff to hierarchy's winnow. Puar is instructive to this project, as she models a way in which we can simultaneously attend to biopolitical upbeats and remain ever attuned to the necropolitical downbeats that subtend them.

Empire is invoked throughout this book simply because empire requires a hierarchy of living existents and a dominant zoerhetorical regime to support this hierarchy. Although I occasionally use the more palatable terms *nation* and *state,* empire underscores the imperialist and colonial qualities of the contemporary US. Many zoerhetorics deployed in the service of empire today "justify the interventions and interests of powerful state and capital forces."[18] Following scholars like Puar and Neel Ahuja, US empire reminds us that we live in a settler nation whose twentieth-century projects of trade, security, military, and territory expansion enjoyed a self-evident support.

One quality of necropolitical thought that nominates it for consideration is that it acts as a rejoinder to the black box of biopolitics. In the work produced by the High Theory names associated with biopolitics (think Foucault and Agamben, as well as Roberto Esposito), there is little empirically grounded explanation for how, exactly, these biopolitical processes occur. In the major biopolitical treatises, which have been cited thousands of times, biopolitical regimes are presented as a black box in which there is an "input" and "output" with little explanation of how they work, how they sustain themselves, or how people are persuaded to participate in them. This book joins the efforts of scholars in sociology, anthropology, and rhetorical studies to share what's inside the mysterious black box of biopolitics. I contend that one set

---

16. Puar, *Terrorist Assemblages,* 35.
17. Puar, *Terrorist Assemblages,* 35.
18. Ahuja, *Bioinsecurities,* 11.

of mechanisms operating inside the box includes the zoerhetorical discourses and practices, always grounded in publics, that transvalue existents.

Corollary to this lack of empirical grounding in High Theory biopolitical scholarship is an inattention to gender and race. Not only does Agamben, for example, employ the generic male for all humans, but he pens nary a word about how bare life may be experienced differently by people of different genders—a "fissure" that Penelope Deutscher declares a "non-accident."[19] Even worse, many of the topics that he writes about, such as the internment camp, exclusion, and dehumanization, have been explored in depth by scholars of color, but Agamben rarely cites these scholars. Alexander Weheliye's critique of Agamben along these lines is particularly damning. He states, "Minority discourses seemingly cannot inhabit the space of proper theoretical reflection," which is why thinkers like Agamben "need not reference the long traditions of thought in this domain that are directly relevant to biopolitics and bare life."[20] Therefore, Agamben's biopolitics are whitewashed. Agamben excludes the contribution of scholars of color and women even as he crafts theories directly relevant to their lives and their scholarship.

Pace Foucault and his *dispositifs*, the biopolitical heavyweights have no truck with rhetoric. They care little for the way that discourse circulates through publics to unevenly and messily maintain and condition the bio-necro hierarchy. Instead, Agamben and Esposito overinvest in the constitutive power of law and etymology. Indeed, in Agamben's body of work, etymological connections, such as those of his *zoe/bios* binary, are granted a nearly mystical explanatory status.[21] While etymology can certainly reveal significant historical connections across concepts, it seems strange to champion the value of etymological histories of words yet virtually ignore their vernacular use, public circulation, and everyday effect on people.

To further explore this inattention to rhetorical productions embedded in publics, let me borrow an example from Mbembe, who, although in many ways is a crucial inspiration to my project, does not have a sophisticated conception of public discourse. He writes,

> Colonial occupation itself was a matter of seizing, delimiting, and asserting
> control over a physical geographical area—of writing on the ground a new

---

19. Deutscher, "Reproductive Politics, Biopolitics and Auto-immunity," 224.

20. Weheliye, *Habeas Viscus*, 9. Weheliye expounds, "If I didn't know any better, I would suppose that scholars not working in minority discourse seemed thrilled that they no longer have to consult the scholarship of nonwhite thinkers now that European master subjects have deigned to weigh in on these topics," 6.

21. Esposito, *Bios*, 183–84.

set of social and spatial relations. The writing of new spatial relations (territorialization) was, ultimately, tantamount to the production of boundaries and hierarchies, zones and enclaves; the subversion of existing property arrangements; the classification of people according to different categories; resource extraction; and, finally, *the manufacturing of a large reservoir of cultural imaginaries.* These imaginaries gave meaning to the enactment of differential rights to differing categories of people for different purposes within the same space; in brief, the exercise of sovereignty. Space was therefore the raw material of sovereignty and the violence it carried with it. Sovereignty meant occupation, and occupation meant relegating the colonized into a third zone between subjecthood and objecthood.[22]

Here Mbembe describes a causal relation between hierarchical differentiation of people and something he calls *cultural imaginaries.* From context clues, we can scrape together a meaning for this term. Cultural imaginaries must be a set of beliefs that circulate within a particular culture. Mbembe contends that these cultural imaginaries serve the crucial function of rationalizing hierarchical differences across categories of people. How do these imaginaries circulate—how do they become widespread, accepted, persuasive, perpetuated? What forms do they take within and across historical moments? With the term *cultural imaginaries,* Mbembe circles around something like the zoe-rhetorical circulation of public discourse.

By providing the narratives that justify necropolitical ranking and sorting, rhetoric acts as a connective tissue and lubrication for hierarchical differentiation. Prior to the biopolitical shifts of the eighteenth century, the sovereign made the decision about who lives and who dies.[23] According to Claire Decoteau's reading of Foucault, the sovereign who decides the exception became decentralized in the advent of the neoliberal era.[24] Decoteau claimed that this decentralization resulted in a distribution of responsibility, thereby giving average people the power to control who lives and who dies. This decentralization would be impossible without the proliferation of public discourses rationalizing hierarchy. Public discourse diffuses necropower across a series of publics. One means by which this occurs is through the construction of status hierarchies. Sometimes these look like stories about why someone belongs in this group or that group, or why someone deserves this or that privilege or punishment. Alexander Weheliye described this process as the "sociopolitical processes of differentiation and hierarchization," of which he considers black-

---

22. Mbembe, "Necropolitics," 25–26; my emphasis.
23. Agamben, *Homo Sacer,* 13–14.
24. Decoteau, *Ancestors and Antiretrovirals,* 105.

ness to be the primary signifier.[25] For Weheliye, as he follows Hortense Spillers, the "hieroglyphics of the flesh, however, remain a potent potential that lingers affixed to the racialized body as not-quite-human, even subsequent to nominal emancipations."[26] Zoerhetorical transvaluations occur beyond and in excess of legal or policy declamations of nominal equality.

Where a living existent resides on such a hierarchy bears radical consequences for the livability of its life. Mel Chen's analogous insight on "animacy hierarchies" thinks through linguistic mediations that adjust the position of various living and nonliving entities along a hierarchy. Often the differences that make a difference for livability occur across the biopolitical fault lines of citizenship, race, gender, sexuality, nationality, or physiological normativity.[27] Even though Chen is a linguist rather than a rhetorical theorist, this book benefits from an *agôn* (in the sense of an "encounter that produces struggle or change"[28]) with Chen. Like Chen's animacy hierarchies, zoerhetorical hierarchies theorize processes of transvaluation in contemporary necropolitical configurations. Zoerhetorical hierarchies depart from Chen in two ways. First, I locate transvaluation not as a linguistic event but as a rhetorical event grounded in particular publics. While Chen's range of focal objects come from popular culture and visual media, Chen does not explain how these focal objects relate to, circulate through, or constitute publics. Second, Chen positions animacy as the dominant mode of making-hierarchy. Dead, inert, lifeless things are at the bottom; agentic, lively existents are at the top of the animacy hierarchy. Animacy may be a useful winnow for hierarchies, but it is not the only predictor; elements like magnitude and habit matter too.

THE RHETORIC OF NECROPOLITICS

At the risk of hyperbole, zoerhetorics are a matter of life and death. While scholars in fields deeply invested in discourse may take little issue with this claim, a conversation I had during graduate school comes to mind frequently. When I tried to explain zoerhetorics to a political theorist friend, he said, "But it's just words. Do words really matter that much? Don't words distract us from the real violence?" His words floored me, but the interaction served as a reminder that not all disciplines steep themselves in the constitutive power of

---

25. Weheliye, *Habeas Viscus*, 5.
26. Weheliye, *Habeas Viscus*, 39.
27. Chen, *Animacies*.
28. Hawhee, "Agonism and Aretê," 185.

public discourse. Far too many scholars, even critical ones, subscribe to a false binary that separates discourse from matter.

Discourse is matter; discourse matters. To rehash the old dichotomy between action and discourse delimits our capacity to apprehend discursive effects. Consider the deadly effects of repeatedly referring to a group of persons as subhumans, like the Nazis did of the Jews—they were literally called Untermeschen, or "under men." They were also referred to as rats and filthy animals. Similarly, during the Rwandan genocide of the mid-nineties, government radio broadcasts characterized the Tutsis as cockroaches and as snakes, insects, and animals to be killed, beheaded or stomped on, and exterminated.[29] In these particular examples, zoerhetorics demoted the value of lives for a group of people, thereby serving a crucial legitimating function for the dominant group. Lynne Tirrell's work on the "language games" that accompany genocides argues that derogatory terms not only have a negative force, "but they also exert a positive power, giving social and material strength to those who wield them."[30] Not all zoerhetorics serve to justify mass killings. But when there are mass killings, I guarantee a consistent zoerhetorical strategy targeted the oppressed group *and* provided a post hoc rationalization to account for the resulting outcomes. In sum, to respond to my naysaying friend, it is too simple to assert that words merely matter. I would go a step further, and argue that rhetorical studies is uniquely positioned to understanding how lives accumulate or lose value through public discourse. Lives can be rendered more or less livable depending on how a group of people are zoerhetorically framed.

A paradoxical relationship with rhetorical studies underpins this monograph. Like many scholarly disciplines, rhetoric has a shameful history of sustaining hierarchical and exploitative relations. Only wealthy aristocrats from Athens could afford the rhetorical training offered by the sophists, thereby limiting whose voices could be heard, or as least deemed credible, in the public sphere. The earliest rhetorical theories were deeply committed to a natural hierarchy of the world, especially along the lines of gender and ethnicity. Like many academic disciplines with long histories, rhetoric has deep roots in settler colonialism and structural racism. At the same time, the affordances of rhetoric are distinctly helpful in making sense of the necropolitical hierarchies that shape existents' lives. This chapter grapples with rhetoric's long-standing servitude to empire, while also making the case that we need its tools in par-

---

29. For an excellent discussion of the action-engendering nature of these derogatory terms, see Tirrell, "Genocidal Language Games."

30. Tirrell, 174.

ticular.[31] If necropolitical regimes require the appearance of differently graded existents, *these transvaluations must occur rhetorically and circulate through publics*. Rhetorical studies can locate and categorize these transvaluations and account for their persuasive effects.

HIERARCHY AS RHETORICAL TRADITION

Whether they are sacred, killable, or inconsequential, the status of all existents is modulated by hierarchy-driven rhetorical practices. Forefigures in the rhetorical tradition provide tools for understanding hierarchy while also justifying a natural hierarchic order to the world. But the latter precedes the former, as I will show. For most of its long history, the European rhetorical tradition labored to justify and teach a natural order to the world. As Terry Eagleton claimed, the Western rhetorical tradition was "utterly inseparable from the social relations of exploitation."[32] I aim to provide in this section a gloss of hierarchy's relationship to rhetoric as it developed in the West.

Before I embark, let me clarify the term *hierarchy*. One of the first documented uses occurred in the sixth century by Pseudo-Dionysius Areopagita. He used it to properly divide the various ranks of angels, developing the word from the Greek *hierarcha*, "rule by priests" or "sacred rule."[33] Historically there have been celestial, ecclesiastical, imperial, and any number of other kinds of hierarchies, but when I use the term I am referring to a consequential sociopolitical hierarchy that evaluates living existents. A zoerhetorical hierarchy is a ranked arrangement of existents who, proportional to their contested position on the hierarchy, experience partisan distributions of livability. Zoerhetorical hierarchies exist in various forms all over the globe. In this book, I am interested in the contemporary zoerhetorical hierarchies in the US.

In one sense, theories of hierarchy begin where rhetoric begins, at least according to the standard Eurocentric narrative—in ancient Athens. From Plato we inherited the seeds of what would grow into the Great Chain of Being in the Middle Ages—a sense of a natural order of the world, with God at the apex. For Plato, all possible kinds of things that could exist did exist. The

---

31. I am familiar with Audre Lorde's oft-quoted intonation about the impotence of the master's tools to dismantle the master's house. However, to assume that the critical, feminist, antiracist scholarly work that I press into service in rhetorical studies today is the same as the rhetorical tradition of the past is to attribute an inappropriately static nature to a field of study. We now have tools that do not belong to the master.

32. Eagleton, *Walter Benjamin*, 101–2.

33. *Oxford English Dictionary*, s.v. "hierarchy."

world was complete in its demonstration of plenitude. Carolyn Miller credits Plato's theory of forms, "the fixed, unchanging, and distinct *eidē* or essences," as importing an essentialism into the Great Chain of Being, which would go on to become a durable influence in multiple spheres, including the early science of taxonomists like Carl Linnaeus.[34] In Plato's narrative, the cookery craft of rhetoric consistently failed to realize the true nature of this hierarchy, compared with her twin, dialectic.

To the complete plenitude of Plato's hierarchy, Aristotle added the elements of continuity and gradation. Aristotle's path-breaking zoology contributed a natural order to the world where each existent was *continuous* (forming an unbroken whole) and *contiguous* (touching and sharing a border) with the next. In addition to this contiguity, this order was also gradient, and included a linearly ranked taxonomic classification of animals, that, of course, placed humans above the rest.[35] Ever since, as Arthur Lovejoy has shown in what is considered the pioneering treatise on the Great Chain of Being, narrative systems of natural orders often feature these three qualities of *plenitude, continuity,* and *gradation.*[36] These three qualities, as I will show here, serve as discursive resources for conditioning and maintaining a rhetorical hierarchy.

Given its durability in Western thought, the Great Chain of Being has been largely overlooked by contemporary rhetoric scholars, with two notable exceptions: George Lakoff and Mark Turner, and some work by Carolyn Miller. Lakoff and Turner dedicate an entire chapter in *More Than Cool Reason: A Field Guide to Poetic Metaphor* to the Great Chain of Being and claim that as a pervasive cultural model, the Great Chain is "widespread, largely unconscious and so fundamental and indispensable to our thinking we hardly notice it."[37] Lakoff and Turner convincingly make the case that thousands of everyday metaphors are underwritten by the Great Chain. Here I seek to extend their argument into territory beyond metaphors.

A recent article in the journal *Poroi* that names the Great Chain of Being in its title only gestures to it in a few sentences. In the section penned by Miller, she writes:

---

34. Miller, "Genre Innovation," 6.

35. Lovejoy, *The Great Chain of Being.* While his contribution is widely revered as the authoritative monograph on the subject, Lovejoy barely addresses how the Great Chain could be used to justify existing unjust social arrangements. Page DuBois makes this critique in her book *Centaurs and Amazons: Women and the Pre-History of the Great Chain of Being,* 59.

36. Lovejoy, *The Great Chain of Being.*

37. Lakoff and Turner, 167. Lakoff and Turner's work on the Great Chain generated more scholarly traction in the field of linguistics than in the field of rhetoric.

This image brings before our eyes questions about the location and distribution of agency, the sources of authority, and the possibility of rhetoric (though the answers it offers likely differ from those we postmoderns would favor).[38]

Miller is right to note that the Chain is the "visual epitome" of Western hierarchies. What's more, she also observes a distribution of agency and authority inherent in the Chain. Given that hers is only a provocative observation, I take up Miller's and Lakoff and Turner's banner here, and pursue a deeper analysis of the Chain in relation to contemporary rhetorical theory.

Selectively the Western rhetorical tradition incorporates or ignores scholars of the Middle Ages in its grand narrative of rhetorical history. With Saint Augustine, Albertus Magnus, and his famous student, Thomas Aquinas, we get the most sophisticated version of the Great Chain of Being. At the pinnacle of the Great Chain resides God, representing the highest degree of perfection. After God and angels (archangels, seraphim, then cherubim) come humans, apes, other animals, plants, and minerals. Humans occupied a unique position in the *scala naturae* (Latin for "nature's ladder") because they shared qualities with divine creatures above them, such as an eternal spirit, but were also condemned to lives of enfleshed desire like those of the animals below them. The Great Chain described the complete universe (plenitude). Augustine's aphoristic response to why God created all things good and bad was "Non essent omnia, si essent aequalia," or, "If all things were equal, all things would not be."[39] In other words, in order for God's world to be perfect, all possible diversity of kinds must be in the world. This is the notion of plenitude, or complete fullness, that Augustine inherited from Plato's metaphysics. In Alexander Pope's famed poem "An Essay on Man," the notion of plenitude is expressed as an admonishment to stay in one's place, lest the whole chain break. "Vast chain of Being!" he begins, "On superior powers / Were we to press, inferior might on ours: / Or in the full creation leave a void / Where, one step broken, the great scale's destroyed." Pope's message is clear: humans are neither to question nor meddle with the perfectly complete God-given hierarchy.

An existent's essential and allegedly immutable status in the natural order of the world determined its position on nature's ladder. In his writing on the duty of the Christian orator, St. Augustine's neo-Platonic commitment to eloquence and truth also bespeaks a nascent natural order to the world. Like all

---

38. Walsh, "The Great Chain of Being," 9. This piece is not a traditional journal article, but instead presents some conversations that resulted from a day-long symposium on agency in scientific communication hosted by ARSTM.

39. Parekh, *Rethinking Multiculturalism*, 23.

kinds of species-types, humans were expected to strain for perfection, and it was the primary duty of Christian orators to teach the way of this perfection, and not to let words themselves obscure truth.[40] In *The Rhetoric of Religion,* Burke noted the verbal hierarchies at work in Augustine's *Confessions.* As a preacher of the "The Word," Augustine mined the linguistic power reserved in god terms (and the term *God*).[41] In the same text, Burke added a Marxist sensibility to the Great Chain of Being, named here as the social ladder and social pyramid:

> By hierarchy we refer to the motive of political order, made possible and necessary by social differentiations and stratifications due to the division of labor and to corresponding distinctions in the possession of property . . . Here is the motive of the social ladder, or social pyramid, involving a concern with the "higher" as an organizing element. . . . (Also, included in such a notion of the "higher" would be the ways whereby the terms of social superiority, coupled with terms of moral strivings and with the "Platonic" forms of a sheerly *dialectical* "ascent," can provide analogies for ideas of "God.") . . . Logologically, begin with an over-all 'God term,' a title of titles, and view everything else *in terms of* that summarizing Word.[42]

As a preacher of the "The Word," Augustine mined the linguistic power reserved in god terms (and the term *God*).[43] God terms are intelligible, and therefore effective, because of hierarchies inherited from Judeo-Christianity.

Great Chain of Being narratives from the Middle Ages prefigure the contestation and boundary work of human-making that I will discuss later. For example, as David Livingstone Smith explained, medieval scholars

> divided humanity into a series of subtypes ranked from "highest" to "lowest." Unsurprisingly, considering their origin, most of these schemes modestly placed Caucasians at the pinnacle of humanity and relegated Native Americans and Sub-Saharan Africans to the bottom, only a hair's breadth away from apes.[44]

The phrase "hair's breadth" is key because it demonstrates another crucial feature of the Great Chain: continuity, or more accurately, contiguity. According

40. Augustine, *On Christian Doctrine.* Here I reference book 4, "On Christian Orators."
41. Burke, *The Rhetoric of Religion,* 49.
42. Burke, *The Rhetoric of Religion,* 41.
43. Burke, *The Rhetoric of Religion,* 49.
44. Livingstone Smith, *Less Than Human,* Kindle edition, Loc. 40.

to Albertus Magnus, borrowing from Aristotle, everything on the ladder was substantively linked, in uninterrupted enchainment, to the existents between which it was sandwiched. In the example Livingstone Smith cites above, Sub-Saharan Africans, then, shared qualities with both the humans above them and the apes below them.

As a rhetorical resource, contiguity underwrites the imbricative fluidity between groups of existents. This fluidity provides a discursive resource by which it becomes possible to metonymically shift entities up and down the hierarchy, accounting for why, for example, racialization occurs in ever-new and rhetorically different ways.[45] When Sara Ahmed described a metonymic slide by which objects come to bear meaning "through their contact with other objects," she asserted the importance of contiguity, or touching, for metonymical operations.[46] What Claire Sisco King called the "associative logic of metonymy," or logic predicated on conditions of relatedness, is crucial here.[47] The opportunity for metonymical sliding together of various existents is a linguistic resource built right into the Great Chain of Being with its principles of continuity and contiguity. I opened this chapter with the metaphor of a necklace to draw attention to the way that different existents can metonymically slide together like beads on a string.

To complete the triad, to the principles of plenitude and continuity/contiguity, the third feature of the Great Chain introduces hierarchy: gradation. With this linear gradation comes evaluation, as each "kind" on the Chain becomes closer to God, or the *ens perfectissimum,* the most perfect thing. The chain's links are ranked, or "forged in relations of superiority and subordination."[48] It is important to recognize that it is possible to have plenitude and lateral contiguity prior to hierarchical valuation. It is only with gradation, then, that valuations (and therefore zoerhetorical transvaluations) can occur. Gradation is often visually represented through the Chain's vertical dimension.

Although the Great Chain of Being sounds absurdly antiquated now, its core ideas persist both as rhetorical resources and as elements that operate on people through contemporary cultural valuations. The Great Chain of Being aspired to legitimacy based on a natural order to the world, and necessarily privileged an elite few as a result. In medieval versions of the Great Chain, the highest-ranking human was the divinely ordained king, followed by land-

---

45. Laura Ann Stoler's recent work *Duress: Imperial Durabilities in Our Times* complicates racism along lines of fixity and malleability.

46. Ahmed, *The Cultural Politics of Emotion,* 87.

47. King, "Hitching Wagons to Stars," 84.

48. DuBois, *Centaurs and Amazons,* 5.

owning lords and then their peasants. Not surprisingly, men as heads of household were placed above women and children. The Great Chain of Being functions as an incredibly convincing way to justify unequal distributions of livability in the Middle Ages and beyond. It offered a coherent narrative that validated and perpetuated inequalities. While it seems like only white supremacists directly reference the Great Chain of Being as authoritative today, the features of social hierarchy of the Chain carry to the contemporary world, albeit in different forms.[49]

The idea of an ordained hierarchy to the world continued in the Western world through the early modern period, the Renaissance, and into the nineteenth century. The European colonization of the Americas, Asia, and Africa in the fifteenth through nineteenth centuries depended on an ascribed "natural" order to the social world. The resulting subjugation of indigenous peoples has been extensively documented in postcolonial scholarship. The history of rhetoric itself more than once served as a platform to justify these oppressive relations. According to Walter Mignolo, "The authority of alphabetic writing and its 'natural' links with history and rhetoric furnished sufficient proof for the Spaniards to look at other cultures as inferior."[50] In this case, the Western rhetorical tradition was used as a cultural high-water mark to rationalize the subordination of indigenous people.

Furthermore, the subjugation of Native Americans, African Americans, and women through the nineteenth century was often underwritten by Christian hierarchies. Susan Romano provided an example of Christian rhetoric in the service of hierarchy work in the New World in her discussion of bilingual sacrament handbooks for the Catholic conversion of Amerindians.[51] Don Paul Abbott further extends this line of inquiry in his analysis of José de Acosta's work. Acosta, a Spanish missionary, argued that conversion rhetorics aimed at native peoples must be fundamentally different from those aimed at Europeans because of the supposed limited intellectual capacity of native peoples.[52]

Similarly, in his sixteenth-century treatise on rhetoric called *Rhetorica Christiana,* Diego Valadés unites his understanding of the classic Greek and Roman traditions with his experience as a mestizo in what is now Mexico. Included in his book are engravings elaborating multiple hierarchies, including ecclesiastical and imperialistic ones.[53] Notably, Valadés's engraving of the

---

49. For more on racism persisting in rhetorically different ways through various paradigm shifts, see Kelly Happe, *Material Gene.*

50. Mignolo, *The Darker Side of the Renaissance,* 112.

51. Romano, "Rhetoric in Latin America."

52. Abbott, *Rhetoric in the New World.*

53. Abbott, *Rhetoric in the New World,* picture inset.

Great Chain of Being is the most commonly circulated visual representation today. An intensely detailed visual work of art, the Great Chain resembles a tree, with a series of ranked rungs or branches. The Chain linking them all derives directly from God's hand (represented in this image as the Holy Trinity), under a banner that reads in faulty Latin "I am the beginning and the end and beyond me there is no God, and all of the Gods of other nations are demons."[54] Anchoring the Chain at the bottom is an image of a louche, spread-eagled devil surrounded by a torturous hellscape.

That the Great Chain of Being would require detailed illustration in a rhetoric manual written for Franciscan missionaries is telling. The logic undergirding the inclusion of the Chain and its accompanying visual images is that in order to communicate effectively with different types of humans, one must understand the hierarchical relations between different types of beings that live in the world. To this end, Valadés and his fellow missionaries used linen screens (*lienzos*) with images like that of the Great Chain of Being to assist their instruction of the indigenous peoples.[55] Without understanding one's position on the hierarchy, as the logic went, one could not understand Christianity.

In this instance, Valadés and others like him were not only spreading the reigning Christian hierarchy of the day, smuggled into their rhetorical teaching. They were also using the Great Chain to make attributions regarding rhetorical capacity, and tailoring their messages as a result. While it may appear that Valadés embraces a multicultural egalitarianism by placing all humans on the same echelon of his version of the Great Chain, his more detailed diagrams elsewhere in *Rhetorica Christiana* clarify his commitment to a racial, colonial hierarchy. Oddly, his representation of the Great Chain departs from most hierarchies by privileging birds and fish above nonhuman mammals.

The persistence and durability of the Great Chain of Being and its linear, hierarchical gradations are evident through the early modern period. I discuss it at length here because the zoerhetorical hierarchy inherits not only the content of the Great Chain but also many of its qualities, including plenitude, continuity/contiguity, and gradation. These qualities are what make the covert biontology of the West (drawing on Povinelli again) available for language users. All existents are measured against one existent, and this one existent is doing the measuring. That all kinds exist as essential beings (plenitude), overlap with two other kinds (often described in the literature as continuity, but

---

54. Archibald, *Aristotle's Ladder, Darwin's Tree*, 3.
55. Abbott, "Diego Valadés."

better expressed as contiguity) and are assigned differing values (gradation), serve as (zoe)rhetorical resources.

Many common rhetorical resources gain traction from the Great Chain of Being. Schema like catacosmesis, as discussed early, are lent intelligibility and therefore effectiveness by the Great Chain. Lakoff and Turner not only argue that the Great Chain "still exists as a contemporary unconscious cultural model," but also assert that the Chain structures metaphors at a basic level. Attributions of higher properties (such as the rational thought associated with humans) and lower properties (such as the self-propulsion associated with insects) inform the production of thousands of metaphors in everyday use. "When the hierarchy of the basic Great Chain is combined with the commonplace knowledge about the Nature of Things," they write, "we get a more elaborated, hierarchical folk theory of forms of being and how they behave."[56] To their credit, Lakoff and Turner are critical of the legacies of dominance and subjugation the Great Chain metaphor smuggles into everyday metaphor.

Even tropes that appear unrelated to hierarchy, such as apostrophe or prosopopeia, are indebted to the Great Chain for their intelligibility. In fact, Kasey Evans locates prosopopeia's power precisely in its ability to "turn the great chain of being into a two-way street."[57] While we are familiar with prosopopeia's upward ascent of granting a human voice to an animal, we must also consider that animating the dead "would be descending the scale, working perversely against the Platonic (and neo-Platonic) mandate to tend toward perfection."[58] In the famous visual rendering of the Great Chain from Valadés, chain links, or *vincula,* vertically connect all the different echelons. This chain closely resembles vertebrae, a fitting representation given the spinal structure that the Chain lends to common language.

The "natural order" of the Great Chain's structure lends power to god terms as well. Regarding god terms, it was not until Kenneth Burke that the rhetorical tradition was provided a systematic theory for how language both draws from and maintains hierarchy. Not only did Burke define man [*sic*] as symbol-(mis)users "goaded by a spirit of hierarchy," but his system of socioanagogic criticism depended on a series of hierarchies. A great example of Burke's eccentric idiolect, the word *socioanagogic* forged together *social* and *anagogy.* Burke borrowed *anagogy* from theology, where it referred to a hermeneutic search for ultimate mystical relevance, often in Biblical texts. From the term's first appearance in *Permanence and Change* through the socioanagogic reading of Shakespeare's "Venus and Adonis" in *A Rhetoric of Motives,*

---

56. Lakoff and Turner, *More than Cool Reason,* 171.

57. Evans, "Prosopopoeia and Maternity," 397.

58. Evans, "Prosopopoeia and Maternity," 397.

socioanagogic criticism provided ways of reading the world through secular appropriations of divinity. A theological employment of anagogy would involve reading, for example, the Old Testament for ways in which eternity was represented. Burke's secular, social anagogy pursued the characteristics of and consequences for language's range of social, political, and religious hierarchies. "Our major concern is to discuss the poem in terms of hierarchy," he wrote in A Rhetoric of Motives.[59] The principles of continuity, identification, god terms, and social order are evident in Burke's socioanagogic analysis:

> Even the world of natural objects, as they figure in poetry, must have secret "identification" with the judgments of status. . . . The veil of Maya is woven of the strands of hierarchy, and the poet's topics glow through that mist. By "socioanagogic" interpretation we mean the search for such implicit identifications.[60]

Burke's legacy of socioanagogic criticism, or his ultimate advice to read for the "enigmatic signature of the hierarchic motive," has not received as much scholarly attention as Burkean ideas like identification or dramatism.[61] At the same time, many of Burke's most crucial concepts, like scapegoating and god terms, rely on hierarchical structuration to make sense.[62] God terms, for example, achieve their rhetorical force from God's position at the top of the hierarchy. Rhetorical agency permeates from the apex of the hierarchy, where resides God, the "title of all titles."[63] Just by mere metonymic association with the pinnacle of the hierarchy, an entity's status can be promoted. Burke is at his most hierarchy-sensitive in the epideictic (and oft-quoted) closing passage of A Rhetoric of Motives, where he notably names Aristotle as a builder of metaphysical hierarchies:

> The mystery of the hierarchic is forever with us, let us, as students of rhetoric, scrutinize its range of entrancements, both with dismay and in delight. And finally let us observe, all about us, forever goading us, though it be in

---

59. Burke, A Rhetoric of Motives, 219.

60. Burke, A Rhetoric of Motives, 219.

61. Burke, A Rhetoric of Motives, 296.

62. Ellen Quandahl pulled a quotation from The Rhetoric of Religion that aphoristically connects scapegoating with hierarchy: "If order, then a need to repress the tendencies to disorder. If repression, then responsibility for imposing, accepting, or resisting the repression. If responsibility, then guilt. If guilt, then the need for redemption, which involves sacrifice, which in turn allows for substitution." Quandahl, "It's Essentially as Though This Were Killing Us," 20.

63. This is but one example from Burke's multipage list in A Rhetoric of Motives of all of the secular things God metonymically replaces, 299.

fragments, the motive that attains its ultimate identification in the thought, not of the universal holocaust, but of the universal order—as with the rhetorical and dialectic symmetry of the Aristotelian metaphysics, whereby all classes of beings are hierarchically arranged in a chain or ladder or pyramid of mounting worth, each kind striving towards the perfection of its kind, and so towards the kind next above it, while the strivings of the entire series head in God as the beloved cynosure and sinecure, the end of all desire.[64]

In this passage, Burke all but names the Great Chain. In *The Rhetoric of Religion,* when Burke introduces his five-part definition of (hu)man, he further explains the importance of hierarchy to human creatures. By definition, according to Burke, humans are symbol-mis/using animals, inventors of the negative, separated from their natural conditions by instruments of their own making, goaded by the spirit of hierarchy, and rotten with perfection. In a footnote, he apologized for the rhetorical flourish of the phrase "goaded by a spirit of hierarchy" and suggested the more neutral phrase of "moved by a sense of order."[65] Whether they are articulated as hierarchy or as order, Burke acknowledges the persistence of ranked arrangements. Later in *The Rhetoric of Religion* he returned again to Augustine, referencing the saint's equation of God's love with ascendance. "By thy gift we are inflamed and borne upward," Burke quotes Augustine. Upon attaining our "proper" level on the hierarchy, we rest.[66] Secularly speaking, the promotional, ascendant capacities of God's love persist.

Burke's socioanagogic criticism and his concept of god terms gave us some tools for understanding hierarchies and how a "natural order" is maintained as a rhetorical resource. Unfortunately, the rhetorical tradition's history of colluding with hierarchies is longer than its development of the tools and practices to understand and critique these hierarchies by thousands of years. Furthermore, some may argue that the dominant Western rhetorical tradition is still in many ways accomplice to social hierarchy, as we use its culturally specific standards to measure all speakers. Consider, by way of example, the way the rhetorical tradition positions language use as that which separates us from the animals.

Because we cannot take for granted that humanhood is self-evident, we need to talk about zoerhetorics across a range of living existents. By a range of living existents, I mean anything that is alive—humans, primates, insects, plants, bacteria. (How is that for unintentional catacosmesis?) I am especially

64. Burke, *A Rhetoric of Motives,* 333.
65. Burke, *The Rhetoric of Religion,* 42.
66. Burke, *The Rhetoric of Religion,* 160.

interested in zoerhetorics around liminal existents whose status is contested. For example, what about potential humans, like human stem cells and human fetuses? What about animals? The animal kingdom perhaps experiences the widest range of zoerhetorical attributions, something I call zoerhetorical sweep. Take mammals, for instance. Mammals can be legally recognized as persons deserving of rights and protections, as dolphins are in India. Mammals can be feted and cared for as cherished companion animals—many of us, including me, treat our dogs with this kind of care and compassion. And yet mammals can also be force-fed the feces and flesh of their siblings and parents as they are raised for slaughter in intensive meat-farming operations. And most of us, including me, eat these animals. Like human mammals, how well we treat nonhuman mammals depends largely on their zoerhetorical transvaluations.

As antiquated as the Chain's rankings seem, they are disturbingly consistent, persistent, and insistent, as this chapter has labored to show. If zoerhetorical patterns move like beads on a string, the string is the Great Chain of Being and it does not rupture. Beads can slide up and down, or break off from a group, but an entire reshuffling rarely occurs. The explanation of contemporary zoerhetorical transvaluation that this book attempts must account for the ongoing presence of the Great Chain. The two scholarly terrains of this book—necropolitics and rhetorical theory—are pressed into service to make sense of the Great Chain. The defection from biopolitics to necropolitics underscores how the Great Chain provides the discursive resources of hierarchical differentiation today. The rhetorical tradition has a distinct historical complicity with the Great Chain of Being that must be acknowledged. At the same time, rhetorical resources like catacosmesis, metonymy, metaphor, and god terms are rooted in the Great Chain's features of plenitude, continuity/contiguity, and gradation.

CHAPTER 2

Human Microbiomes
in Popular Science

IN MAY 2013 the *New York Times* published a long form article by popular American food journalist Michael Pollan about the several hundred microbial species with whom we share a body. The article, titled "Some of My Best Friends Are Germs," mobilized leading-edge scientific research on the human microbiome to make a powerful claim about the nature of human life. According to scientists, a *microbiome* refers to the aggregate genetic material of microbial life within a particular environment, and the *human microbiome* describes the combined genomes of all microbial life on or within the human body. In his essay, Pollan urges us to think of ourselves not as singular individuals but instead in the "first person plural—as a superorganism."[1] Indeed, in his signature accessible style, Pollan relays a rather contested fact that has reached mantra status of the popular science around microbial life: the majority of living cells inside our human bodies contain no human DNA but instead are harmless or even beneficial species of bacteria, archaea, and fungi that compose the human microbiome. Or, as it is more popularly stated, we are only 10 percent human.[2] Pollan proceeds to share his hope that the

---

1. Pollan, "Some of My Best Friends Are Germs."
2. This oft-quoted "10 percent human" fact can be a head-scratcher. Microbial cells may outnumber human cells, but our human (eukaryotic) cells are ten times bigger than bacterial (prokaryotic) cells. The 10 percent human statistic, then, may be true by *number* but not by *mass*. It is a little like claiming that the main residents of my home are spiders. More recently, a

results of microbiome research will bear on a wide range of ailments that plague the West, including obesity, asthma, allergies, and some chronic infections and inflammation. Like many popular science writers, Pollan cautions us that the research is in too early a stage to recommend specific protocols, yet advises the cultivation of a diverse range of microbial species in our guts. As he frames it, Americans ought to consider caring for the "interior wilderness" of the "impoverished Westernized microbiome."[3]

We are living in a microbiome moment. Pollan's 2013 article surfed the crest of what would become, in the ensuing seven years, a tidal wave of scientific and popular science publications on the human microbiome. In 2016 President Obama launched the National Microbiome Initiative, promising millions of dollars to microbe research among multiple ecosystems, including the human microbiome. The same year witnessed the creation of the *Human Microbiome Journal,* signaling a proliferation of scholarship in this area. Alongside research, popular science writing on the human microbiome flourished as well. Headlines like "Unlocking the Secrets of the Microbiome" (*New York Times*) and "Getting to Know My Microbiome" (*Washington Post*) have become commonplace. The last six years also saw a range of popular science books on the human microbiome. A sampling of their titles demonstrates the sense of wonder that popular science writers bring to this topic. Consider Alanna Collen's *10% Human: How Your Body's Microbes Hold the Key to Health and Happiness* and Ed Yong's *I Contain Multitudes: The Microbes Within Us and a Grander View of Life.* These news articles and books, which often read like paeans to our gut microbes, arrive amid a raft of other popular media artifacts, including cookbooks, TED talks, podcasts, blogs, and online summits centered on our microbiota. Instructions on how to cultivate, restore, feed, and otherwise manage our gut bugs pervade health magazines and websites, and the popular MOOC purveyor Coursera runs a course called "Gut Check: Exploring Your Microbiome." The American Gut Project, currently the largest citizen-science project in the world, charts the human microbiome by collecting samples of fecal matter. At the same time, Second Genome, a privately held biopharmaceutical company specializing in translating microbiome science into medical products, has secured millions in venture funds (and happens to be a sponsor of the American Gut Project). Microbiologist Jonathan Eisen's apt neologism and hashtag *microbiomania* simultaneously confirms this moment of microbe fervor and critiques its hype.

---

number of sources have critiqued the 10 percent human fact as imprecise or exaggerated, what Ed Yong calls a "back of the envelope calculation" that happened to go viral. See Yong, *I Contain Multitudes,* 10.

3. Pollan, "Some of My Best Friends Are Germs."

This chapter offers a two-part argument. First, the master metaphor of immune-system-at-war structures contemporary popular discourse on the human microbiome, albeit in a slightly new way. Instead of the prevailing microbe-as-enemy military metaphor, we are now invited to preside as invested, beneficent rulers over our microbial others. Said another way, instead of framing the microbes with which we come into contact as enemies requiring annihilation, we have switched to framing these microbes as subordinates requiring supervision. In the emergent popular microbiome discourse, while the vehicle of the metaphor might pivot from war to peace, it does so within the same worldview built by the initial, master metaphor. Our gut microbes may be undergoing a zoerhetorical promotion but, importantly, the overall relation between human existents and the human microbiome remains both discrete (that is, these existents are considered separate from one another) and ranked (that is, the initial relation of domination persists). It is no mere coincidence that this change closely mirrors the historical shift in how developed countries approach the Global South: broadly speaking, the racist imperialism of the colonial era gave way to the subordinating paternalism of the postcolonial era.[4] The second part of the argument excavates the ongoing constraints of this circumscription, including the colonial impulses in contemporary microbiome discourse. As they emerged in the US in 2013–18, popular science discourses of the human microbiome function as a project of empire-building. The analogous relationship between bodily dominion (over microbial others) and national dominion (over racialized others) is, again, no coincidence. Rather, it is an outcome produced by a commitment to a foreclosed discursive pool for apprehending microbial life as it relates to human existents. In our current moment of microbiomania, we are entreated to conceive of the human body as a mini-empire—with all the relations of hierarchy, resource extraction, and racialization concomitant with empire.

The popular science discursive artifacts that circulate within the public of our current microbiome moment furnish significant probative value for zoerhetorical theory. The microbiome moment marks a time when the biopolitical management of microbial life must shift to accommodate the emergent significance of our tiny others. Zoerhetorics are the discursive strategies by which this shift occurs; to chart the zoerhetorics of the microbiome moment is to begin to map the way that existents (in this case, microbes) are rendered intelligible to bio-necro regimes of hierarchy. Zoerhetorical theory maintains

---

4. For a sustained discussion of the paternalism inherent in settler colonialism, see Singh, *Sweet Talk*. For a discussion of the ways in which bacterial and viral colonies operate in ways analogous to human colonies, see Veracini, *The Settler Colonial Present*.

that to be attributed liveliness—to be thought of as alive and as significant to human life—means to be absorbed into biopolitical hierarchy. While we have known about microorganisms since the 1600s, and we have known that they live inside us since the 1800s, this emergent fervor around the human microbiome signals a demonstrable shift in human–microbe relations. Paxson, following Bruno Latour, names this the shift from Pasteurian to post-Pasteurian approaches to microbial life. In her book *The Life of Cheese,* Paxson offers *microbiopolitics* to characterize the "means of social regulation carried out through control of microbial life."[5] The utility of new concepts like microbiopolitics attest to that fact that, after years of living in relative ignorance of our microbial symbionts, we are now compelled to consider the significance of microbes as lively companions. The microbial moment provides an opportunity to watch the way the biopolitical hierarchy must shuffle and reorganize to accommodate new life—or at least new approaches to new life.

In addition to its freshly effusive quality, microbiome discourse is also significant for zoerhetorical theory because it models a process of *zoerhetorical inclusion.* Unlike other figures featured this book, like the human fetus, human gut microbes themselves are not nominated for humanhood, but rather the existing dominant notion of humanhood must stretch and shift to incorporate (literally, in-corporate) an understanding of itself as "10 percent human," that is, as profoundly constituted by microbial others. If we are now, as some wags wager, *homo microbis,* then what does that mean for how we live our lives? Charting this discourse of inclusion or absorption into humanhood is crucial to the development of zoerhetorical theory, for it registers the process of redrawing the borderlines of humanhood itself. In this microbiome moment, the boundaries that constitute humanhood are upset, however briefly—only to powerfully reassert their domination again.

This chapter is organized as follows. First, I describe the rhetorical context in which popular discourse on the microbiome is situated, and the narrative fields of nationhood and war to which is it bound. Second, I provide an overview of my focal archive, which consists of the American Gut Project (AGP) and the blog posts of scientists affiliated with the AGP. Third, I use the zoetrope of somatopeia to name the ways in which empires and humanhood-attributed existents co-constitute each other. The discourse and practices that circulate within the popular science public on the human microbiome provide em-bodying, or somatopeic, functions with implications far beyond any one person's belly.

5. Paxson, *The Life of Cheese,* 160.

MICROBIAL OTHERS IN RHETORICAL CONTEXT:
THE INESCAPABILITY OF WAR

Notwithstanding recent advertisements about "good" bacteria in yoghurt, I am schooled in recognizing my meetings with bacteria as military encounters—invasion and defense—between my (nonbacterial) individual self and disease (bacteria). That is, the pathogen matrix overwhelmingly defines the parameters of animal meetings-with bacteria.

—Myra Hird, *The Origins of Sociable Life*, 2009

The human immune system is a registry of modern fears.[6] Immunity discourses in the contemporary US provide windows into national neuroses. The pathogen matrix that Hird describes in the epigram above primes us to consider our immune systems (and therefore our bodies) as capable of being invaded, encroached upon, and swarmed. Adversarial pathogens and foreign enemies perpetually swap roles as vehicles and tenors in metaphors of biological and national immunity. Emergent popular science discourses on the human microbiome are about much more than the good gut bugs living in our bellies. Our bacterial others—their diversity, their numbers, their fundamental participation in our physiological processes—are poised to be conceptually, even paradigmatically, challenging to us. If, as Donna Haraway suggested, immune system discourse constructs bodily boundaries, then it is not exaggeration to state that our conceptions of microbes inform our current relationship to humanhood.[7] Where does my selfhood end? Where does otherness begin? The dominant biological model of immune function insists that the immune system first separates self from nonself and then attacks what it deems as nonself. (As we will see, gut microbiome research is causing scientists to reconsider this model.)

The epigram from Hird identifies the metaphor dominating our relationship to microbes: bodies at war. Militaristic defense is the conceptual foundation by which humans conceive of their relation to microbial life. Invasion, battle, enmity—these terms ground modern medicine's approach to pathogens and, as a result, fundamentally structure our relationship to the beneficial microbes with whom we share a body. As Gronnvoll and Landau demonstrate in an exploration of genetic metaphors, metaphors and their entailments powerfully condition thinking and have "material consequences."[8] To demonstrate

---

6. For this sentence, I am inspired by John Durham Peters's oft-quoted "Communication is a registry of modern longing," *Speaking into the Air*, 2.

7. Haraway, "The Biopolitics of Postmodern Bodies."

8. Gronnvoll and Landau, "From Viruses to Russian Roulette to Dance," 62.

the inescapability of the war metaphor, consider, by way of example, the first sentence of Wikipedia's page on the immune system: "The immune system is a *host defense system* comprising many biological structures and processes."[9] In both scientific and popular accounts of microbes, war rules the day. This literature review documents a key implication of the inescapable defense metaphor for human immune discourse: the persistent associative logic metonymically linking bodies to nation-states. The significance of this consistent metonymical linkage across artifacts? Even when we are speaking of microbial friends rather than of enemies, a nationalistic subordination still dictates our understanding of bacterial meetings-with. After all, the word *colony* describes clusters of both bacterial and human bodies, lending connotations of subordination and otherness to both associations.

A wealth of scholarship demonstrates the ubiquity of defense as a foundational concept for our relations to microbes. Arguably, in order to understand the meanings entangled in our current microbial moment, we must first understand the ubiquity, power, and implications of this metaphor. Generally, immunity rhetoric follows this formula: The immune system must rally around an intrusion from a foreign agent, the pathogenic microbe. We marshal white blood cells as "soldiers" who attempt to defeat the enemy in the ensuing battle. Even though hostile intruders (pathogens) constantly threaten to invade our borders, we are (sometimes) protected by our vigilant immune systems. Implications of this metaphor's ascendancy influence nearly every aspect of medical research, education, and practice. As Catherine Waldby wrote in a study of HIV, "The immune system is habitually and comprehensively figured through military metaphor."[10] The result is something that Waldby calls the immunological nation-state.

Let's explore the positioning of the individual body as sovereign nation-state (or empire) implicit in the war metaphor. According to Ed Cohen, whose work is foundational to this argument, the immune system's primary charge is to separate self (this is me) from nonself (this is not me). Although Cohen argues that this is ultimately an incoherent conception of human immunity, it remains dominant.[11] The biological winnowing of self from nonself in immunity discourse has an analogous operation on the political level. Who belongs, and who does not belong, in our imagined community? It is no accident that the opening paragraph of Susan Sontag's famous *Illness as Metaphor* likens the immune system to nationality. Sickness, she wrote, is a "more onerous citizen-

---

9. *Wikipedia*, s.v. "immune system"; my emphasis.
10. Waldby, *AIDS and the Body Politic*, 52.
11. Cohen, "Self, Not-Self, Not Not-Self But Not Self."

ship," and "stereotypes of national character" permeate public understandings of sickness.[12]

Emily Martin discussed at length the positioning of the body as autonomous nation-state, noting the implicit racial and gendered hierarchies at work in what she calls the "central image" of both scientific and popular discourses of the immune system.[13] Importantly, Martin's focal object consisted of popular mass-mediated accounts of sickness and health, bringing an important vernacular dimension to the discussion. The fixedness of body-as-nation, as Martin documents, surfaces an interesting question. Which came first—the body at war, or the body as a nation-state (at war)? While both metaphors complement each other, does one have cardinal or architectural status over the other?

Ed Cohen would argue that the war metaphor is primary and that the body-as-nation-state metaphor is a secondary effect or implication. Cohen's influential book *A Body Worth Defending* questioned the naturalness of the immunity-as-defense metaphor from a biopolitical perspective. He writes, "Most of us remain ignorant of a basic historical fact: biological immunity as we know it does not exist until the late nineteenth century. Nor, for that matter, does the idea that organisms defend themselves at the cellular and molecular levels."[14] Cohen showed that immunity, as it emerged as an eighteenth-century medical concept, derived "from Western legal and political accounts . . . for the complex, difficult, and at times violent manner that *humans* live among other *humans*."[15] Immunity-as-defense was a metaphor for human interaction long before it was a medical metaphor, yet biology and medicine depict the immunity-as-defense paradigm as obvious and self-evident. He goes on, "In fact, modern biomedicine embeds modern political ideology when it represents the singular, epidermally bound organism which defends itself against a relentlessly pathogenic environment as a universal fact."[16] For Cohen, immunity is a metaphor first derived from human politics that "helps us reconcile ourselves to the fateful microbes."[17] Cohen's contribution is inestimable here, for his monograph provided the foundation for theorists like me to de-naturalize immunity, to think outside the war metaphor's inevitability.

In a later essay, Cohen continued to trouble the naturalness of the immunity-as-defense metaphor, but this time with the example of autoim-

12. Sontag, *Illness as Metaphor*, 3.
13. Martin, "Toward an Anthropology of Immunology."
14. Cohen, *A Body Worth Defending*, 3.
15. Cohen, *A Body Worth Defending*, 3; emphasis in original.
16. Cohen, *A Body Worth Defending*, 274.
17. Cohen, *A Body Worth Defending*, 5.

mune disorders. As he deftly demonstrates, there is a striking paradox at the heart of the cluster of diseases (including diabetes, multiple sclerosis, lupus, ulcerative colitis, and Guillain-Barré syndrome) designated as autoimmune disorders. If the immune system's primary task is to sort "self" from "non-self," Cohen asks, then isn't a model of disease in which "self-mistakes-self-as-not-self" a contradictory impasse?[18] Cohen persuasively points out that health care providers and medical researchers actually have no idea what triggers autoimmune etiologies. His message is that perhaps we have stuck too long and too doggedly to the defense metaphor, despite its decreasing explanatory value. As Cohen's body of work shows, the war metaphor is (to turn to another metaphor) bankrupt, both ethically and epistemologically. Despite its limited explanatory value, the war metaphor still seems inescapable.

Not only does the war metaphor govern domestic talk about health and disease, but discourses of microbes at war are often pressed into the service of US imperial expansion. Neel Ahuja charts how the defense metaphor materializes across living bodies in uneven states of precarity, arguing that US imperial expansion has been shaped by the attempts of military *and health* officials to control the interactions of humans, animals, viruses, and bacteria at the borders of US American influence. Ahuja's case study of the carceral quarantine of Haitians at Guantánamo Bay in the early nineties showed how US empire biopolitically constituted the HIV-positive Haitian body as "human-viral hybrids" as well as "racial dependents; an excess of movement, contagion, plasticity" that must be contained by military intervention.[19] As they are positioned at the nexus of critical race studies, biopolitics, and affect theory, Ahuja further reminds us that "viruses and bacteria must be approached as world-making species rather than simply as dangerous pests demanding eradication."[20] Ahuja's key contribution is not only that the defense metaphor structures the body's internal "fight" with a disease but also that discourses of health and disease, in turn, structure our national peripheries by generating investments in the imperial state as protector of life.

Ahuja's exhortation to apprehend microbial life as world-making species would be well met within rhetorical studies. Although they do not address microbes, in an essay that charts the world-making effects of genetic metaphors, Marita Gronnvoll and Jamie Landau encourage attunement to the consequences of talking about medical terms in certain ways.[21] Discourses of germs and disease register persistent concerns about "contamination, national

---

18. Cohen, "Self, Not-Self, Not Not-Self But Not Self," 29.
19. Ahuja, *Bioinsecurities*, 171–72.
20. Ahuja, *Bioinsecurities*, 11.
21. Gronnvoll and Landau, "From Viruses to Russian Roulette."

identity, and Otherness," as Cara Finnegan and Lisa Keränen explain in a review essay.[22] Indeed, rhetorical analyses like Huiling Ding's on SARS and Priscilla Wald's on typhoid explain how the rhetoric of a disease is as influential in its spread or treatment as its biological contagion.[23] According to Wald, rhetorics of outbreak affect both survival rates and contagion routes; that is, the way we narrate our interactions with microbes affects how microbes themselves move and work.[24]

As is evident, rhetorical scholars focus nearly exclusively on *pathogenic* microbial others. And for good reason, given the painful experiences and suffering that accompany infectious disease. However, we also need to develop methods to apprehend meetings-with so-called good or neutral microbes. Furthermore, we must be attuned to our microbes in a way that charts our own effects on them. As Hannah Landecker explains, "The bacteria of today are not the bacteria of yesterday, whether that change is registered culturally, genetically, physiologically, ecologically or medically. Bacteria today have different plasmids and traits and interrelations and capacities and distributions and temporalities than bacteria before modern antibiotics."[25] Microbial species are neither static, nor entirely pathogenic pests, nor isolated from human practices—all important lessons for scholars in the humanities to bring to microbial research.

In 2014 Heather Paxson and Stefan Helmreich were the first to identify the advent of the current microbial moment. They were both intrigued by and wary of the ways in which "dominant representations of microbial life have shifted from an idiom of peril to one of promise," noting that microbial life is being held up as a model for interdependent ecosystems. When Paxson coined *microbiopolitics* in 2008, she used the term to extend Foucauldian biopolitics to "recognize and manage human encounters with the organic agencies of bacteria, yeast, fungi, and viruses."[26] Paxson's empirical project focuses on artisanal cheese, although I would argue that the concept of microbiopolitics can be fruitfully used for bacterial relations beyond foodways. As Paxson assists us in considering, a bio/necropolitical hierarchy governs the relations of all living existents, from the microbial to the macrobial.

What is often neglected are critical (rhetorical) treatments of the ways in which popular science discourses of the human microbiome are predicated on gender and race. Jessica Houf is an exception here. Her essay comparing the rhetorics of vaginal and penile microbiomes demonstrates the gendered

22. Finnegan and Keränen, "Review Essay," 225.
23. Ding, *Rhetoric of a Global Epidemic*; Wald, *Contagious*.
24. Wald, *Contagious*.
25. Landecker, "Antibiotic Resistance and the Biology of History," 21.
26. Paxson, *The Life of Cheese*, 160.

nature of microbiome discourse.[27] Looking specifically at reproductive morphology, Houf shows how the vaginal microbiome is positioned as a more appropriate target for microbial colonization than the penile microbiome. Ultimately, Houf argues that these gendered discourses function to maintain our contradictory relationship to microbes as both threats and saviors. Houf models a crucial intervention in her article. Not only is the human microbiome narrowly apprehended in relation to the war metaphor; it is also structured by gendered and sexualized expectations and exclusions.

Even in moments of potential paradigm shift, the war metaphor still forecloses other possibilities for making sense of microbes. Jamie Lorimer's work is an interesting example here. Lorimer draws attention to the way that scientists are reworking the old, entrenched medical binaries, as well as the immunity-as-defense metaphor, in their approach to helminth therapy. Helminths are hookworms that some people purposefully infect themselves with to help with autoimmune disorders. However, it is notable here that while Lorimer allegedly works to undermine the old binary, the shift that he champions is a modest one. Lorimer's tone is sanguine, even celebratory, of this new model of immunity and awareness of multispecies assemblages. "Understood this way, parts of the immune system are not at war with invaders. Instead they are involved in continuous processes of communication, modulation, and diplomacy."[28] That Lorimer would shift the metaphor of warring nation-states to peaceful nation-states supports the overall argument of this literature review; instead of creating a new metaphor, much of human microbiome research is still operating from an old notion of interacting countries. This supports my hypothesis that despite the promises of a paradigm shift, traces of the old defense paradigm seem inescapable.[29]

In sum, the war metaphor pervades science and popular science discourses of health and disease. This results in a rather ironic set of circumstances where, according to Neel Ahuja and others, diseases understood as battles become mobilized to justify actual battles and American exceptionalism. While rhetorical studies developed an impressive body of work in the last twenty years documenting pathogenic rhetorics, we have few conceptual resources available to apprehend our mutualistic or commensal microbial others. Developing this conceptual language would need to incorporate Landecker's recommendation that we understand microbial life as the result of histories of human practices. We would also do well to follow Houf's example

27. Houf, "The Microbial Mother Meets the Independent Organ."

28. Lorimer, "Gut Buddies," 67.

29. Although I do not substantively engage theories of the trace here, I am inspired by Jacques Derrida's "Signature, Event, Context" as well as Christopher Peterson's *Bestial Traces*.

of charting the gendered (not to mention sexualized and racialized) narratives surrounding human microbiome discourse, while eschewing Lorimer's appropriation of the war metaphor into a metaphor of diplomacy. Smuggled into the militarized war metaphor are a host of problematic assumptions about how our human-identified bodies can relate to microbial others.

THE FOCAL ARTIFACT: THE POPULAR SCIENCE OF THE AMERICAN GUT PROJECT

One of the reasons I opened this chapter with Pollan's article is that he cites his experience with the American Gut Project as a turning point in his interest in the human microbiome. The American Gut Project is the largest crowdsourced citizen-science experiment in the world. Aiming to "shed light on the connections between the human microbiome and health,"[30] the American Gut Project operates by recruiting participants (that is, "citizen scientists") to swab their own fecal matter and send the samples to labs in Boulder, Colorado (or, now that Rob Knight has moved his laboratory, to La Jolla, California) for processing. In return, a participant receives information about their personal microbiome. Since 2014 the AGP has processed over ten thousand samples. In fact, according to Pollan, it was after he received by email the "huge, processor-choking file of charts and raw data" from the AGP that he began to think of himself as a "superorganism, rather than a plain old individual human being."[31] In his narrative, Pollan gained a new appreciation for the composite nature of his "self" at precisely the moment when he received a large electronic file from the American Gut Project. This file contained information about the species of microbial life that live in his mouth, on his skin, and inside his intestines, and how his microbial makeup compares with the "average" American human's microbial makeup. As Pollan tells the story, it was upon witnessing this scientific attempt to map his personal "vast uncharted wilderness" that he felt humbled in the face of his own multispecies body.[32] Pollan has authorized the AGP to use his microbiome results for educational and comparative purposes. Everyone who sequences their microbiome with the AGP has the opportunity to compare their guts with Pollan's.

Among the hundreds of artifacts of popular science discourse on the human microbiome that have appeared in the last six years, I take the American Gut Project and its affiliate websites as my primary focal object. The AGP

30. Homepage. http://americangut.org/
31. Pollan, "Some of My Best Friends Are Germs."
32. Pollan, "Some of My Best Friends Are Germs."

is not only the biggest citizen-science project in the world; it often serves as the public face of gut microbiome discourse across multiple media. For example, it is featured or mentioned in a number of books, TEDtalks, a free online course offered by Coursera, and in news articles like Pollan's that I used to open this chapter. In addition to its popular appeal, I am drawn to its hybridity as a genre, as it must straddle the overlapping publics of science and popular science. Consider, on one hand, the rhetorical demand of recruiting tens of thousands of participants and persuading them to pay at least one hundred dollars to participate in the study. On the other hand, scientists at the AGP must not only compel an audience of non-experts but also translate the results of the study into empirical research for an expert audience.

The American Gut Project investigates the relationship between the bacteria in our guts and human health. Here's how it works. To sign up, the AGP directs users to its Fundrazr site. (The AGP also used to have a page on Indiegogo; both Indiegogo and Fundrazr are online platforms for crowd-sourced fundraising.) The AGP crowdsources not only the "biomass" but also some of the costs of the project, with charges beginning at $99.00 to process one sample. As of this writing, the Fundrazr site has raised over $1.8 million and processed over twelve thousand samples—including my own—in the last six years. After payment is collected, the AGP snail-mails participants a kit, which includes sterile swabs and instructions on how to collect a sample. There are options to pay more money (called "claiming perks" in Fundrazr's language) for more comprehensive sampling. For example, $129 will purchase "You Plus the World," a package that funds the processing of your sample along with someone from "either Africa, South America or Asia."[33] At the high-roller end of the spectrum, twenty-five-thousand dollars will net "ultra-deep sequencing of your microbiome sample aimed at generating as many individual bacterial genomes as possible."[34] Claiming this perk would allow an individual to "be among the first in the world to get the most detailed map of your gut microbiome and help us push the state-of-the-art in high-throughput sequence technology of microbial communities." After completing a detailed form online that includes diet and lifestyle information, participants mail their sample to the lab. At the lab, bacterial DNA are isolated and analyzed. An individual's data is aggregated with over ten thousand other samples from humans across the world. The AGP also sends participants a complex document detailing their personal microbial makeup. Participants can compare their microbial

---

33. Fundrazr, "American Gut Project."
34. Fundrazr, "American Gut Project."

profile with those of people with similar BMIs, similar diets, or, of course, with Michael Pollan.

Euphemistic reference to "biomass" does not erase the actual act of shitting on a stick that the AGP requests of its participants. Membership in contemporary civil society generally requires the concealment of one's bowel movements. If shitting is, as Josh Gunn contends, "that erotogenic pleasure that one is to first repress for membership in a given public,"[35] then participation in the American Gut Project reverses the rule. To become a "citizen scientist" of the American Gut Project, a participant must collect and share fecal matter. What's more, they must circulate fecal matter through the public postal system. Perhaps at least some of the popular appeal of the American Gut Project resides in the transgressive pleasure one might take in the exhibitionist act of sharing fecal matter. I certainly found it delightful.

The American Gut Project must be understood in the context of the artifacts and discourses circulating within the popular science public of the human microbiome. Parsing the popular science of the gut microbiome into genres can get messy. What I identify as the recently developed popular science public on the human microbiome shares an important quality with many contemporary pop science publics that center on a particular topic: earnest and careful explanations of research exist alongside pseudoscientific claims exaggerated for headline clickbait or to peddle "alternative" or "natural" health therapies and products. Indeed, referring to these pseudoscientific claims, science journalists like Kavin Senapathy warn us to "keep calm and avoid microbiome mayhem."[36] Here Senapathy describes events such as the online "Microbiome Medicine Summit" which featured, among other entrepreneurs, new-age author Deepak Chopra asserting that our gut bacteria listen to our thoughts. Often earnest and faithful explanations of the recent scientific research (I would put Ed Yong in this camp) blend indistinguishably with the hyperbolic claims of the profit-seekers (like Chopra). For example, Jeff Leach is a scientist who researches the human microbiome, maintains a personal blog, and has professional links to the American Gut Project. Like many participants in the microbiome moment, Leach straddles multiple publics. While I believe it is crucial to distinguish between these genres as a practice of critical rhetorical consumption, both the earnest and the quackery genres circulate around my central artifact of the American Gut Project. To be sure, the digital presentations of these artifacts are arranged and delivered in ways that invite users to make no distinction between these genres. This seems true of

35. Gunn, "ShitText," 81.
36. Senapathy, "Keep Calm and Avoid Microbiome Mayhem."

most pop science publics, but especially so for the contemporary pop science public of the human microbiome. My intention here is not to offer criteria for making distinctions between these genres but to emphasize their ongoing and varied angles of juxtaposition with one another. The messy hybridity of this pop science public is especially compelling to me as a researcher because it is the gateway through which an "average person," perhaps casually Googling the human microbiome, would enter the public.

While the researchers, laboratories, and data processing methods conform to the genre of scientific research, the AGP is necessarily built to interface with a public, insofar as it is dependent on this public for participation by virtue of its research design. Therefore, the AGP produces discourse for a non-expert public, including its website, published interviews with lead researcher Rob Knight, and links to scientific blogs. By way of example, AGP's FAQ page claims, in an informal bro-speak, "Science is coolest when it informs our daily lives and what could possibly be more daily than what goes on in your gut?"[37] In this quotation, we see a rhetorical device often observed across these artifacts—a shift downward in decorum to achieve emphasis. The AGP's rhetoric courts the non-expert by explicitly engaging an informal register. Furthermore, just a few clicked links away from the AGP's website, the curious citizen-scientist might find a range of plans and products for purchase, promising healthier gut microbes. The AGP is a unique hybrid of multiple discursive genres that constitute the popular science public of the human microbiome.

Perhaps the vibrant new-age, self-help industry blossoming around human microbiome research can be attributed to the simple fact of the human microbiome's range of possible promises. While no judicious scientist would agree with, for example, Chopra's claim that our gut bacteria can hear our thoughts, it is easy to see how the romantic promise of the human microbiome has helped produce an active pop science public. In short, the human microbiome intimates promises of curing much of what ails the Western world. Research suggests that our gut microbes work in tandem with our immune systems to the extent that a depletion or "lack of diversity" of microbial species may cause a range of autoimmune and mental health disorders, susceptibility to certain kinds of infection, and even obesity.[38]

Specific artifacts under consideration in the following analysis includes objects such as the AGP's website and affiliate links; websites, products, and other popular science publications by AGP-affiliated personnel; and AGP's

---

37. American Gut Project, "FAQ."
38. Pollan, "Some of My Best Friends Are Germs."

material provided for participants (including recruitment material, text and video instructions, and personalized results). Specifically, I also look at Jessica Green and Karen Guillemin's TED-Ed lesson entitled "You Are Your Microbes," because the AGP's blog links to it. Furthermore, I consider Jeff Leach's blog, because he is one of the co-founders of the American Gut Project. Leach produces a lot of microbiome-related content and frequently references and links to the AGP. With the exception of my personalized gut microbe sequencing results, each of these artifacts is easily accessible for public consumption.

ANALYSIS: *SOMATOPEIA* AT THE AMERICAN GUT PROJECT

This section explores the implications of the war metaphor's sticky inevitability at the American Gut Project. If human bodies are mini-empires, then the necropolitical processes by which empires parse lives can be extrapolated to microbial others. First, I document the way that the American Gut Project collapses microbial Others with human Others—a move made possible by the overarching master metaphor of war. By implication, the relationship between an ideal (white) human body-nation and its inner microbial life is one of postcolonial dependence and control. Furthermore, at the American Gut Project and its affiliated artifacts, microbial life is directly and indirectly conflated with people of color and people of lower socioeconomic status throughout the discourses of the microbiome moment. The ultimate result is the preservation of white supremacy and privilege within American-identified empire.

This chapter explains the zoetrope of somatopeia to name the tropological attribution of a body intelligible to necropolitical ranking. When I refer to *somatopeia* as a zoetrope, I broaden the scope of the classical definition of *somatopeia* to name the tropological means by which we "make body." In the case at hand, there are two important registers of somatopeic manifestation: the individual human body and the national body. Zoetropological theory is useful insofar as it allows us to witness moments where existents are transvalued according to the demands of biopolitical regimes. To become em-bodied, we must be em-bodied somewhere, in hierarchical relation to other bodies *and* in relation to empire. To govern biopolitically is to govern within a hierarchical arrangement. An existent can only be controlled, governed, or measured if that existent has a body that is controllable, governable, or measurable. To be drawn into biopolitical regimes, bodies must become intelligible to biopolitical regimes. Once an existent can be assessed, that existent joins the constant demand of bio/necropolitical winnowing. Some bodies are intelligible to biopolitical fields of vitality-raising (like Pollan's superorganism); some bodies are intelligible to necropolitical fields of killing. Many bodies waver indefinitely in between these two poles. The important thing to recognize here is first that somatopeic embodiment prefigures biopolitical processes, and, therefore, within biopolitical regimes, to be em-bodied is to be em-bodied in relation to an empire. For this reason, this chapter takes this popular science public of the human microbiome as a worthy focal object because the discourses composing this microbiome moment tell a story of how an emerging set of existents becomes intelligible to a biopolitical field of vitality.

In 2016 Ed Yong published *I Contain Multitudes,* one of the best-selling and most enthusiastically reviewed popular science books on the human microbiome.[39] Rob Knight of the American Gut Project is interviewed in Yong's book, as well as Jack Gilbert, Faculty Director of the Microbiome Center of the University of Chicago. When Yong describes Gilbert's project, he unwittingly recapitulates a body-as-empire metaphor:

> Our microbiomes have wide-reaching tendrils that root us in the wider world. Gilbert wants to understand those connections. He wants to be an all-seeing border officer for the human body, who knows exactly which microbes are coming in (and their point of origin), and which ones are leaving (and their destination).[40]

Nations employ border guards to enforce the security of a nation's boundaries. In this metaphor, Gilbert's panoptic ("all-seeing") border officers proffer a new twist on the standard body-as-empire metaphor. Knowledge is linked to power, as the goal of knowing *exactly* which microbes come in and out (a fantasy, of course) is likened to knowing exactly which people come in and out. Yong's use of this metaphor is interesting given the post-Trump national context in which we currently live. Yong's border officers may seem benign, or even friendly, given that their intent is merely to *know,* and not to, say, control, or annihilate. Yet border work, that is, events or practices that make distinctions between existents, unavoidably transvalues.

The title of Yong's sixth chapter beautifully, if unwittingly, underscores my argument about the shift from war to diplomacy. Called "Mutually Assured Success," this chapter explains the various ways in which microbes help organisms digest food, confuse prey, or "otherwise succeed where other species fail."[41] The overarching argument is that mutuality between microbial and

39. Yong, *I Contain Multitudes.*
40. Yong, *I Contain Multitudes,* 253.
41. Yong, *I Contain Multitudes,* 167.

other species supports success for both on an evolutionary scale. Employing a bait-and-switch rhetorical strategy, Yong relies on the reader's knowledge of the phrase *mutually assured destruction* to complete the pattern with a surprise: the substitution of the opposite of destruction, success. A cold war–era concept, *mutually assured destruction* assumes that the global annihilation that would result from a full-scale nuclear attack is in itself an effective deterrent. As in other permutations of the master metaphor, human bodies are nations and microbes are enemies-turned-allies.

At the American Gut Project, the human body and the national body exist in metonymic relation to each other; in other words, they are called on as shorthand to reference each other in a circular relation. First, consider the title itself—American Gut Project. The project is nominally predicated on the discoverable characteristics of a national population, even one whose borders are porous and perhaps even meaningless regarding the composition of gut microbiota. I am not disavowing the utility of the knowledge generated by tracking gut microbiota by geographic region; rather, I suggest that the term *American* in the American Gut Project does more than merely denote a neutral geographical region. Empires are never neutral. The *American* in the American Gut Project intertextually adjoins patriotism, citizenship, belonging, and empire. By way of comparison, consider that the American Gut Project and its sister experiment, the British Gut Project, are hosted under the broader Earth Microbiome Project. Despite the adjective *American* in its title, the AGP actually welcomes samples from around the world. Yet the American Gut Project is American-identified in provenance and execution.

When linked with the concept of *citizen* science, the American Gut Project accrues additional nationalistic overtones. Citizen science describes scientific research projects that enlist "the public" with help with, for example, data collection. There has been a boom in citizen science research projects. The Obama White House hosted a citizen-science day in 2015, and this crowdsourcing of the scientific process has a certain democratic appeal. As James Wynn has documented, we are living in a moment of citizen science.[42] At the same time, we also live in a moment where citizenship indexes a privileged status within an empire. Unfortunately, Wynn does not engage the robust rhetorical literature on critical citizenship in his book on citizen science in the digital age. At face value, I admire the democratizing ethic behind placing knowledge advancement in the hands of the many. I understand that the term *citizen science* is *meant* to imply that everyone pitching in helps scientific

---

42. Wynn, *Citizen Science in the Digital Age.* Presumably because of the digital focus of his book, Wynn does not comment on the American Gut Project, despite its (admittedly, self-proclaimed) status as the largest citizen science project in the world.

advancement, and that we are invited to be citizens *of* science (rather than citizens of a particular nation). As an index of belonging and privilege in the US, ignoring the implications of citizenship as more than a legal status enacts a certain wishful ignorance. I concede that the American Gut Project invites people to become *citizen* scientists, not *citizenship* scientists. Yet the unreflective use of the term *citizen* (endemic to all citizen science projects, not just the AGP) is problematic because citizenship is "intricately implicated with borders and alienage."[43] I am concerned that the citizen of "citizen science" takes on inclusionary/exclusionary properties specifically in the context of the American Gut Project.[44]

The AGP's title addresses the bodily boundary with the term *gut,* marking the inside (and therefore the outside) of the human body. It addresses national boundaries by the term *American,* marking the inside (and therefore the outside) of the nation. However, these boundaries are further explained by Rob Dunn on the AGP's FAQ page: "Your gut is actually, developmentally speaking, the outside of your body, but it has evolved many intricacies that make it seem like the inside. Your gut starts with your mouth and ends with your anus."[45] In the phrase *American Gut Project, gut* can operate both as adjective and noun. As an adjective (as the researchers likely intended), both *American* and *Gut* describe the noun *Project.* However, as a noun, a collective *American Gut* modifies *Project.* In this second permutation, the fiction of one, singular *American Gut,* presumably the compilation of the gut microbes of all American citizens, becomes problematic. The project itself makes no distinction between these two vacillations of *gut.*

As KC Councilor writes, metaphors of digestion are commonly invoked to explain American relationships to the other. Here again we have a somatopeic conflation—human *and* national bodies are both engaged in a process of digestion. Although Councilor's essay focuses on Progressive-era immigration rhetoric, we still today can see the way that a fictitious "american gut" is a central metaphor for how our nation meets with others. Often American-identified rhetorics belie a fear of being consumed themselves. Councilor explains,

> Because eating is necessary to sustain life, and because of the physical vulnerability inherent in the act of eating, anxieties over racialized encounters often emerge as anxieties about foreign foods and strange eating cultures.

43. Cisneros, "Rhetorics of Citizenship."
44. For a different take on citizen science, see Ruha Benjamin, *People's Science.*
45. Dunn, "FAQs." For the sake of underscoring the ways in which these artifacts are networked together, note that there is a link to the FAQ page on both the official AGP site and Leach's blog.

This anxiety is frequently about what happens *after* a person eats or drinks, not only about the act of eating in the moment, but what happens in someone's gut over the next hours and days—a space where there is a lack of control, where the body's processes take over. Digestion is particularly salient because of the ways that race in the United States has always been constructed through discourses that center on and through the body.[46]

In sum, Councilor's description of eating and digestion as acts of vulnerability show how bodies meeting others (in this case, immigrants) serve as a metaphor for how nations meet others.

Alongside the title of the American Gut Project, and its citizen-science status, consider the logo. The AGP's logo, stamped on most of its physical and virtual materials, features five man-shaped icons of varying colors (exactly the same as the classic male toilet icon, except arms are slightly raised). The words "american gut" are in all lower-case letters, suggesting a desire for instant brand readability. The first four crudely index an array of skin tones—brown, sienna, yellow, beige. The fifth male icon is patterned with the bright stars-and-stripes of the American flag. The American-flag-patterned male icon also presents as catachresis, or deliberate error. The series reads from left to right: person of color, person of color, person of color, white person, American-flag-colored person. The last of these clearly departs from the pattern. The deliberate error conflates race (as depicted by different skin colors) with nationality (as depicted by the American flag). Importantly, the flag-patterned person punctuates the series, communicating that no matter the color on the outside, participants of the project are all American on the inside. In other words, to be American is its own race. The AGP, therefore, is in the business of colorblindness. While they collect racial identification as a part of their demographic questionnaire, race as an experience of structural violence and exclusion is dismissed. The logo hints at a broader assumption undergirding the AGP, which is that skin color (i.e., "race") is a shallow, surface-level difference, and that inside, we all have the same processes and relations of gut bacteria.

At the same time, the AGP is premised on the idea that each of us has a unique microbiome, occasionally referred to as a microbial fingerprint. The AGP's technology is required to "see" this difference. The implicitly male icons are arranged with their hands just barely touching, or about to touch, which I read as a reference both to the hand-to-hand exchange of bacteria and to the together-we-achieve-more ethos of citizen science. Taking it at face value, one could say that the AGP's logo appeals to diversity and equality. That was

---

46. Councilor, "Feeding the Body Politic," 143.

likely the intention. But to invoke a colorblind approach while simultaneously invoking American empire (in the case of the flag) centralizes American-identified belonging. The AGP's logo appeals to a facile notion of biodiversity. However, instead of diversity being shorthand for the inclusion of people of color, it is about the inclusion of multiple different microbes.

Catchphrases often heard alongside diversity, such as "revitalization," are common at the AGP. The AGP posted a TED-Ed video on their Fundrazr site called "You Are Your Microbes." In this four-minute animated short, we learn that our guts are "teeming metropolises of interacting microbes." As the video goes on, they develop a blue-collar career metaphor whereby each microbe is well-suited to its particular job:

> Food made of complex molecules like an apple requires lots of different microbial workers to break it down. But if a food is made of simple molecules like a lollipop, some of these workers are put out of a job. Those workers leave the city, never to return. What doesn't function well are gut microbial communities with only a few different types of workers. . . . We don't fully understand the best way to manage our individual microbial societies, but it is likely that . . . eating a varied diet of complex plant-based foods can help revitalize our microbial ecosystems in our gut and across the entire landscape of our body.[47]

As a woman's voice narrates this script, we see a set of cartoon mini-blob "workers" get carried away on a factory lift at the mention of a lollipop diet, and then returned to the worksite on the same lift at the mention of a varied, plant-based diet. On the "bustling streets" of our guts, each species of microbe is visually portrayed as having a different low-skill job, such as breaking down cellulose (depicted as cartoon blobs with hammers). In this particular case, if the tenor of this metaphor is gut microbes, the vehicles are specialized *blue-collar workers* living in *cities*.[48]

To spell it out, the diversity of gut microbes is equated with the diversity of people living in a city. Nascent in this analogy, then, is the second-person "you" toward whom the video is addressed. "You" must necessarily be a white-collar citizen, in charge of city-level planning. "You" are someone with a *noblesse oblige* duty to care for your gut microbes. Considered in this light,

---

47. Green and Guillemin, "You Are Your Microbes."

48. When she compared immune system discourses in 1992 to those of global capital, Emily Martin ("The End of the Body?") noted that both discourses emphasized flexible accumulation and time/space compression. This is very different than the old-timey factory model reproduced in this video about human gut microbes.

a clear ethic of paternalism emerges. As Green narrates in the video, "Our bodies are homes to millions of different microbes, and we need them just as much as they need us."[49] Like colonial paternalism, practices of care ultimately stand to benefit the colonizers just as much as, if not more than, the colonized. Rarely do arguments advocating microbial diversity frame the benefits as for the microbes themselves.

Othering Microbes

Thus far I have observed the subtle ways in which microbial life and people of color are metonymically linked in discourses at the American Gut Project. The rest of this section explores a more directly racially charged discourse. One co-founder of the AGP, a biologist named Jeff Leach, publishes a blog linked from the AGP's website. Some of the AGP's content links to his blog, and his blog often pronounces the successes of the AGP. I discuss Jeff Leach's writing at length here not only because he is a significant node of the popular science microbiome public but also because of the racist sentiments in which he traffics. While it would be tempting to indict Leach as well-meaning but clueless regarding global and national histories of oppression, my aim lies elsewhere. Jeff Leach's racist microbiome rhetoric underscores the empire-building impulses circumscribed in the master metaphor of war.

One of Leach's blog posts is called "Going Feral: My One-Year Journey into Acquiring the Healthiest Gut Microbiome in the World." In this post, Leach describes his travel to Tanzania, to live among the Hadza people and study and sample their microbiota. As he explains, biologists are interested in Hadza microbiomes because the Hadza live a hunter-gatherer lifestyle, and therefore their microbiomes may be similar to our "ancestral" microbiomes. The Western diet and pervasive antibiotic use have led to an impoverished Western gut that lacks the rich microbial diversity of our "ancestral" microbiomes. As Leach expounds:

> My little experiment coupled with a steady flow of papers suggesting diet and lifestyle can dramatically impact your gut microbial composition in short period of time, has led me to my 2014 goal of acquiring and *catching* the healthiest gut microbiome in the world. By catching, I mean it's not all

---

49. Green and Guillemin, "You Are Your Microbes."

about what you eat, but how and where you live—and whom you live with—
and your interaction with the microbial world around us.[50]

In this excerpt, Leach appropriates his emphasized verb *catch* cleverly. Used
colloquially, we "catch" colds and other illnesses, or more precisely, we "catch"
the viruses or bacteria that lead to colds and illnesses. Leach stretches the col-
loquialism to imply that we can also "catch" other kinds of microbial life, even
beneficial and neutral microbes.

Across many of Leach's publications (including his book, *Rewild: You're
99% Microbe*), people of color are represented as animals. Leach describes his
time with the Hadza as "going feral." The *Oxford English Dictionary* supplies
two definitions for feral. The first reads, "(especially of an animal) in a wild
state, especially after escape from captivity or domestication," and the second
reads, "resembling a wild animal." As a descriptor, feral unavoidably implies
nonhuman animal life. To live like the Hadza, for Leach, is to live like an
animal. There is a long and well-documented history of discursively linking
racialized others to animals. Describing Hadza people as feral also rehashes
the bogus postcolonial distinction between culturally advanced and civilized
white people and backwards, primal, dark others. Unfortunately, Leach is
deeply invested in this advanced/primitive distinction, describing the Hadza
people as a "free living population that is still intimately connected with
nature."[51] It is not only the Hadza who are animalized. In his book (which is
mostly a collection of his blog posts), Leach titles a chapter "Slumdog Microbiome More Diverse."[52] The "slumdogs" he refers to here are children from
Bangladesh. In his publications, Leach unwittingly endorses the racialized
hierarchy that is the incessant work of necropolitics. The affordance of naming this "going feral" as somatopeia first draws attention to it as a trope, as
a figure of speech. Just as sin, in our previous example, is given a particular
embodied form by "crouching," a collective "we" are given an embodied form
in relation to ferality. Bodies are made intelligible, and then again newly intelligible, through zoetroping.

In Leach's blog, the metonymical elision of person of color with simian
traffics in both textual and visual registers (see figure 2). Accompanying the
"going feral" post is an image of Leach sitting on a rock next to a small, brown,
presumably Hadza child. While they do not seem to be communicating with
each other, their encounter is a close one. Their proximity in the image—their
legs may be touching—visually supplements Leach's notion of "catching" a

---

50. Leach, "Going Feral."
51. Leach, "(Re)Becoming Human."
52. Leach, "Slum Dog Microbiome More Diverse."

⌂ Home / Human Food Project / Going Feral: my one-year journey to acquire the healthiest gut microbiome in the world (you heard me!)

GOING FERAL: MY ONE-YEAR JOURNEY TO ACQUIRE THE HEALTHIEST GUT MICROBIOME IN THE WORLD (YOU HEARD ME!)

🍴   Jeff Leach   January 19, 2014   Human Food Project   319 Comments

FIGURE 2. Screenshot of Jeff Leach's *Human Food Project* blog. By permission of Jeff Leach.

more diverse microbiome through Hadza contact. Here the brown child may be read as a less developed, more "primitive" human in comparison to the white adult. Their juxtaposition, with the child on the left and Leach on the right, is a reminder that all elements of the Great Chain of Being are contiguous with each other. This contiguity, or sustained categorical "touching," is a resource for zoetropological movement. Reinforcing this barely there tease of a touch is a sidebar advertisement of Leach's book, *Rewild*. The book's cover features a drawing of a white male human hand on the left barely grazing the fingers of a dark brown simian hand on the right. Like its referent, Michelangelo's famous painting *The Creation of Adam*, the image infuses the power of touch (contact) with the great potential of the *creation* of new life—albeit very tiny life. Recall that this trace of touch is also represented in the stick figures holding hands on the AGP's official logo. As Neel Ahuja reminds us, "The racialization of transborder epidemics—the use of the media to activate the feeling of bodily risk through the touch of foreign bodies and environments— played an important role in generating public optimism in the imperial state as protector of life."[53] In science blogger Jeff Leach's symbolic universe, rubbing up against other elements on the Great Chain of Being (God abutting man, chimpanzee abutting human, brown child abutting white adult) creates pathways for seeding new microbial life. However, instead of generating affective investments in the imperial state as protector, as is the case with Ahuja's trans-

---

53. Ahuja, *Bioinsecurities*, 5.

border epidemics, we are invited to generate affective investments in microbial science.

The diverse, microbial others of our gut inhabit a landscape very similar to the romanticized "dark Africa." The gut is consistently referred to a lush rainforest. "Not many people get to go to the rainforest to search for, much less discover, a new kind of monkey, but a new kind of bacterium, well, it is within (your toilet paper's) reach."[54] Compare this with Pollan's description of our "interior wilderness" and Rob Dunn's insistence on the "wild life" inside of our bodies.[55] Jeff Leach also writes of the "slimy vastness" of our intestinal tracts.[56] In the classic *Wilderness and the American Mind,* now in its fifth edition, Roderick Frazier Nash unpacks wilderness etymologically, sharing that *wilder* is a collapse of *wild-deor,* or wild beast; that is, creatures far from the civilizing control of man.[57] This beastly origin of wilderness coalesces with colonial notions of indigenous savagery and of people of color living in the "completely wild and untamed state" far from humanhood.[58] Central to the argument at hand, as Nash demonstrates later in his book, are claims to wilderness uniquely grounded in American nationalism.

There is a crucial slippage here regarding (bio)diversity. Pollan, Leach, and others lament the lack of biodiversity in the "impoverished" Western gut. Indeed, even when popularizers of science caution that we do not yet know enough about our gut microbiota to start manipulating them, they seem to agree that diverse gut microbes equal healthier humans. To resolve this lack of diversity in his own gut, Leach turns to people of color living in the Global South—to the Hadza or Bangladeshi children. In seeking out the Hadza in order to diversify his gut, he conflates racial diversity (as both neoliberal catchphrase and ethical call) with microbial biodiversity. In both cases, the call for (bio)diversity is understood as an unconditional public good as well as a practice of inclusion that must be managed by an implicitly white human existent.

At one point (and, as he confesses, against the better advice of his colleagues), Leach decides to perform a fecal transplant on himself. In a blog post entitled "(Re)Becoming Human," Leach explains, "I wanted to know if my western diet and lifestyle could rapidly destroy this newly acquired diversity in a short period of time."[59] He locates a Hadza man of roughly his same age, and they use a turkey baster to insert the Hadza man's fecal matter into

54. American Gut Project, "Overview."
55. Dunn, *The Wild Life of Our Bodies.*
56. Leach, "(Re)Becoming Human."
57. Nash, *Wilderness and the American Mind,* 1.
58. Blake, *The African Origins of Rhetoric.*
59. Leach, "(Re)Becoming Human."

his own anus. In a reversal of Freudian anal retentiveness, we have an example of anal consumption, shown here as a white man anally consuming the enviable (bio)diversity of what he conceives as the feral other. Mouth and anus are conflated as modes of consuming something other than oneself. After his experiment, he writes, "So how did I feel after the transplant? Not that much different other than—as it was pointed out to me by my girlfriend—I seemed to be farting a lot less—a lot less! Didn't really notice any change in my mood or my bow hunting skills either!"[60] One image on the blog shows Leach leaning forward to drink from a puddle with a caption that describes the action as drinking "that flavorful baboon shit laden water."[61]

The gut microbes of both the so-called slumdog children of Bangladesh and the Hadza people—and, by extension, other racially, geographically, or economically othered people—are positioned as an extractive resource available for use by whites. While Leach is unclear about how exactly he recruited his fecal donor, I presume that larger questions of who owns a group's microbiome, which includes microbes and their genetic material, were not considered. By way of comparison, consider Jenny Reardon and Kim TallBear's discussion of genomic science's attempts to access the DNA of indigenous peoples in the Human Diversity Genome Project. Regardless of the good intentions of researchers, both the Hadza sampling project and the Human Diversity Genome Project maintained "old links between whiteness and property."[62] The predictable attributions of authority represented by the Great Chain of Being remained intact as well. In these cases, science is attributed more authority and more access to the realm of truth than indigenous knowledges.

In this hierarchy, feral humans living close to nature (as opposed to culture) offer the key to a host of modern Western health ailments. Eating for microbial diversity expresses a nostalgia for a time when human dietary practices better supported human physiology. In this way, the discourse of microbiome diversity compares closely to another current trend: the Paleo(lithic) diet. As Adrienne Rose Bitar observes, locating civilization as the cause of ill health and endorsing the return to a mythic "primitive" utopia is somewhat of an American dietary tradition. This mythic utopia is a "prehistoric dreamland characterized by health, community, friendship, and a natural division of leisurely labor," as Bitar writes in an analysis of Paleo diet guidebooks.[63] As Leach lives and works among the Hadza, he locates the Hadza as occupying this temporal space of vague before-ness. When Leach refers to "my donor's ancestral

60. Leach, "(Re)Becoming Human."
61. Leach, "Microbial Diversity."
62. Reardon and TallBear, "Your DNA Is Our History," S234.
63. Bitar, *Diet and the Disease of Civilization,* 44.

microbial ecosystem," this temporal positioning allows Leach to romantically and longingly imbue the Hadza with the secrets to health.

Resonant chimes with sex and sexuality pervade the blog. Leach jokes, subtly and parenthetically, about his friends buying him the largest turkey baster they could find for his fecal transplant. This jokey homophobia twins with homophobic desire, as one imagines Leach's friends thinking about inserting a larger rather than smaller object in his anus. Furthermore, turkey basters are the colloquial low-tech solution to artificial insemination, often associated with lesbian parenthood. In a queer doubling of the pregnant body, Leach's post-injection bodily position mimics the iconic position of a woman trying to not let semen leak out of her vagina: "I pedaled an imaginary upside down bicycle in the air to pass the time as I struggled to make sure my new gut ecosystem stayed put inside me."[64] Substituting fecal matter for semen, Leach's "transplant" belies longing for a queer life to take hold. As Gunn, invoking Jacques Lacan and Slajov Zizek, writes of the "fecal gift," the problem of what do with feces marks the distinction between human and animal.[65] Leach's punchy prose seems gleefully aware of what Gunn would call the erotogenic pleasures of transgression regarding shit.

To clarify, I do not believe it was Leach's *intention* to participate in or perpetuate a racialized hierarchy; his intention was to invite people to read his blog posts. But despite his intentions, there are consequences not only for people of color but also for the Westerners invited to "go feral" along with him. Going feral, or what Leach also calls "rewild[ing]," for a privileged, Western body, kindles nostalgia for a simpler way of being that we have somehow collectively left behind. Repeatedly, Leach refers to the Hadza's microbiome as our collective "ancestral" microbiome. In this case, Leach's somatopeic conflation presumes first that our Western bodies are not feral, or are no longer feral, and therefore are civilized humans.

Furthermore, Leach should not be considered a rogue actor or an unintentionally racist person amid otherwise well-intentioned scientists. On the contrary, he is embedded and respected within a scientific community that produces a number of peer-reviewed research essays on microbial work. His website formally affiliates him with the American Gut Project. Given that Leach himself is a scientist writing for both scholarly and popular audiences, his blog epitomizes the hybridity of these mutually embedded discourses. It would be a mistake to assume that gut microbiome scientific discourse is neutral while the popular culture responses to it are racialized; instead, both

---

64. Leach, "(Re)Becoming Human."

65. Gunn, "ShitText," 89. It is interesting to juxtapose Leach's shit talk with President Donald Trump's recent description of many countries in the Global South as "shithole countries." Both discourses use feces to racialize.

expert and lay discourses participate in the racialization of gut microbiomes, albeit on different registers. It is important to acknowledge here that while Leach represents one example of popular culture taking up microbial life, he should not be dismissed as an aberration but rather seen as an example of the racialized discourses nascent in human microbiome research.

When an entity is somatopeically embodied, or shifted, one of the questions we can ask is, "What kind of body is being made here; what are its features, limitations, acts, and habits?" In the case of Jeff Leach's quest for somatopeic re-forming of his own body, the body being formed here is well resourced and knowledgeably cultivates its own microbial garden with benevolent affection for its garden's inhabitants. In another blog post, Leach writes that all of us, "every last one us, are in varying stages of gut dysbiosis." After reading about his descriptions of the Hadza gut, one can see that the Hadza are not invited into the not-so-inclusive *us* that Leach uses here. The resonances between this body and the national body obtain. If nation and body are somatopeically conflated in the American Gut Project rhetoric, what kinds of body, and what kind of nation, are idealized? The answer to these questions, respectively are *white bodies* and *white nations*.

The precise affordance of somatopeia as a zoetrope is to mark the moment where figurative devices of language are uniquely conducive and persuasive to the hierarchy-making necessary for the necropolitical machine. The American Gut Project demonstrates the inescapability of war as a metaphor for immunity. Even when the scientists at the AGP want to promote an understanding of microbes as friends rather than enemies, they still sip from a well of meaning in which war defines how a nation-state approaches Others. While it may seem like the friend/symbiont approach to microbes is actually the opposite of the enemy/pathogen approach, both approaches still employ *the same exact metaphor*. To wit, in both cases the tenor of the metaphor is the immune system, or more broadly the structures and processes of the body that function to protect an entity. The vehicle of the metaphor is the nation-state. Whether we approach microbes with war or with diplomacy, the mood of the metaphor may change but its entailments remain the same. In our current microbiomania moment, we are consistently invited to understand the human body as an empire in miniature—with all the relations of hierarchy, resource extraction, and racialization concomitant with empire.

CONCLUSION: MAKING MULTISPECIES HUMANHOOD

We are much less human, and much more microbial other, than we think. Yet somehow we are able to meet our microbial others agog with feverish awe and wonder. I submit that this is because we are invited to manage our microbial others in a way that is sharply reminiscent of the way the first world rules the rest—from a subordinating domination to a subordinating paternalism. Broadly concurrent with Black Lives Matter and Donald Trump's xenophobic presidential campaign and early presidency, the microbiome moment operates within a time of high national anxiety about race. (Tellingly, there is even a Facebook account entitled "Microbial Lives Matter.") The nascent link between microbial others and people of color exists in the rhetoric of much of the popular science public on the gut microbiome, and rises to fever pitch in the musings of one particularly careless blogging scientist.

In the emergent popular science discourse on the human microbiome, the national body and the human body are often co-constructed simultaneously; to make a nation is to make bodies in which to govern. The zoerhetorics by which we absorb our gut microbes are an opportunity to track the rituals of confirmation and repudiation that humanhood must continually undergo. In the narrative I have told here about the gut microbiome, humanhood has rhetorically absorbed gut microbes, thereby temporary redrawing the borders of the human. Importantly, the means by which we craft and recraft these borders are not arbitrary or neutral; rather, they are recrafted to favor power. In other words, the absorption of gut microbes into the status marker of humanhood yields or maintains more power than any logical alternatives by preserving a paternal/colonizing relation to the other. The "other" here is a metonymically shifting cast of microbes, people of color with the US, and people of color from other countries. The rhetorics of destruction and annihilation that have worked in the past for both microbial others and racial others work no longer; and microbes model a rhetoric of absorption that preserves power relations.

When I first began sniffing out the subtexts of race and ethnicity in the discourse of popular science on the human microbiome, I was convinced that the microbiome was acting as a proxy for these divisive contemporary issues. That is to say, I assumed that American-identified publics were struggling through the fraught contemporary issues such as demographic shifts and immigration as they discussed the human microbiome. While I still believe this is true to some extent, what is even more profound, as I have discovered over the course of this research, are the ways in which a racial ontology structures the discourse of the human microbiome in the first place. Given the long history of subordinating human relations, perhaps this should not be surprising. When researchers talk about discursive resources, they often use the metaphor of a body of water: a *pool* of discursive resources. Language users engaging with the human microbiome seeming to be pulling the same hideous fish out of the pool, over and over again. That hideous fish? Dominance and subordination.

A tenet of zoerhetorical theory states that to be attributed liveliness immediately means being absorbed into necropolitical regulation. How are the gut microbes of American-identified humans necropolitically regulated? They are regulated by discourses of in/corporation into an existing regime of living (the human body), dominated by the metaphors of acquisition ("catching") and cultivation ("growing"). This incorporation is then conditioned by zoerhetorical appeals to the diversity and health benefits of gut microbes—appeals that closely mirror appeals to diversity and health in public life. Note that the benefits of gut microbes are not available for all American-identified humans. Instead, they are available for the privileged humans whose lives are nourished toward vitality.

Zoetropological theory offers a pathway for understanding how some lives come to matter and some lives fail to matter. If necropolitical regimes function as machines for producing bodies nourished toward life, neglected for deterioration, and targeted for death, then zoetropes are one means by which these inequalities are publicly justified and legitimated. They are a set of mechanisms by which we are compelled to participate in these inequalities. Existents on the necropolitical hierarchy are attributed a status superimposed from the exterior, and then subject to the series of status contestations demanded of hierarchical differentiation. In this chapter, I read the American Gut Project partially for its implicit *pedagogical* directives. The AGP *teaches* people how to interact with, understand, and ultimately curate their gut microbiota. As such, the AGP produces and encourages particular understandings of gut microbiota, such as where "we" end and our microbiota begin. And because talking about boundaries and borders *always* means talking about power, the AGP reproduces particular power relationships between humans and other existents.

The next chapter engages a case study of different existents that, welcome or not, reside in abdomens: fetuses. While the gut microbe is rhetorically absorbed into the human body as one superorganism (or, sometimes, supraorganism), the fetus is rhetorically separated and *addressed* as a separate human. While popular science rhetoric on the gut microbe is fairly emergent and new, the fetus is marked by its historical and ongoing political intractability. And finally, while the discourse of cultivation permeates the popular science public of human gut microbes, we usually conceive of the human fetus in terms of care rather than cultivation, or obligation rather than war. Fetal life is swept into an altogether different set of zoetropological forces, marked not by paternalistic bodies-as-empires but instead by gendered imperatives of motherhood.

CHAPTER 3

Fetuses at the National
Memorial for the Unborn

My precious babies in Heaven—I will be your voice!
—Hannah Rose Allen, on a letter left at the National Memorial for the Unborn

I am so sorry to have aborted you. But I guess that's life. Or not life, in your case.
—Anonymous, on a postcard sent to the National Memorial for the Unborn

AT THE CENTER of one of the most intractably deadlocked public debates, the fetus floats silently. As the target of political, legal, medical, vernacular, and religious communicative practices that address its flourishing as well as its termination, the fetus is among the most publicly contested existents of the twenty-first century. The fetus as an object of reproductive control has occupied controversial political space in the US since at least the 1800s,[1] but the debate's recent instantiation since the 1980s as a recurring issue of the "culture wars" continues to divide political factions today. As I write this, the *New York Times* is running a headline that locates abortion, and therefore fetal life, as a key point of friction in the most recent round of national health care debates: "Abortion Adds Obstacle as Republicans Plan to Unveil Health Bill."[2] On the state level, in just the last two years, over one thousand provisions have been introduced to ban abortion, grant embryos or fetuses legal personhood, or

---

1. Linda Gordon, in her comprehensive history of birth control, *The Moral Property of Women: A History of Birth Control Politics in America*, 58, 106, cites the early nineteenth century as a time of increased fetal contestation. But we can cast the net back as far as antiquity: Aristotle's writing on the "potency" of human embryos and their sequential acquisitions of "sensitive" and then "rational" souls marks early debates around fetal becoming. See Ford, *When Did I Begin*, 37.

2. Pear and Kaplan, "Abortion Adds Obstacle as Republicans Plan to Unveil Health Bill."

restrict the efforts of abortion providers. At the same time, 21 percent of all pregnancies in the US end in abortion, and over one million legal abortions occur in the US every year.[3]

Amid this fray, in the past twenty years, pro-life communities have developed and embraced the practice of fetal memorialization, the commemoration of aborted or miscarried unborn babies. Central to these fetal memorial practices is the National Memorial for the Unborn (NMU) in Chattanooga, Tennessee. The NMU is not only the largest and oldest facility in the United States dedicated to unborn memorialization but also the only one to declare a relationship to the nation in its title.[4] Since 1994 the NMU has been open seven days a week to provide a space where the nation's unborn can be remembered and grieved. Meanwhile, an adjoining office in the crisis pregnancy center next door provides an online presence and logistical support for at least fifteen smaller memorials to the unborn scattered across the country. Installed on the NMU's imposing fifty-foot granite Wall of Names are hundreds of inscribed brass nameplates, each dedicated to an unborn baby.

The NMU heavily invests in the status of the fetus. This contestation over the fetus stands to tell us something important about how humanhood is rhetorically mediated across publics. For its rhetorical force, fetal memorialization relies on the rhetorical construction of the fetal entity as a full-fledged human. The theory of zoetropes that I advance here attempts to explain how the assessed social worth of fetal existents is rhetorically transvalued upwards toward the consequential status threshold of humanhood. The *zoe-* prefix of zoetropes derives from the ancient Greek word for all living beings. The term *zoetrope* shares a name with a Victorian-era toy that serves as a useful metaphor for zoetropological rhetorics. Just as the optically illusive device creates animated "life" in the movement of its turning, life is also "created" in the turning/troping movement of zoetropological rhetorics. In this chapter, I seek to understand the rhetorical practices that modulate the social status or value of various existents as they occur within the National Memorial for the Unborn. At the NMU, the unborn rhetorically accumulate or solidify humanhood in iterable, prescriptive, and tropological ways.

More recently, the fetal rights movement has been absorbed into a broader right-to-life movement that also includes within its purview the rights of stem cells and brain-dead persons.[5] But it is not just these existents whose social

---

3. Guttmacher Institute, "Fact Sheet."

4. See Fixmer-Oraiz, *Homeland Maternity,* for a discussion of the ways in which reproductive anxieties, maternity, and US patriotism are enmeshed.

5. The National Right to Life organization includes health care rationing and euthanasia, in addition to abortion, among the issues for which it advocates.

worth is rhetorically mediated or politically contested. And even though most scholars of rhetoric would agree that the status, value, or worth of various living entities is rhetorically mediated and constituted, there is not yet a clear theoretical framework for understanding the material-discursive formations through which these transvaluations occur. Furthermore, it is not farfetched to claim that these transvaluations are a matter of life and death, as the extent to which existents are valued in the public sphere largely determines the manner in which they are treated. Perhaps no group knows this to be true more than the pro-lifers, whose consistent and often successful rhetorical strategy has been the attribution of humanhood to fetal existents.

The chapter proceeds as follows: after a chronospatial tour of the NMU, I collate four ways in which fetal existents are attributed humanhood at the NMU. I call these four zoetropes that promote the status of the fetal entity naming (antonomasia), en-voicing (apostrophe), en-facing (prosopopeia), and em-bodying (somatopeia). Zoetropes, or rhetorical devices that modulate an entity's social status, demonstrate the constitutive nature of tropes in biopolitical regimes. But before I embark, I want to discuss candidly the perils and pleasures of doing field work in a pro-life community, and how to "figure the fetus" in a way that is true to my pro-choice, feminist-identified political project.

HOW TO FIGURE THE FETUS

The fetus is among the most politically contested existents in the US, and for good reason—high stakes accompany how we approach fetal life. Feminist political projects strive to strike a balance between adequately addressing and inadvertently recentering fetal life. On one hand, there is a palpable fear that comes with any feminist discussion of the fetus, almost as if any acknowledgment grants fetal life the substantiality of humanhood that the pro-life community claims for it. The effort to avoid the substantiality of fetal life is understandable, but can be taken to the extreme. For example, some feminists dismissively attribute a false consciousness to women grieving an abortion or a miscarriage, thereby disregarding the lived experiences of these women.[6] We would be obdurately wrongheaded to think that the fetus—as public icon, index of cultural values, and yes, even vital social actor—could be willed out of existence by the magic of our inattention.

---

6. Keane, "Foetal Personhood and Representations of the Absent Child."

On the opposite hand, some scholarship attends to fetal life but fails to orient inquiry around an ethical project attuned to the lived and embodied experiences of fecund persons.[7] Like the first camp, scholars in this camp may unwittingly omit the lived experiences of people with uteruses.[8] A common critique leveled at this camp might be, "Whither the woman?"[9] Despite these difficulties, figure the fetus we must, precisely because we are invested—for many of us, invested at a visceral level of embodiment—in fetal zoerhetorics.

How do we navigate between the Scylla of avoiding the fetus and the Charybdis of centering it at the expense of women? Jane Bennett's "thing power" and the assemblage approach more generally allow me to sidestep this debilitating tension in feminist approaches to the fetus. I conceive of the fetus as an object with thing power in the same way that my heart or my liver matter and act in the world.[10] In other words, the fetus is a vibrant actant that participates in any number of material-discursive assemblages. This allows us to grant the fetus substantiality as an actor without falling into discourses of humanist obligations such as "fetal rights." For the public in which the NMU persuasively circulates, the fetal entity is a potent actor indeed. In sum, when I use the terms *unborn* and *baby*, I deeply fear and respect the political consequences of these terms for fecund persons.

To further illustrate the complex political ground here, consider the stakes of using any of the available names for the entities commemorated at fetal memorialization sites. There is no publicly circulated term for the fetal entity entirely void of status investments. Consider the forces at work in the following ranked list of public names, both medical and vernacular, for current or former fetal entities: zygote, embryoblast, embryo, fetus, aborted baby, unborn baby, baby, child. (Technically, embryologists refer to the embryo as a fetus roughly eight weeks after fertilization, or ten weeks after last menstrual period.[11]) The plurality of available names for the embryonic/fetal entity is made possible by the conceptual elision, or what John Lynch called the "metonymic

---

7. I recognize that *people with uteruses* and *fecund persons* are awkward discursive constructions. However, I want to explicitly acknowledge that persons with a range of gender identifications can be fertile, such as a transman or a gender-nonconforming person. Moreover, not all "women" are fertile, or will be fertile, or have been fertile. When I use these constructions, I refer to persons who have the physiological capacity to bear fetal life.

8. Jason Edward Black's "Extending the Rights of Personhood, Voice, and Life to Sensate Others" exemplifies this camp for me.

9. Jacqueline Rhodes levels such a critique against a previous version of this chapter. Rhodes, "Counterpoint: Calling Out Publics."

10. Bennett, *Vibrant Matter*.

11. Zygotes become structures called blastocysts about five days after fertilization, the inner cell mass of which is referred to as an embryoblast. In humans the formation is technically called an embryo from the first cell division until eight weeks after fertilization (or roughly

reduction," of all embryonic/fetal entities, regardless of their state of development.[12] This conceptual collapse provides the foundation for a wild vacillation of status assignations for the fetal entity. This vacillation is evident in the range between, on one end, the term *zygote* (a single diploid cell, often considered the beginning of life in pro-life rhetorics) and, on the other end, referring to the embryonic/fetal entity with a first name or even nickname. Throughout this chapter, I follow the standard ethnographic practice of using the terms emic to the field site when making references regarding the NMU. For example, like the NMU itself and the women I interviewed there, I refer to fetuses as the unborn or as unborn babies.

My feminist-identified political project resists the inclusion of fetal entities into the threshold of humanhood, especially when already-born people often do not enjoy such broad and inviting norms of inclusion. As I develop below, humanhood is perhaps the most consequential, yet also the most furiously debated, status threshold. Fetal entities, especially, are rhetorically contested around the threshold of humanhood. While attributions of humanhood come to fuller fruition when a fetal entity is given a name, as is the encouraged practice at the NMU, attributions of humanness are also evident in terms like "aborted baby" and "unborn baby." In order to be a baby, one must be human. Depending on political orientation, "unborn babies" or "aborted babies" are either sacred children, foolish oxymorons, or somewhere in between. For approaching fetal memorialization writ broadly, I find political traction in a term that feminist reproductive theorists have been using since the eighties: the public fetus. I find analytical traction in a term coined by Nathan Stormer: prenatal space.[13]

THE PUBLIC FETUS IN PRENATAL SPACE

As a public icon, the fetus serves as an index of cultural values around innocence, medical risk, femininity, and maternity in the public sphere. The concept of the public fetus reminds us that fetal photographs, ultrasound images, and even the mutilated fetuses pasted on anti-abortion billboards have not always saturated the national stage in the immediately intelligible ways that they do now. As Donna Haraway observed in 1997, "It is almost impossible to get through the day . . . without being in communication with the public

---

ten weeks after last menstrual period). After this time, embryologists refer to the structure as a fetus. See Sadler, *Langman's Medical Embryology.*

12. Lynch, *What Are Stem Cells?*, 54.

13. Stormer, "Mediating Biopower."

fetus."[14] Some scholars point to the development of visualization technologies such as ultrasound and fetal photography to explain the recent ascendance of the public fetus.[15] Others argue that the public fetal entity was in ascendance long before the advent of these technologies.[16]

Across its representational forms, the public fetus is indelibly linked with women and power. Feminist scholars have interrogated political permutations of the public fetus through the practice of ultrasounds (Lisa Mitchell), fetal surgery (Monica Casper), vehicle advertisements (Janelle Taylor), maternal self-management (Anne Balsamo; Deborah Lupton), and racialized maternity (Dorothy Roberts; Angela Davis).[17] These scholars often observe that when the fetus is foregrounded into what Susan Bordo called a "super subject," the gestating woman is backgrounded.[18] As a national figure in the US, the public fetus paved the way for the construction of the nation's unborn as it occurs at the NMU. Like the public fetus more generally, the fetus at the NMU is marked by ascriptions of innocence, appeals to maternal protection, and attributions of sacredness.

Rhetorical scholarship tends to approach the human fetal entity obliquely, often through analyses of the formal argumentation strategy of both pro-life and pro-choice abortion rhetorics. Celeste Condit's *Decoding Abortion Rhetoric* tracked the rhetorics of pro-life and pro-choice movements from 1965 to 1985 within a social movement framework. Studies in this vein have analyzed rhetorics of *Roe v. Wade* (Kate Gibson), the ideographs of "life" and "choice" (Sara Hayden), constitutional disputes around abortion (Edward Schiappa), and philosophical abortion arguments (Chris Kaposy).[19] The emphasis on argument often forgoes analysis of the public fetus itself, with some important exceptions. Recently, John Lynch described the public fetus as a demonstration of "biorhetoric." *Biorhetoric* is John Lyne's term for the discursive strategy that smuggles moral injunctions into statements of apparent biological fact. In the case of the public fetus, which Lynch, following Condit, identified as a

---

14. Haraway, *Modest–Witness*, 201–2.

15. Petchesky, "Fetal Images," 263; Stabile, "Shooting the Mother," 178.

16. Seigel, *The Rhetoric of Pregnancy*, 46, 96; Stormer, *Articulating Life's Memory*.

17. Mitchell, *Baby's First Picture*; Casper, *The Making of the Unborn Patient*; Taylor, "The Public Fetus and the Family Car"; Balsamo, "Public Pregnancies and Cultural Narratives of Surveillance"; Lupton, "'Precious Cargo'"; Roberts, *Killing the Black Body*; Davis, "Racism, Birth Control and Reproductive Rights," 355.

18. Bordo, *Unbearable Weight*, 80.

19. Gibson, "The Rhetoric of *Roe v. Wade*: When the (Male) Doctor Knows Best"; Hayden, "Revitalizing the Debate between <Life> and <Choice>"; Schiappa, "Analyzing Argumentative Discourse from a Rhetorical Perspective"; Kaposy, "Proof and Persuasion in the Philosophical Debate about Abortion."

"metonymic construction borrowed from the abortion debate," the allegedly neutral language of science is mobilized to make value claims for the substantiality of the fetus as a person.[20]

In his formidable body of rhetorical work on reproductive politics, Stormer has used the fetus as an entryway into critical theory. Importantly, Stormer coined the term *prenatal space* in 2000 to identify the ways in which the fetus has "become part of the cultural landscape" as a *site* for discourse.[21] Prenatal space is the material and discursive site struggled over and shaped by rhetorics of reproduction and life. An emphasis on prenatal space rather than the public fetus offers two clear advantages. The first reminds us that the public fetus is located within the ongoing matrix, scene, and context of the womb.[22] In other words, while the concept of the public fetus can inadvertently recoup the primacy of the fetus, prenatal space reminds us that the fetus lives *somewhere,* within the condensed site of consequential discourse that is prenatal space. The second advantage of prenatal space is its resonance with biopolitics. Ten years after coining the term, Stormer returned to prenatal space as a demonstration of biopower:

> There are certainly other spaces of great importance for biopower, but prenatal space has been of special import in the struggle to embody regimes of living. Prenatality parses space and time within life itself to create a mediating environment in which biopolitical arrangements can be forged. Historically, the pregnant body was the space of generative capacity to be managed and, therefore, was foundational to the renewal and growth of all regimes of living. Due to the pivotal status of pregnancy, how prenatal space was governed became a heuristic for stratifying more or less advanced regimes of living on a timeline of civilization. This is especially apparent within biomedical rhetoric about abortion.[23]

Here Stormer has located prenatal space as an example of biopolitical mediation. Reproduction, articulated through biopolitics, is a means of parsing civilizations as primitive or advanced.

Despite the persistent public visibility of the fetal entity and the consequential gravity of its representations for women's lives, a robust rhetorical literature has not yet formed around the human fetus (with Stormer's work as the exception). The dearth of critical rhetorical treatments of the fetus goes

20. Lynch, "Stem Cells and the Embryo," 322.
21. Stormer, "Prenatal Space," 136.
22. Stormer, "Prenatal Space," 117.
23. Stormer, "Mediating Biopower," 10.

beyond an endemic male bias in the rhetorical tradition or the overdetermined intractability of the abortion debate. Rather, I submit that the fetal entity is undertheorized also because of its capacity to trouble assumptions dear to the rhetorical tradition. As Stormer observed, the emphasis on individuality as a frame for understanding fetal life exposes the poverty of individuality as a frame for the rhetorical tradition.[24] The fetus disrupts the nearly universal assumption that one human body equals one human person and disturbs the boundaries between human/nonhuman and speech/silence.

The human fetus causes trouble for even the most inclusive of rhetorical theories. For example, in *Inessential Solidarity,* Diane Davis described a fundamental rhetoricity inherent in the vulnerability of corporeality, a rhetoricity available to humans and animals alike.[25] Yet unlike an animal, the fetus is both corporeally exposed (that is, it has the capacity for injury, just like my liver or a giraffe's heart) and enfolded within another corporeality, upon whom it is entirely dependent (again, just like my liver or a giraffe's heart). As a field, we have just begun to assemble the conceptual toolbox needed to think through the fetus as a productive existent while maintaining a feminist political project. In sum, rhetoric has focused on the arguments around the abortion debate rather than on the fetus itself, or has inadvertently recentered the fetus at the expense of the woman, or has failed to account for how the fetus requires perturbing some dearly held assumptions of the rhetorical tradition. Given the emphasis on *life* in representations of the fetus, it is instructive to follow Nathan Stormer's lead and approach the public fetus through biopolitics, the diverse field of critical studies that regards *life itself* as a mode of regulation.

Classically, the sovereign made the decision of who lives and who dies.[26] But in contemporary late liberalism, the sovereign who decides the exception is decentralized.[27] This is where rhetoric enters. Public discourse articulates (in both senses of the term) necropower across a series of publics. One means by which this occurs is through the construction of status hierarchies, or what Alexander Weheliye described as the "sociopolitical processes of differentiation and hierarchization," of which he considers blackness to be the primary signifier.[28] Mel Chen's analogous insight on "animacy hierarchies" thinks through linguistic mediations that adjust the position of various living and nonliving existents along a hierarchy. Where an existent resides along

24. Stormer, *Articulating Life's Memory,* xi.
25. Davis, *Inessential Solidarity,* 36.
26. Agamben, *Homo Sacer,* 13–14.
27. Decoteau, *Ancestors and Antiretrovirals,* 105.
28. Weheliye, *Habeas Viscus,* 5.

the biopolitical fault lines of citizenship, race, gender, sexuality, nationality, or physiological normativity bears radical consequences for the livability of its life.[29] Zoetropes are one means by which these differences become consequential across various publics.

The theoretical framework with which I approach the fetus is attuned to the rhetorical construction of various existents along such a necropolitical hierarchy. Again, my intention here is not to claim that the millions of aborted fetuses in the US rank among the racialized necropolitical injustices listed above. Rather, I call for a rhetorically attuned inquiry into exactly *how* lives are disciplined into "full humans, not-quite-humans, and nonhumans."[30] Because the social status of all existents is rhetorically mediated across a diverse set of publics, the fetus, given its malleability and high political stakes, offers an instructive case study regarding these contested movements.

Judith Butler offered the concept of frames as representational modes that permit or fail to permit the representability of the human.[31] Concerned with depictions of Palestinians and "enemy combatants" in the so-called war on terror that failed to represent their humanness, Butler urged us to interrogate the radical inequality that characterizes "the difference between grievable and ungrievable lives."[32] Butler asserted that not all entities who deserve the benefits of humanhood are invited "under the sign of the Human."[33] How did the fetal entity become a human in some public spheres? In the face of humanhood's radical and shocking exclusions, how did human fetuses become legitimate candidates for humanhood in some publics?

A particularly malleable quality of the public fetus lends itself to these attributions of humanhood. Claudia Castañeda made claims about the changeability of "the child" that are also true of fetal entities:

> What is distinctive about the child is that it has the capacity for transformation. . . . This implies that the child is also never complete in itself. It is precisely this incompleteness and its accompanying instability that makes the child so apparently available: it is not yet fully formed, and so open to re-formation. The child is not only in the making, but also malleable—and so can be made.[34]

29. Chen, *Animacies.*
30. Weheliye, *Habeas Viscus,* 81.
31. Butler, *Frames of War: When Is Life Grievable?*
32. Butler, *Frames of War: When Is Life Grievable?*, xxii.
33. Butler, *Precarious Life,* 49.
34. Castañeda, *Figurations,* 2–3.

I approach the fetus as a mutable existent whose multifarious framings invite consequential renderings of social worth. Therefore, the fetus joins other existents whose impassioned zoerhetorical contestation is central to their public representation: animals, brain-dead persons, the ecosystem, and historically oppressed groups of human-identified existents. Yet among all of these groups, the fetus alone enjoys the most "zoerhetorical sweep," or range of status attributions. The fetal entity ranges from either nothing (a clump of cells, a blob of tissue) or a supercitizen (an unborn child deserving human rights and protection that supersede those of the mother) depending for the most part on how we talk about it. The unique zoerhetorical instability of the fetus likely fuels much of the social anxiety and handwringing about it. Because of this span of status assignations, and because each of these status assignations demands a different ethical obligation to the fetus, the fetus furnishes a crucial case study for zoerhetorics.

An existent's position on the hierarchy largely determines the extent to which that existent experiences nourishment toward life or abandonment toward death. Its position also bears a correlation to the extent to which it is granted rhetorical agency or "animacy." Although there are a number of zoerhetorical thresholds, such as the contested grounds between animal and human, or nonliving and living, the most salient and status-laden threshold on the zoerhetorical hierarchy is humanhood. It is precisely this threshold around which zoerhetorics of the fetal entity concern themselves. It follows, then, that the most patent zoerhetorical movements at the NMU are those that address precisely this burden of establishing the unborn as a human "person" or "life." Humanity, an identifying marker and performance, is one of the stickiest thresholds of the zoerhetorical hierarchy. Like Butler's "congealed" performances of gender, humanity, too, sticks to us like a thick pelt.[35] If the NMU is a place committed to making humans out of fetuses, how exactly does this happen? I argue that humans are partly made in a series of tropes—iterable turns, movements, displacements—that function to raise or lower the status of a particular entity. In order to elaborate the contours of these status investments at the NMU, I will first provide a description of the site of itself.

TOURING THE NATIONAL MEMORIAL FOR THE UNBORN

Nestled in the suburbs east of Chattanooga, Tennessee, and gated with minimal signage visible from the road, the National Memorial for the Unborn doesn't get much incidental foot traffic. It came to my attention as I imagine

---

35. Butler, *Gender Trouble*, 43.

it does for most people: through web-browsing affiliated sites. This is how I "discovered" the NMU. Familiar with my interest in fetal rhetorics, Professor Jerry Hauser, a member of my doctoral committee, alerted me to a public controversy ignited by a local Boulder church. The Sacred Heart Memorial Wall for the Unborn (located at Sacred Heart of Mary Catholic church) came under scrutiny in 2005 when it was discovered that their pro-life committee had been secretly burying fetal abortion remains surreptitiously stolen from a local mortuary by an employee of the mortuary. When the secret burial ceremonies were revealed in 2005, the left-leaning Boulder community reacted with outrage. Dr. Warren Hern, a famous pro-choice activist, medical scholar, and one of the few late-term-abortion providers in the country, called the church's actions a "macabre death ritual."[36] Most of the fetal ashes buried at Sacred Heart came from his clinic. To this day the Sacred Heart of Mary Church maintains a website for its Memorial Wall for the Unborn and lists the NMU as an affiliate on its website. The website boasts, "Since 1996, the ashes of approximately 5,500 aborted babies have been buried at the Memorial Wall for the Unborn located at Sacred Heart of Mary Cemetery at 6739 South Boulder Road in Boulder, Colorado."[37] Interestingly, the NMU is ranked on the popular web-based travel site TripAdvisor as "#54 of 108 things to do in Chattanooga."[38]

I found the NMU through a link from Sacred Heart's abortion memorial website, in the relatively mindless act of clicking on one of the "Relevant Web Links." I remember sitting up a little at my desk when I landed on the NMU's homepage—*how interesting*, I thought; *this fetal memorialization stuff is a bigger deal than I thought*. It was not until much later that I would fully understand the friendly and financial connections between Sacred Heart and the NMU. One woman I interviewed at Sacred Heart said that all plaques requested from the state of Colorado are both displayed at the NMU and on Sacred Heart's Wall. Sacred Heart's website instructs viewers to use the resources of the national body while also keeping it local:

If you are ready to order a plaque for the Memorial Wall for the Unborn, please click on the link below to connect to the National Memorial for the Unborn website and order form. If possible, please note you would like the plaques sent to Sacred Heart of Mary Church.[39]

36. Kelly, "Church Plans to Bury the Ashes of Fetuses from Abortion Clinic."
37. Sacred Heart of Mary, "Memorial Wall."
38. TripAdvisor, "National Memorial for the Unborn."
39. Sacred Heart of Mary, "Memorial Wall."

Many fetal memorials display the customized bronze nameplates of which the NMU is the sole manufacturer, demonstrating its centrality in the unborn memorialization community. Although the NMU's website and social media presence have matured in the past four years that I have been a regular web visitor, many core components have remained in place. It is likely that the website mediates most people's first experiences (and perhaps only experiences) with the NMU, as it did mine. At the same time, visitors and volunteers at the NMU with whom I spoke also heard about the NMU through their church or friends. For the local Chattanooga community, the NMU holds a series of events such a sing-alongs, memorial ceremonies, and pro-life rallies. A series of photographs of the site cycle along the homepage's banner, and the opening text welcomes visitors:

> A Burden Lifted. The National Memorial for the Unborn, located in Chattanooga, Tennessee, is dedicated to healing the generations of pain associated with the loss of aborted children. On this site where 35,000 babies have died, the memory of unborn children is honored.[40]

As the website details, the NMU is located on the site of a former abortion clinic. The story of the NMU's provenance is also retold in two recently published books: *101 Stories of Answered Prayers* and *Empty Arms: More Than 60 Stories of Hope from the Devastation of Abortion*. By dint of luck, the Pro-Life Majority Coalition of Chattanooga (also known as ProMacc) discovered a last-minute opportunity to purchase the building that the clinic occupied. In less than forty-eight hours, ProMacc raised $294,000, which allowed them to outbid the "abortionist" and take possession of the building. Later, a reporter asked ProMacc's Patricia Lindley why they overpaid for a building worth only about $189,000. Lindley's reply condensed the classic pro-life stance that amplifies the fetus at the expense of the gestating woman: "You can never put a price tag on the value of even one human life."[41] This 1993 takeover of an abortion clinic would later serve as the template for other pro-life communities shutting down or outbidding others for clinic sites.[42]

As a result of these events, proponents of the NMU understand the site as a landmark victory in God's battle against abortion. "We prayed and the Lord

40. National Memorial for the Unborn, "Homepage."

41. Williams and Caldwell, *Empty Arms*, 6.

42. For example, a clinic in Kansas detailed in this 2007 editorial exemplifies such a takeover. The editorial mentions an abortion clinic in Baton Rouge, Louisiana, taken over by a pro-life group and renamed the "American Holocaust Memorial." See Harkinson, "The Exorcists: Pro-Life Activists Take Over an Abortion Clinic and Cast Out the Demons Within."

answered," is a common refrain.[43] NMU founders estimate that 35,000 babies died on-site. The website claims that each of these babies is now remembered by one of the 35,000 rocks in the "rock garden." As another woman I interviewed told me, "God's hand is all over this place." A plaque in the rock garden states: "The glory of this latter house shall be greater than of the former, saith the Lord of hosts, and in this place will I give peace. Haggai 2:9." Founders and proponents call the site a holy ground of America, "as much as a Civil War battlefield is holy because of the lives lost there."[44]

The most salient feature of the NMU's website is the Virtual Wall, where a user can search for the plaque for his or her baby or the baby of a loved one. Although it is impossible to ascertain online how many brass nameplates honor unborn babies at the NMU, searches for common Christian names can yield tens of results. The website also features a photo gallery, a document that offers a "tour" through the NMU, a contact page, a video that takes the viewer on a tour, an online store, and an order form for a $40.00 brass nameplate or brick paver.

A sophisticated and compelling narrative of healing and repentance accompanies the NMU. The homepage of the website sells a book called *Empty Arms: More Than 60 Life-Changing Stories of Hope from the Devastation of Abortion* by Wendy Williams and Ann Caldwell.[45] Williams and Caldwell were involved in the formation of the NMU in the mid-nineties and still maintain seats on its governing board. Free copies of their book are distributed to women who seek pregnancy care at the Choices pregnancy center next door to the NMU. Most of the stories feature a young woman who chooses abortion when faced with an unplanned pregnancy. As she gets older, she realizes with the help of a Bible study or abortion recovery group that she is dealing with the symptoms of post-abortion syndrome. She grieves her abortion (often with the help of folks at the NMU), and God gives her the peace of knowing that she will see her baby in heaven. Each story begins with the NMU nameplate dedicated to that particular woman's unborn baby and ends with a Bible quote. In the narratives offered in this book, the NMU "stepped in to bring hope and healing" to the multitudes of women with "deep wounds and unresolved emptiness in their heart [sic]."[46]

In these two books, and circulating within the NMU's public more broadly, abortion is portrayed as an event that often results in deep grief, drug abuse, infertility, depression, divorce, and heartache. Ann Caldwell confirmed her

---

43. Williams and Caldwell, *Empty Arms*, 6.
44. Williams and Caldwell, *Empty Arms*, 7.
45. Williams and Caldwell, *Empty Arms*.
46. Williams and Caldwell, *Empty Arms*, back cover.

anti-abortion stance clearly in the book's preface: "One purpose of this book is to show that all women who have had abortions suffer afterwards."[47] I was troubled by the disinformation that this book promoted about abortion. I was even more disturbed that the book promulgated the myth of post-abortion syndrome, a "disease" widely discredited by the psychological establishment. Proponents of post-abortion syndrome maintain that abortion causes psychological damage not only to the woman who received the abortion but also to other people involved, like the baby's father or grandparents. Caldwell's book conforms to the narrative of post-abortion syndrome that suggests that while the woman may initially feel relief, a depression or trauma will slowly sneak up on her, sometimes many years later—unless of course she repents. As Eva Dadlez and William Andrews argue, in the cases when there is psychological trauma resulting from abortion, it can be attributed to the shaming practices of pro-life post-abortion counseling, a practice that the crisis pregnancy center adjoining the NMU participates in.[48] Kimberly Kelly aptly observes that the grassroots efforts of crisis pregnancy centers themselves—such as the one adjoining the NMU—spread harmful disinformation about the existence of post-abortion syndrome.[49]

Guided by instructions from the website, I sojourned to the Wall in May of 2012 and August of 2013 to conduct interviews with volunteers and visitors. My first visit coincided with Mother's Day, and I arrived at the NMU that Sunday during when I thought would be the prime post-church rush. Much to my surprise, there was no one there. The NMU promotes active subsidiary branches all over the country, a fact that belies the quietness of the actual physical site. A person entering the gates is greeted with a sign that says "Welcome . . . The gates and doors of the National Memorial for the Unborn are always open . . . please enter in peace." An Ebenezer Rock of Deliverance bigger than my compact rental car circumvents passage to the main built structure. According to its placard, the rock is an Old Testament symbol of God's victory. As former NMU executive director Carol Martin explained of the massive rock, "It represents the deliverance of this property from death and despair to hope and life."[50]

Inside the NMU, the most commanding feature is the fifty-foot marble Wall of Names, which consists of hundreds of small plaques, each dedicated to an aborted baby. The oblong shape of the built structure invites bodies to mill back and forth across the space in front. As I walked to and fro, I let my

---

47. Williams and Caldwell, *Empty Arms*, xviii.
48. Dadlez and Andrews, "Post-Abortion Syndrome."
49. Kelly, "The Spread of 'Post-Abortion Syndrome' as Social Diagnosis."
50. National Memorial for the Unborn, "Homepage."

eyes run over the hundreds of nameplates on the Wall, stopping to read the ones that caught my attention. With each iteration of this alternating movement, I "discovered" new nameplates. It became clear to me with this initial skimming that the following words appeared over and over again on the Wall: angel, baby, John, love, mommy, and sorry.

Above the Wall, Psalms 51:17 is quoted in large black print: ". . . a broken and contrite heart, O God, thou will not despise." (The first part of the sentence omitted in the quotation reads: "The sacrifices of God are a broken spirit . . .") Crowded together colorfully across the shelf under the Wall are hundreds of gifts, letters, and other "remembrance items" for the unborn. Hand- and typewritten notes on ripped loose-leaf, Hallmark cards, postcards, bespoke stationery, and even the backs of medical documents are among the many epistolary vehicles for textual communication with the unborn. Among the notes cluster stuffed animals, plastic figurines, candles, jewelry, baseball gloves, dolls, Mylar balloons, and other objects intended as gifts for the unborn babies. Sometimes gifts were placed directly under their corresponding nameplate, but other times there was no nameplate in sight that matched the names on the notes and letters below.

Participants and volunteers at the NMU curate a sophisticated narrative of sin and repentance, supported by pro-life books, websites, and events. At no point was the consistency of this narrative clearer than during moments where an event or item "broke" from the script. During an interview at the site, I had the privilege (and I will admit, the pleasure) of witnessing a volunteer named Leah "mend" the broken narrative. I had asked Leah which of the gifts left at the Wall was her favorite. At one point, as we were strolling back and forth in front of the Wall discussing the remembrance items, she paused with furrowed brow, drawing my attention to a postcard that I would have otherwise passed over. The postcard's handwritten text, which I used as an epigraph to open this chapter, said: "I am sorry to have aborted you. But I guess that's life. Or not life, in your case." This note, neither addressed nor signed, has led me to wild speculations about its provenance and purpose. Was it intentionally disruptive, perhaps left by a funny, irreverent feminist like me? Or does its flippancy mask a deep painful regret? Regardless of the answer to these questions, when Leah removed this postcard from the display, she removed a discourse-object that deviated from the requisite abortion-contrition-forgiveness script. The NMU actively and purposefully curates discourse-objects that fit the narrative and culls discourse-objects that do not fit the narrative. This careful curation creates the overall impression that multiple voices unite with one single message at the NMU. To know that not all voices or participants shared this message was, frankly, heartening.

With a ten-foot wooden cross suspended from the ceiling and thoughtfully placed tissue boxes on a half-circle of chairs around a lectern, the indoor space feels simultaneously like a church and a funeral home. To the right side of the Wall hangs a pair of plaques signed in 1997 by Norma McCorvey (the anonymous Jane Roe of *Roe v. Wade*) and Sandra Cano (Jane Doe of *Doe v. Bolton*). More than twenty years ago at an event at the NMU, McCorvey and Cano publicly recanted their involvement in their respective high-profile abortion-rights court cases and committed themselves to the sanctity of life. Both women claimed that their attorneys manipulated them and that the pro-choice movement used them as pawns. The declaration on McCorvey's plaque acknowledges the restorative and sacred properties that many people experience while visiting the NMU: "In this place of healing, the National Memorial for the Unborn, I stand with those who honor the worth of every unborn child as created in the image of God. I will strive, in the name of Jesus, to end this Holocaust." This event, and the plaques that mark it, are significant insofar as they tie the NMU to mini-celebrities of the pro-life movement, and affirm the NMU's importance as a site where significant events occurred.

Although there are a few generic or nameless plaques that repeat themselves throughout the Wall (such as "Our Baby, Mommy's Sorry," and "My Beautiful Baby"), a number of nameplates rise to this unusual rhetorical occasion. Many plaque writers choose not to provide a first name or a surname: "Fourth Baby Newton," "Eighth Baby Newton," "Sibling of Brian and Megan." Some plaques supply surnames, most of which sound European, like the plaques in remembrance of "Angel VanDyke" or "Abigail Grace Rothgery." Some plaques are not from parents but from other family members, such as "Irma's Grandbabies / I cried for you together / now in heaven." One plaque's paratext offers a cryptic statement of absolution that hints at past coercion: "Baby Ernst / 1974 / I forgive my ex-husband."

Participants have the option to select up to 75 characters of text distributed over three lines on their baby's brass nameplate. While a few choose to acknowledge an unborn baby with one line (such as the nameplate that says only "Baby Martinez"), most participants engage the opportunity to supply more text. Quoting Biblical passages is one of the most common textual practices for nameplates. Among the hundreds of passages quoted are Luke 1:50, Matthew 5:9, and Psalms 27:3.[51] Some plaques are intended to represent the

---

51. Here are these Bible passages in the King James version that the NMU favors: Luke 1:50: "And his mercy is on them that fear him from generation to generation"; Matthew 5:9: "Blessed are the peacemakers: for they shall be called the children of God"; and Psalms 27:3: "Though an host should encamp against me, my heart shall not fear: though war should rise against me, in this will I be confident." This is just a sampling from the hundreds of Biblical passages referenced on the nameplates at the Wall.

combined abortion loss for a family ("Mendy's two babies") or even an entire institution ("In memory of the babies / of Maryland General Hospital / 1965–1972—a nurse"), while some families maintain a distribution of one aborted baby per plaque. The Roy family, for example, commissioned separate plaques for Brian Andre Roy, Rebecca Christina Roy, Joshua Roy, and Gabriella Roy.

Except for me, no one visited the Wall during that Sunday afternoon on Mother's Day of 2012. At that moment, I felt misled by what now seemed like the self-aggrandizing title of "National" Memorial for the Unborn. The NMU's founders wanted the American-identified cultural cache that indexed the biggest and most influential memorial for the unborn with the word *national,* a word that I naïvely thought would deliver as many daily visitors as other "national" memorials I have visited. To be fair, the NMU assemblage is "national" to the extent that the spokes issuing from its hub reach across the US. The NMU provides resources for smaller state-affiliated memorials to the unborn, such as the Kentucky Memorial for the Unborn, as I have mentioned earlier. Said former director Carol Martin in a video on the website, "It's our prayer that one day we will have affiliates in every state in the nation." They even offer an affiliate site package to start a memorial in your own area. Despite these facts, at that particular moment, the self-bestowed title "national" seemed more aspirational than actual, and even a little disingenuous.

Barbara June,[52] a long-time volunteer at the NMU and at the Choices pregnancy care center next door, sat with me for about an hour on a week-day inside the NMU during my second visit. She explained the relationship that the NMU shares with its sister ministry, the Choices Pregnancy Resource Center next door. Although they are located in the same building, they have separate entrances, mission statements, 501(c)3 statuses, websites, executive directors, and parking lots. At the same time, the administrative offices for the NMU are housed on the Choices side of the building, and the volunteers for each site overlap considerably. To reach the NMU from the pregnancy center, you have to walk outside and around the large gated yard. The Choices Pregnancy Resource Center, like many pro-life pregnancy centers, is "fake" (my words, not Barbara's) because they advertise guidance about "choices" but with a hidden political agenda to counsel against or discourage abortion. Reproductive health activists condemn these institutions for using deception and misinformation that threaten women's health.[53] Given that the NMU endeav-

---

52. This is a pseudonym. The University of Colorado, the institution whose review board approved this research, required that I use pseudonyms, even though many of the women I interviewed encouraged me to publish their real names.

53. Mertus, "Fake Abortion Clinics."

ors to appear apolitical and supportive to women, it is key to not overlook its connection to the crisis pregnancy center. As one woman wrote on the NMU's TripAdvisor site, "Let's not politicize grief and loss, but show respect for this memorial which is meant in large part to support the mothers as well as the child. Viewed in that way, isn't this memorial a terrific idea?!"[54] The NMU gains credibility, as this comment demonstrates, by its façade of political neutrality.

Standard operating procedure at the crisis pregnancy center entails inviting women seeking care for a tour of the NMU next door. The volunteers I interviewed identified this practice as particularly moving and persuasive for women considering abortion, although they did admit that some women refused to take the tour. As one volunteer explained, "It's really important for women considering abortion to see how many people regret it later." This practice underscores that there is much more to the NMU's mission than what is stated on their main web page: "The NMU is dedicated to healing generations of pain associated with the loss of aborted and miscarried children." As a mission statement, this is only partially true. To dissuade pregnant people from choosing abortion is also one of the NMU's goals—although language stating this goal never appears anywhere officially.

I asked Barbara June, Leah, and a number of other volunteers specifically about their relationship to the broader pro-life movement. They were tired of being associated with an angry, shaming, and even violent pro-life movement that uses shock-and-awe tactics like images of bloody babies on huge billboards. They wanted the NMU to embody what they saw as an important shift toward *caring* for all women. "We are pro *every* life, and that includes the mother," one visitor at the Wall told me, in an interesting appeal to biolegitimacy that attempts to equate the zoerhetorical status of woman and fetus. As the director explained to me, the NMU's mission has evolved away from *shaming* and toward an ethic of *caring*.

Finally, it was only through speaking with women at the NMU that I was able to briefly experience an affective commingling that allowed me to see, just for a moment, how other women may experience the Wall. When Leah was talking about how often the siblings of unborn babies can really "see" and "feel" their lost brothers and sisters, I briefly "caught" her emotional intensity. Her wide, wet eyes, urgent vocal delivery, and eager grip on my arm showed me that many people experience the Wall's shiny, reflective surface as magical and mysterious. When she told me that some women report seeing fleeting

---

54. Hubbynfather, "Powerful, if you permit yourself to think and reflect." https://www.tripadvisor.com/Attraction_Review-g54946-d4428157-Reviews-National_Memorial_for_the_Unborn-Chattanooga_Tennessee.html#REVIEWS.

glimpses of the ghosts of their babies in the Wall's lambent reflection, I found myself checking the Wall for fugitive shadows out of the corners of my own moist eyes. I experienced a momentary connection with Leah in a way that somehow briefly superseded even my staunchest pro-choice political commitments. I doubt that affective contagion like this would have been possible if I had not physically visited the Wall and spoken with volunteers and participants in person. This experience allowed me to understand the Wall as some of its visitors do, as a moving, persuasive, rich experience. The Wall is not merely reflective but also productive and surprising—a topos you can visit to generate an experience, a place to project your hopes and longings.

ZOETROPES AT THE NATIONAL MEMORIAL FOR THE UNBORN

Because of its wide-ranging zoerhetorical sweep, the fetal entity provides a unique case study for advancing a theory of zoetropes. How does the promotion of the fetal entity occur at the nation's premier fetal memorialization site? Although the fetus is certainly a special case, attuning to the rhetorical processes by which the fetus is made into a human can shed light on how all human-attributed existents are zoetroped into humanhood. Rather than using the Latin term of personification, which acts as a sort of definitional umbrella for many of the tropes I cite here, I use the more specific Greek figures instead. The tropes I explore below serially constitute the fetus as a human, each with a different material-discursive effect: naming (antonomasia), en-voicing (apostrophe), en-facing (prosopopeia), and em-bodying (somatopeia). If tropes conjure liveliness, then once an entity has been rhetorically animated, or given life, through figuration, that entity is immediately subject to biopolitical and necropolitical regulation.

Antonomasia: Naming the Unborn

Within pro-life narratives of healing from an abortion, giving your baby a name is often cited as one of the first steps of repentance that ultimately lead to healing. The back matter of *Empty Arms* states: "Healing is possible through claiming one's child, naming one's child, and honoring one's child."[55] Naming is not only one of the first acts that inaugurates a newborn into human

---

55. Williams and Caldwell, *Empty Arms*.

society, but for Kenneth Burke, naming, as an act of condensation, is one of the central social acts of language.[56] As an interpretive act, naming shapes profoundly the significance of the thing named. Each of the brass nameplates on the Wall (or the brick pavers reserved for miscarried babies in the garden outside) represents an opportunity for NMU's publics to engage in or observe the powerful act of denomination. Searching for any popular name on the NMU website's "Virtual Wall" yields many results. For example, a search for "John" yields fifty-four search results of nameplates with babies named John or plaques that quote from the Biblical book of John.

Similarly, Raymie McKerrow centered the power of naming on the "power of language to constitute subjects."[57] Here we can make a linguistic distinction between common and proper nouns, the latter of which are reserved for subjects. Participants at the Wall engage in both types of nominalization. Fetal entities are "named" common nouns such as *baby* or *angel* as well as proper nouns such as Charles, Joseph, or Elizabeth. As Chen wrote of nominalizations, "[They] function to fix, stabilize, and most crucially, enable bounding . . . and hence—this is no minor consequence—to render identities finite."[58] When participants of the Wall name the unborn, they engage in subject-forming, identity-bounding acts.

Arguably, the Vietnam Veterans Memorial in Washington, DC, inspired the commemorative practice of permanent inscription of names of the dead, a practice that Blair, Jeppeson, and Pucci described as uniquely attentive to the *individuals* commemorated.[59] The names of the veterans were physically engraved in granite, lending them a permanence and importance. Casting the unborn as individuals is exactly the effect that the NMU intends to achieve. Like the Vietnam Veterans Memorial, the Wall of Names is reflective and thus "quotes whomever and whatever is within its reflective range."[60] In other words, both sites mirror back distorted images of their observers and surrounding objects. At the NMU, confronting your image at the Wall bears the additional significance of "confronting yourself" with the consequences of a singular abortive act (perhaps your own) or the cumulative abortive acts of the nation. Intertextuality with the Vietnam Veterans Memorial is not lost on the volunteer staff at the NMU. A quoted testimonial on the website asserts that the NMU is "as significant as the Vietnam [Veterans] Memorial."[61]

56. Burke, *On Symbols and Society*, 61.
57. McKerrow, "Critical Rhetoric," 105.
58. Chen, *Animacies*, 74.
59. Blair, Jeppeson, and Pucci, "Public Memorializing in Postmodernity," 278.
60. Blair, Jeppeson, and Pucci, "Public Memorializing in Postmodernity, 273.
61. National Memorial for the Unborn, "Testimonials."

Broadly conceived, the zoetrope of naming at the NMU is metonymical, insofar as something is given the name of something else. Kenneth Burke named metonymy as one of the four master tropes, following a thread of identifying master tropes that emerged from Petrus Ramus in the sixteenth century and that continued through John Smith in the seventeenth and Giambattista Vico in the eighteenth centuries.[62] As one of Burke's four master tropes, metonymy conveys "some incorporeal or intangible state in terms of the corporeal or tangible."[63] Burke's example of saying the "heart" rather than the "emotions" demonstrates this displacement of the incorporeal for the corporeal. This understanding of metonymy as a progression toward material substance, toward the touchable or fleshy or real, is crucial for the production of the fetus as human. Under the umbrella of metonymy, we can also call the naming zoetrope at the NMU antonomasia, "the use of on epithet or patronymic, instead of a proper name, or the reverse."[64] Yet, perhaps the most descriptive trope for naming unborn babies is catachresis, a deliberate misnaming or strained use of a word or phrase. De Man defines catachresis as the trope "which coins a name for a still unnamed entity, which gives face to the faceless."[65] In naming those who have never been born, participants at the Wall use catachresis to invite recognition of the humanhood of the fetus, and their subsequent loss.

Importantly, just as the statuses of the fetal entities are raised through naming, the statuses of family members performing contrition are raised as well. Rather than just constituting the unborn as subjects, the brass plaques and the antonomasic practices associated with them also constitute subjects interacting with the Wall as mothers, fathers, and general heaven-bound protectors and guardians of the unborn. As the unborn and their families at the NMU are named and promoted, the absent demoted Others includes families who are not publicly grieving abortions.

It is not just the plaques that nominalize through antonomasia, but also practices and events promoted by the NMU. According to one woman's testimony, the effects of naming were realized during a memorial service at the NMU:

You see, when you have an abortion, you want to deny that your baby exists, and you don't want anyone to know about him. The memorial service was

---

62. Fahnestock, *Rhetorical Style*, 101.
63. Burke, "Four Master Tropes," 424.
64. Lanham, *Handlist of Rhetorical Terms*, 17.
65. De Man, *Resistance to Theory*, 44.

one way I could recognize my child was a real person with a name and identity, and restore him to the dignity that I had taken from him.[66]

Because many names are gender-specific, naming an entity often goes
hand in hand with gendering the entity. A human is not identifiable as such
until *she* or *he* has not only a name but also a gender; gender is a condition for a subject's emergence. To be fair, participants at the Wall require a
gendered pronoun to avoid the periphrastic "he or she" construction, or the
unwanted objectification effects of "it." Yet there is more invested in gendering the unborn than just utility at the level of sentence building. Rather, at
the NMU, hegemonic gendering is also a practice by which the fetus attains
status. Referring to infants, Butler observed that when a "girl is girled" she is
brought into the domain of kinship.[67] In the context of fetal memorialization,
this "girling" or "boying" is fascinating given that most abortions occur before
ten weeks, when the embryo has no distinguishing genitalia, but rather devel-
ops (around six weeks) what is called a "genital tuber," or a tiny protrusion
that will eventually become labia majora, a penis, or something in between in
the case of intersex presentations. To be clear, I am not claiming that gender
identity necessarily and logically follows from the assignment of biological
sex. Rather, I bring this up to acknowledge that for most abortions, it would
have been impossible to receive any kind of medically sanctioned assignment
of sex—much less any inkling of the gender identity (nonbinary, woman,
man) that the entity would eventually develop. This results in a difficult tension for language users wishing to human-ize the fetal entity.

Some participants manage the gender tension by choosing gender-neutral
names. One woman I spoke with purposefully requested the gender-neutral
Jordan for her baby's nameplate. Other participants simply provide two names
for one unborn baby, like the plaque that reads "Melody Ellen or Noah."
Another woman I interviewed said that it came to her in deep prayer that her
baby was a boy. This prayer-driven or intuitive knowing seems to be the most
common way of sexing the unborn. As Stephen Whittle has noted, a chief
part of being recognized as "human" is being recognized as normatively gendered.[68] Further, reflective of a worldwide preference for male babies, there are
more traditionally masculine than traditionally feminine names on the Wall.

Of course, across American-identified culture, gendering operates in complex ways. The assignment of gender may not always be a status promotion,
but the attribution of a normative, hegemonic cisgender may be. Indeed, the

66. Williams and Caldwell, *Empty Arms*, 43.
67. Butler, *Bodies That Matter*, xvii.
68. Whittle, "Foreword," xiii.

"binary phallocratic founding myth by which Western bodies and subjects are authorized" is in full cry at the NMU.[69] These distinctions are also evident in the gender-specific toys left under the Wall. Dolls and pink stuffed animals are left for baby girls, and baseball gloves and blue stuffed animals are left for baby boys. Yet naming and gendering are mere baby steps in the accumulation of personhood, given that we name and gender pets and vehicles. After an existent has a name, she can be addressed. Returning to our bicycle metaphor, the iterative tropological effects of naming (pedaling) are a precursor to and precondition for the more powerful effects of address (shifting gears).

Apostrophe: En-Voicing the Unborn

To the fetus's mutability we can at least partially attribute muteness. At least, the fetus is mute within the traditional definition of speech. Because of this silence, the fetus requires rhetorical mediation if it is to become a social actor—mediation that no shortage of willing parties have supplied. I suggest that apostrophe, or the tropological address to an absent or distant other "as if they had a voice with which to respond," operates at the Wall as another way of promoting the fetal entity.[70] Often described as fractured address, etymologically apostrophe "turns away" to address an absent entity as a way of addressing a broader public.

Fetal entities are addressed at the NMU in a number of distinct forms. First, the unborn are addressed on hundreds of the engraved plaques affixed to the Wall. Underneath the aborted baby's name is additional text that often hails the unborn directly, such as these: "Dance with Jesus until I come"; "Forgive me angel for robbing you"; "Your sister loves you"; and "I do love you now." Some of this additional text seems to address the wider public rather than the unborn, often in ways that explain or apologize for the abortifacient action: "I didn't have Jesus then"; "1946 was a tragic time"; "Foolishness of our youth."

Second, the unborn are addressed in the hundreds of open letters strewn underneath the Wall. These epistolary rhetorics are addressed directly to the unborn but, by virtue of their public placement, also "turn away" to address the broader audience of NMU visitors. The following excerpts from letters underneath the Wall exemplify the genre. The first excerpt is from a stepmother, the second from a father, and the third from a sister of different

---

69. Stone, "The Empire Strikes Back," 231.
70. Hartelius, "Face-ing Immigration," 314.

unborn babies memorialized at the Wall. Original spelling and punctuation are maintained:

> This letter is to let you know we all think about you. We love you. We (Laura, Corbin, Brendon, and I) came to Chattanooga to see Chandler, Sydney, & Tyler and you. Well, your name & plates & stones. Your father is very sorry for what happened and I have not talked to your mother but I know by her actions she is sorry as well. All children are precious and we would love to have you here with us. That choice can not be changed unfortunately but we know we will see you and the other "babies" in heaven.

> Hey little one, this is your dad. This might be the hardest letter I've ever had to write. . . . You would've been the apple of my eye, whether I was showering you with all the things a little princess could ever want to teaching you to hunt and fish. I also know deep in my heart I would have been the greatest dad ever. But god needs all the angels he can get. I also know that your mother would also have loved you very much. We were very young and I was fool of vinegar. I'm so so sorry. We had boy and girl names picked out and had big plans. . . . Love, your daddy Josh 7/14.

> I don't even know what to say . . . I miss all the silly little arguments we would get in. When you taught me how to drive because mom and dad were too afraid. You would love dad, I picture you just like him, strong, laidback. I'm about to have a boyfriend, sure wish you were here to chase him off. I miss you. . . . a lot. I need you . . . more. I don't know why mom kept me and not you. 5 years later she was in the same spot but chose me . . . why? I ask God that a lot. Well whatever the reason don't worry I'll make you proud! Living for the both of us . . . miss you. Love, you little sis Jess 6-27-12.

Immediately remarkable in all these letters is an informal chattiness combined with strictly gendered familial roles. The unborn are addressed not only as human persons but more specifically as hegemonically gendered boys and girls. The boys even go fishing and intimidate their little sister's (potential) boyfriends. Taken together, the three excerpts demonstrate the instability of this relatively new rhetorical practice of memorializing the unborn. Understandably, the authors of these letters seem unsure of how exactly to address the unborn. This uncertainty is clear not only in the first excerpt's placement of "babies" in scare quotes (as if to ask, "are you actually babies?") but also in the vacillating attributions of omniscience to the unborn. The first letter patiently explains who is visiting "you" today, suggesting that the unborn baby does not know. By way of contrast, in a guestbook entry, Eli's parents attribute a near-omniscience to him. I have italicized these examples below:

> 1-13-13. Hello Eli, *As you know* it is mom and dad. We came on the bike it is very cold outside. Eli I am sorry I have not talked to you at home a lot of the last few weeks or have not been able to come see you a lot. Your Aunt Jackie has been down, then we drove to Kentucky with her which was a nightmare (*but I know you already know all of this as you know I still miss you everyday*).

A few months later, Eli's father signed the guestbook again: "Hey Eli, Sorry for being so Long in coming. Mom is sick and I miss you a lot. Jesus forgive us for not allowing a bright new life upon this earth." Two weeks after that, he wrote again, updating Eli on his mother's health: "4/13 My Dear Eli, Mom is better. I miss you. I have had to forgive myself for what I did to you." If Eli already knows, why write these letters and guestbook entries? Because they are not only for the babies. They also "turn away" to address the NMU's public in a ritual of repentance.

There is an oft-repeated refrain at the Wall that conforms to the mode of apostrophic address. "I will hold you in heaven" not only appears on over two hundred nameplates on the Wall but also is the name of both a centrally featured painting at the NMU and a book distributed for free at the crisis pregnancy center next door. The phrase "I will hold you in heaven" implies an increase in status (matched by a literal ascendant upward movement, toward heaven) for both the addressed fetal entity *and* the speaker. The implication is that by asking for forgiveness, the persons who committed the act of abortion will be redeemed and forgiven. Just as is true with the zoetrope of naming, apostrophizing the unborn raises the status of not only the fetal entity but also the speaker.

In a prescient 1986 essay, Barbara Johnson explored the political consequences of addressing the fetus. For Johnson, addressing fetal entities was a way to animate them into being: "Apostrophe is a form of ventriloquism through which the speaker throws voice, life, and human form onto the addressee, turning its silence into mute responsiveness."[71] More recently, Lauren Berlant described the potential of apostrophe to conjure subjects, calling apostrophe a "phenomenologically vitalizing movement of rhetorical animation." Berlant remained critical of apostrophe's political implications for subjectifying fetuses. Referring to it as "fake . . . intersubjectivity," she was wary

---

71. Johnson, "Apostrophe, Animation, and Abortion," 30.

of the suspended optimism of speakers who engaged in apostrophic address.[72] Here she describes those speakers while playing with the "turning away" etymology of apostrophe:

> The present is made possible by a fantasy of you, laden with x qualities I can project onto you, given your convenient absence. Apostrophe therefore appears to be a reaching out to you, a direct movement from place x to place y, but is it actually a turning back, an animating of a receiver on behalf of the desire to make something happen *now* that realizes something *in the speaker*, makes the speaker more or differently possible.[73]

Just as the phrase "I will hold you in heaven" suggests, an apostrophic address of the fetal entity hails into being not only the fetal entity as a human but also the speaker as an ethical subject (and heaven-bound protector). The zoetrope of apostrophe animates not just its direct or indirect addressees but also its speaker.

In a similar engagement with apostrophe, Johanna Hartelius argued that apostrophe and prosopopeia are tandem rhetorical operations. If apostrophe is addressing an existent as if it had a voice with which to respond, prosopopeia is addressing an existent as if it had a face with which to respond. And "that which has been 'faced'—or that which has experienced enfacement, can be acted on and toward in the social world."[74] Following Paul de Man, Hartelius described the two tropes of apostrophe and prosopopeia as inextricably linked operations, so I turn my attention next to prosopopeia.

Prosopopeia: En/Facing the Unborn

The classic definition of prosopopeia is when a nonliving existent is represented "as having human attributes and addressed or made to speak as if it were human."[75] As Megan Foley observed of Terri Schiavo, a clamor of voices was willing to speak for her in an attempt to fill the silent void left by her brain death.[76] When these voices started imagining what Schiavo might say, Foley identified it as prosopopeia, the tropological attribution of voice.[77] Similarly,

---

72. Berlant, *Cruel Optimism*, 25.
73. Berlant, *Cruel Optimism*, 25–26.
74. Hartelius, "Face-ing Immigration," 315.
75. Lanham, *Handlist of Rhetorical Terms*, 123.
76. Foley, "Voicing Terri Schiavo," 396.
77. Foley, "Voicing Terri Schiavo," 381.

Michael Riffaterre defines prosopopeia as "staging, as it were, absent, dead, supernatural, or even inanimate beings. These are made to answer as is our wont."[78] However, what these voice-centered definitions of prosopopeia miss, as Hartelius asserts, is the importance of *face* for prosopopeia.[79] Paul de Man enchained apostrophe with prosopopeia as the tropological attributions of voice and face, respectively, through etymological evidence: "Voice assumes mouth, eye, and finally face, a chain that is manifest in the etymology of the trope's name *prosopon poien,* to confer a mask or a face (*prosopon*)."[80] For de Man, the face as the "locus of speech" is necessary to the constitution of the speaking subject.[81]

Evidence of prosopopeic enfacement at the NMU includes any rhetorical event in which the unborn have faces or are generally considered social actors. For example, when Jessica Renee wrote of her unborn baby in the *Empty Arms* book, "In her very short lifetime, she changed my life," her unborn baby is prosopopeically enfaced as an agentic, change-making human actor.[82] One handwritten note from pro-life activist Hannah Rose Allen demonstrates an apostrophic promise to quite literally speak-for: "My precious babies in Heaven—I will be your voice!" Here Allen publicly commits to retelling her baby's story, while also en-voicing her baby. In this case, prosopopeia via apostrophe is the milestone of successful person-ification.

If these are the prosopopeic promotions at the NMU, what are the corresponding demotions? Davis (here following Paul de Man) recognized the multiple movements inherent in prosopopeia when she rhymed that it *"defaces* and *effaces* precisely to the extent that it *enfaces*."[83] Although Davis was referring to the defacement and enfacement of the same speaking subject, we can also extend her observation to the dynamic quality of zoetropes. In the case of the NMU, as the unborn are enfaced, women whose reproductive practices do not conform to the NMU's regime of living are effaced. These women are effaced at the NMU by means of exclusion from a life-loving public sphere. Further, because of the Wall's shiny granite surface, visitors can see their shadowy reflections in it. Therefore, visiting the Wall means "facing yourself"— and therefore facing the murderous effects of your reproductive decisions. As

---

78. Riffaterre, "Prosopopeia," 107. This is presumably Riffaterre's own translation of Pierre Fontanier.

79. Hartelius, "Face-ing Immigration," 314.

80. De Man, *Resistance to Theory,* 76.

81. De Man, *Rhetoric of Romanticism,* 89.

82. Williams and Caldwell, *Empty Arms,* 53.

83. Davis, *Inessential Solidarity,* 43; emphasis in the original.

the unborn, then, are prosopopeically en/faced at the Wall, visitors of the Wall "face" themselves, and perhaps their past actions, literally and figuratively.

The face-making movement of prosopopeia finds its opposite in the lesser-known *antiprosopopeia*. Notably, when the pro-choice side might describe an embryo or fetus as a "clump of tissue," they conform to the common definition given for antiprosopopeia, or "using inanimate objects to represent humans."[84] Of course, the *prima facie* assumption of humanhood in this definition glosses over the effects of zoetropes to condition our tendencies to attribute human-hood to some existents and not others. The point here is not to demonstrate both the promotional and demotional capacities of zoetropes for one existent but instead to underscore that there are no existents outside of zoerhetorical (un)making.

Somatopeia: Em-Bodying the Unborn

Jeanne Fahnestock relegates somatopeia to a list of cognates for personifica-tion, as do many rhetorical handbooks throughout the ages.[85] But I would like to revive somatopeia from relative obscurity because the meaning mani-fested in its etymology, *somato poein,* to make body, is important for zoe-tropes and necropolitical figuration. Somatopeia serves as the logical next link in de Man's tropological enchainment. If "voice, therefore face" links apos-trophe with prosopopeia, then "face, therefore body" links prosopopeia with somatopeia.

The common practice of leaving gifts under the Wall can also be under-stood as somatopeia, especially insofar as many of the gifts imply absent bod-ies, much more so than absent voices or faces. The embodied habits of play that these gendered gifts entail, of throwing and catching a baseball with a baseball glove, of dressing a doll, serve to embody the unborn as social actors. Stuffed animals are the most commonly gifted items at the Wall. What is it implied that the unborn children do with teddy bears, doe-eyed lambs, or even the one iridescent-winged dragon left at the Wall? They cuddle with them. They hold them in their hands; they hold them to their bodies. In so doing, their bodies are zoetropologically manifested as not just any bodies but as the bodies of small, active, gendered, and able-bodied children. In so doing, somatopeic embodiment transvalues existents, promoting fetal life in the necropolitical hierarchy.

---

84. Howard, *Dictionary of Rhetorical Terms,* 36.
85. Fahnestock, *Rhetorical Style,* 170.

There is an uncanny acceleration and cessation of time that occurs at the NMU that can be explained by the demands of somatopeic mediation. Ray Harvey's original painting, encased in glass on the left side of the Wall, is titled "I will hold you in heaven." The painting depicts an alabaster woman holding a large baby. The visual rendering of the fetal entity's face marks a moment of prosopopeic enfacement, but it is the size of this baby that best represents the demands of somatopeic embodiment. Most abortions occur before ten to twelve weeks, at which point the embryo/fetus is roughly the size of a cocktail shrimp.[86] In the circulating mythology of the NMU, sometime between the abortion and the fetal entity's arrival in heaven, the baby balloons to over 500 percent of its original size, growing into a fully developed, even large, infant. Then, it remains this size—conveniently, the size of an intelligible baby—as it waits to rejoin her family in heaven. This one-time "growth spurt" occurs because it is impossible to enface the fetal entity at its actual size when aborted. Because we do not have an existing cultural frame for recognizing inch-long entities as enfaced human actors, the fetal entity goes through a logic-defying growth spurt to meet the demands of somatopeic embodiment.

The interlocking, symbiotic power of apostrophe, prosopopeia, and somatopeia carries with it human-izing zoetropological effects. Although each of these zoetropes occurs simultaneously at the NMU, I have presented them in the logical order of the accumulation of humanhood. First name, then voice, then face, then body. An entity is rendered as most human when mediated prosopopeically and somatopeically. To social actors successfully "enfaced" and "embodied" as humans, we attribute rhetorical agency. At the NMU, the unborn are zoetropologically attributed faces and bodies, resulting in human-ized social actors toward whom we have an ethical obligation.

To return to the metaphor of riding a bike, consider the sheer accumulation of zoetropes required to get somewhere. Each of the thousands of nameplates across the country equals one pedal stroke. Metonymic sliding or shifting—the gesture of calling something by a different name in a way that changes its status—is like the simple, light pressure of a foot against the pedal of a bicycle. You will not make much progress in one rotation of the pedals, but repeating the movement over and over will get you somewhere. Put another way, zoerhetorics are consequential insofar as they are iterative. Mechanically, these repeated pedal strokes are a precondition for the more powerful effects of shifting gears. Address (either apostrophic, prosopopeic, or somatopeic) is the more mechanically efficient movement required to "shift" an entity over a contested status threshold like humanhood. Like turns of the

86. Guttmacher Institute, "Fact Sheet: Induced Abortion."

pedal, the tropes of shifting achieve measurable effects only when accumulated en masse in a particular public. Just as a bicycle gains momentum, the tropological effects mutually reinforce one another. Like riding up a hill, a more mechanically efficient movement is required to "shift" an entity over a contested status threshold like species or race. The same principle of iteration works here too. To cover ground, a rhetoric needs to circulate multiple times, gaining traction and momentum across the terrain of a particular public.

CONCLUSION: THE ZOETROPOLOGICAL ACCUMULATION OF HUMANHOOD

As we saw with the hegemonic gendering practices at the NMU, the unborn are not just zoetropologically transvalued toward enfaced humanhood. Rather, they are also raised toward a prescriptive American-identified hegemonic humanhood. The fetal entities at the NMU are not *just* babies, infants, children, or persons; they are "Holy Innocents," "martyrs," "soldiers," and "angels." The NMU does not just remember the unborn; the NMU is an encomium to the unborn. When participants at the Wall make humanizing attributions to the unborn, they appropriate a hierarchy similar to the Great Chain of Being, hitching fetal entities to those existents with higher statuses, such as angels. When Susan Squier observed that the public fetus almost always seemed to be "white and male," she was remarking on the raced and gendered nature of this hierarchical differentiation.[87]

Many voices attempt to speak for the fetal entity, perhaps the most contested entity in the contemporary US. One of these public voices that "speak for" the fetal entity is the National Memorial for the Unborn, which promotes fetal memorialization, an active component of the pro-life movement. The NMU is invested in the rhetorical construction of the fetal entity as a sacred unborn life. As I have shown, a series of zoetropes name, en-gender, en-voice, en-face, and em-body the unborn as "persons." These seem to build on one another in a gradual and mutually reinforcing accumulation of social status. First, most primally, naming calls them into being. Gendering makes them one of "us" in kinship. Apostrophe humanizes by turning them into addressees, prosopopeia humanizes by imagining voices and therefore faces, and somatopeia manifests human bodies. Toys like baseball gloves somatopeically lend them gendered, embodied, and even American-identified habitual practices like playing catch with a baseball. Of course, one promotional zoetrope does

---

87. Squier, "Fetal Subjects and Maternal Objects," 530.

not a human make. Rather, it is a process that happens across diverse iterations at the NMU and in conversation with the broader pro-life movement.

The NMU is by no means the first organization to promote fetal entities.
In fact, merely the existence of a memorial to the unborn suggests that we are
well into a historical period of fetal inflation, of which the NMU is only a late
but critical marker. Because these zoetropes have reached beyond the pro-life
movement and into broader sets of American-identified publics, the fetus is
rendered intelligible as a subject worthy of protection. The implications of
these renderings for the current political environment are profound, especially given the ongoing attack on abortion rights in the US. The Planned Parenthood Federation of America categorizes these attacks into six categories:
unconstitutional abortion bans, attacks on Planned Parenthood patients, the
targeted restriction of abortion providers, nonsurgical abortion bans, biased
counseling, and "personhood" measures.[88] Large swaths of the US have been
called "abortion deserts" because restrictive laws force women's health clinics
to shutter. Fetal promotion is strongly implicated in these pervasive threats to
women's health and bodily autonomy.

We can certainly recognize the rhetorical devices of antonomasia, apostrophe, prosopopeia, or somatopeia without the concept of the zoetrope. Beyond
the mere identification of the rhetorical device, the precise affordances that
zoetropes bring to the table are twofold. First, zoetropological theory recog-
nizes the ways in which "life itself" is tropologically embedded in language.
Just as the trope "quickens" or comes to life in the moment that it turns from
its literal meaning, so too does the entity. Second, this quickening or animation simultaneously makes liveliness and positions its object within a biopolitical hierarchy. To be recognized as alive or recognized as human is to
live-in-hierarchy, to be subject to a series of status differentiations. Zoetropes
conceptually link the quickening capacity of rhetorical figures to the parsing
demands of biopolitical regimes.

Zoetropological theory offers a pathway for understanding how some lives
come to matter and some lives fail to matter. If necropolitical regimes function
as machines for producing bodies nourished toward life, neglected for deterioration, and targeted for death, then zoetropes are one means by which these
inequalities are publicly justified and legitimated. Just like a human entity,
the human fetal entity is superimposed from the exterior, and then subject
to the series of status contestations demanded of hierarchical differentiation.
At the same time, not all human-identified existents share the qualities of the
fetus that make it so "available" for zoetroping. The malleability and silence of

---

88. Planned Parenthood, "Types of State Attacks on Abortion."

the human fetus invite voices to "speak for" it. Further, humanhood may be the most consequential status threshold for zoetropological enfacement, but a host of existents are zoetroped into being as well. We can think of all human-identified existents as embedded within accumulated effects of zoetropes.

Earlier I compared zoetropes to the Victorian toy with which they share a name. Like the toy, zoetropes "make life" in the moment of turning. Also like the toy, zoetropological rhetorics involve a sleight of hand or misdirection. Often zoetropes draw attention to a particular movement (such as the promotion of fetal existents) as a means to draw attention from another movement (the demotion of a less visible Other). In the case of the NMU, these less visible Others are often women whose reproductive practices do not conform to the specific maternity practices prescribed there. In Kasey Evans's words, "When the dead or inanimate gain a voice or a face through prosopopeia, they do so at the risk of the living."[89] As the fetal entity is promoted at the NMU, women with a diverse range of reproductive practices are demoted.

Contemporary necropolitical regimes parse sets of bodies vitalized toward life, neglected toward deterioration, and abandoned toward annihilation, often along the fault lines of race, gender, sexuality, and physiological normativity. Zoetropes, as they traverse legal, medical, religious, and vernacular publics, are but one means by which these cleavages become persuasive and legitimate. While this chapter investigates the ways in which necropolitical hierarchies become persuasive in one pro-life community institution with a national audience, the next chapter turns to the ways in which necropolitical hierarchies become persuasive at a very different set of sites: two fitness facilities in Boulder, Colorado.

---

89. Evans, "Prosopopoeia and Maternity," 397. Evans makes a fascinating case for prosopopeia as a "masculine privilege, an arrogation of the prerogatives of maternity," 411.

CHAPTER 4

Vital Biocitizens at the Gym

We may define a good thing as that which ought to be chosen for its own sake, or as that for the sake of which we choose something else; or as that which is sought after by all things. . . . One thing may entail another in either of two ways—simultaneously or subsequently. Thus learning entails knowing subsequently, health entails life simultaneously. Things are productive of other things in three senses: first as being healthy produces health; secondly, as food produces health; and thirdly, as exercise does—i.e., it does so usually. . . . Further, health, beauty, and the like, as being bodily excellences and productive of many other good things: for instance, health is productive both of pleasure and life, and therefore is thought the greatest of goods, since these two things which it causes, pleasure and life, are two of the things most highly prized by ordinary people.

—Aristotle, *On Rhetoric*, Book 1

IMAGINE THIS SCENE. A group of men and women gather for a regular Tuesday exercise-and-beer evening. On this night, four friends bring their carbon fiber racing bicycles and bike trainers to Blaine's house for a favorite activity: viewing the hit cable television show *The Biggest Loser* while racing each other for mileage.[1] This group of fit, white, attractive, professional thirty-to-forty-somethings, a few of them semiprofessional athletes, call *The Biggest Loser* the "best fitspo." (Fitspo is a portmanteau of "fitness inspiration.") They all agree that host Jillian Michaels—famously known as the "mean" host—provides the most motivation. "I don't care if you both die on this floor. Let's go! You better die looking good," Michaels shouts at two large-bodied contestants doing push-ups.[2] Blaine and his friends pump their legs harder as they watch on-screen a large man gag exercise-induced vomit over an arrangement of indoor

---

1. A pseudonym, a practice repeated throughout this chapter.
2. This Jillian Michaels quote is immortalized in many DIY fan mash-up videos of *The Biggest Loser* on YouTube, like this one, called "The Wrath of Jillian": http://www.youtube.com/watch?v=ovfW59st9xc.

foliage. After the ride, they chat about their PR (personal record) goals for their next races over locally brewed craft beer that tastes better "when you've really earned it." Before they part, they confirm plans to meet at the outdoor pool at the local athletic club for a Masters swim class at 5:30 the following morning.

When I retell this story, it reliably produces grimaces. People say, "That's *so* Boulder," roll their eyes, and generally find something at least mildly objectionable about the way that the fit bodies *use* the fat bodies as motivation, or as a kind of visually mediated prime-time fuel for enhanced exercise performance. Further grounds for reproach include the ways that the fit bodies have the opportunity to experience the double pleasure of simultaneous identification with (Jillian Michaels is shouting at *me*!) and disidentification from (Look how much fitter *I* am!) the show's contestants. I began with this scene, as it was casually recounted to me in an interview, because it summarily imparts a number of themes that define the local Boulder, Colorado, subculture in which I found myself halfway immersed from 2010 to 2014: aspirations toward fitness, antipathies toward fatness, exercise-oriented socialization, flesh-gazing (that "gets off" toward cardiovascular arousal), orientations to "earning" food, and preoccupation with measurable personal performance, all wrapped inside class-specific performances of consumption, leisure, whiteness, and athleticism.

In an attempt to understand the consequential rhetorics of these fitness practices, I conducted field method research, including participant observation and interviews, at two athletic clubs in Boulder, Colorado, reputed to exemplify this subculture of vitality. One was a full-service gym with a self-claimed "country club feel"; the other was a top-billed indoor climbing and fitness facility. The above anecdote exemplifies a central contention of this chapter, present in observations across both sites—that populations encouraged toward vitality (here, the fit bikers) are in a hierarchical relationship with populations marked for deterioration (the large-bodied contestants). Zoerhetorical theory attempts to understand the ways in which these unequal distributions of privilege and status are encouraged, enforced, and legitimated in biopolitical regimes of living.

It is a truism of biopolitical theory that regimes of living form ethical subjects. What (or who) counts as "good" or "ethical" ties intimately with biopolitical mandates. Didier Fassin named this phenomenon, as it operates on the level of the nation-state, *biolegitimacy,* or the recognition of the sacredness of life itself. According to Fassin, the imposition of biolegitimacy is crucial to the "moral economies of contemporary societies."[3] Fassin situates biolegitimacy

---

3. Fassin, "Another Politics of Life," 50.

within biopolitical theory as both rejoinder and revision to Foucauldian bio-power. When Michel Foucault famously identified the eighteenth-century shift from sovereign power (letting live and making die) to biopower (making live and letting die), he forsook an emphasis on "life itself" in place of popula-tion regulation.[4] As Fassin observes, the meat of Foucauldian biopolitics—demography, epidemiology, psychological institutions, public health—operates at the level of the population. Fassin's intervention supplants the emergence of biopower with the "imposition of biolegitimacy."[5] He explained, "It is not so much the power over life which is at stake here but rather the power *of* life as such."[6] Focusing on biolegitimacy rather than biopower emphasizes "the con-struction of the meaning and values of life instead of the exercise of forces and strategies to control it."[7] Biolegitimacy names this power *of* life itself.

I propose that we define biolegitimacy as the rhetorical strategy by which rhetors align themselves with humanitarianism by appealing to "life itself" in various forms.[8] A successful appeal to biolegitimacy may function to bolster credibility, gain good will, or justify violent actions. Crucially, it is not just particular bodies—human, animal, sick, healthy—that can be considered bio-legitimate. Nation-states and other organizations can achieve biolegitimacy; but in this chapter, I am concerned with the performances of biolegitimacy at the individual level. Persons engaging in successful performances of vitality (later I make a pitch for identifying them as "vital biocitizens") are marked by the cluster of qualities associated with properly internalized regimes of self-care—goodness, virtue, discipline, self-control, responsibility, and so on.

Of course, not everyone has access to life-building biolegitimate prac-tices, and herein lies the problem. In *Pedagogies of Crossing*, M. Jacqui Alex-ander asked a question that provided me a guiding heuristic for this chapter. She queried, "What do lives of privilege look like in the midst of war and the inevitable violence that accompanies the building of an empire?"[9] The daily practices of vitality at the nonpareil athletic clubs of Boulder, Colo-rado, are poised to supply an answer to this question. In fact, it is difficult for me to imagine lives more dramatically embedded in the privileges of vitality and well-being than those of these biocitizens. Alexander's question challenges the attributions of innocence and virtue associated with vitality-building practices like going to the gym. Her question even indicts the daily

4. Foucault, *History of Sexuality*; Foucault, *Society Must Be Defended*.
5. Fassin, "Another Politics of Life," 48–49.
6. Fassin, "Another Politics of Life," 50.
7. Fassin, "Another Politics of Life," 52.
8. Rowland, "Life-Saving Weapons."
9. Alexander, *Pedagogies of Crossing*, 1–2.

habits of Boulderites like Blaine and his biking pals (who, of course, act as substitutes for myself and my community of friends and acquaintances—no one is let off the hook here). Following Alexander leads me down a terrifying road, a road shockingly counterintuitive to most well-meaning white liberals. American-identified vitality practices are crucially bound to the formation of empire.

That vitality practices, especially as enacted by privileged populations, operate to maintain a hierarchy will be a starting assumption of this chapter. As daily, embodied, life-building habits, vitality practices both perform biolegitimacy and accumulate privilege, such as the very tangible privilege of a body that more closely conforms to the fit, slender, hyper-able ideal. Biolegitimate rhetorics and practices cluster in Boulder, in microbreweries, brunch joints, Whole Foods, and yes, gyms. The intensely demanding regimes of self-care in this small city feel compulsory and compulsive.

The chapter proceeds as follows. First, I elaborate the theoretical framework with which I approach vitality at the athletic clubs, centered around complementary threads of biopolitics and the growing scholarly corpus that positions itself "against health." From here I extrapolate the figure of the vitality-performing biocitizen—the privileged person whose life-building, zoerhetorically ascendant practices accumulate and store embodied privilege. To answer Alexander's question, these practices are what lives of privilege look like in the formation of empire. Next, I describe how vital biocitizenship is articulated in specific modes and moments at each site. Vital biocitizens use rhetorics of *training* and *whiteness* to encourage and justify the accumulation of embodied privilege—an accumulation that occurs at the expense of populations who are, in Lauren Berlant's words, slowly wearing out.[10]

THE ZOERHETORICS OF VITAL BIOCITIZENS

In *Losing It with Jillian*, the short-lived reality television spin-off of *The Biggest Loser*, host and trainer Jillian Michaels temporarily moves in with larger-bodied families to help them establish the exercise and nutrition patterns they need to "recover their health" and lose weight. In the pilot episode, a moment of exercise-induced exhaustion prompts family matriarch Agnes Mastropietro to say "Jillian, you're killing me!" The grave-faced Jillian shakes her head. "No," she responds, "you're killing you."[11] This moribund exchange marks clearly the

---

10. Berlant, *Cruel Optimism*.

11. Michaels, *Losing It with Jillian*, television program, NBC, season 1 episode 1, 2010.

stakes of performing health in contemporary regimes of living. To be healthy is to reach toward life; to be unhealthy is to slide toward death. If you are not performing biolegitimacy, you are dying. This section explores scholarship around regimes of living that suture performances of vitality to what it means to be a "good" citizen.

According to Foucault's genealogy, biopolitics has been the primary mode of governmentality since the late eighteenth century. The two interlocking poles of biopower, the disciplinary control of the individual body ("anatomo-politics," or care of the self) and the regulatory control of the population en masse, collaborate to render bodies both docile and useful.[12] Ethical subjects are formed by regimes of living, or what Andrew Lakoff and Stephen Collier call the "configurations of ethical elements—forms of practice, norms, modes of reasoning" concerned with the social and biological life of individuals and collectives.[13] In our specific historical moment, regimes of living form ethical subjects through performances of vitality. In other words, we tend to attribute positive qualities to persons performing biolegitimacy, or persons who demonstrate a commitment to "life itself" through health practices.

Biopolitics is system of managing populations. When citizens internalize practices of health and self-care, the state benefits biopolitically (that is, on the level of population) as well as economically. The "health" of a nation is roughly equated with the health of its worker-citizens, because sickness under capitalism means an inability to work.[14] The state, then, institutes a range of public programs and policies by which it encourages "health." Yet, as a growing body of necropolitical scholarship shows, not all groups of persons are subject to these liberal modes of governance that encourage flourishing and longevity. To echo Achille Mbembe, it is not an *accident* of biopolitical governance that some populations are nourished toward vitality and others are targeted for death. Rather, it is a *necessity* for the maintenance of domination—a necessity in the building of empire. To summarize this aphoristically, and probably too simply: all health is stolen.

What Mbembe called necropolitics described the ways in which regimes of power create populations targeted for *both* life and death. While Foucault and other biopolitical theorists like Roberto Esposito thought that some sort of rupture had to occur before biopolitics became lethal, Mbembe maintained that the life-giving and life-taking qualities of biopower were continuous with each other. Whereas persons of privilege are encouraged toward life in life-worlds, dispossessed persons are targeted for death in deathworlds. Like Jac-

12. Foucault, *Care of the Self.*
13. Lakoff and Collier, "Ethics and the Anthropology of Modern Reason," 427.
14. Harvey, "The Body as an Accumulation Strategy."

qui Alexander, Mbembe demands that we consider the populations targeted for death on which populations targeted for life both materially and symbolically rely. Yet, while a concept like Mbembian deathworlds might be indispensable for a zoerhetorical analysis of, say, drone strikes in Pakistan in the war on terror, it is less useful for understanding populations that aren't being directly targeted for death.

Enter Lauren Berlant and her theory of "slow death," which makes sense of less spectacular and more everyday biopolitical distributions of livability. In *Cruel Optimism,* Berlant identified a conceptual blind spot in Mbembe's necropolitics. What about, she asked, the many groups of people just slowly, unremarkably dying? She appended Mbembe's dramatic necropolitics with a theory of the daily, slow neglect and deterioration of populations. While Mbembe's deathworld inhabitants were Palestinians living in Israeli-occupied territories, Berlant's slow deathworld inhabitants were the fat working poor in the US. Rather than the attention-grabbing spectacles of murder and war, populations neglected toward "slow death" experience an unremarkable, daily deterioration.[15] In the same year that Berlant talked about slow death in *Cruel Optimism,* Rob Nixon debuted a similar concept of "slow violence" as a kind of violence of attrition, spread out over time and space, that is not spectacular and instantaneous but rather "incremental and accretive."[16] Both slow death and slow violence are useful counters and supplements to Mbembian deathworlds.

If Berlant's fat working poor experience *slow death,* we might think of the persons who work out at the Boulder athletic clubs as experiencing *slow life.* While Berlant focused on the everyday movements of US Americans who are slowly wearing out or "life-expending," I focus on the everyday movements of their counterparts: Americans who are slowly "getting better" or "improving" through what Berlant called "life-building" practices.[17] Indeed, rhetorics of self-improvement abound at the health clubs. Many people are attempting to improve their overall physical fitness, health, and well-being. The minute, daily, slow accrual of various components of physical fitness stands in sharp relief against the frenetic work of exercise itself—exercise intended to enhance muscle endurance, muscle strength, agility, flexibility, and cardiorespiratory fitness. These biometrically measurable indicators of vitality are forms of stored body privilege. This privilege might later result in desirable payoffs like longevity, attributions of physical attractiveness, or survival in the

---

15. Berlant, *Cruel Optimism.*

16. Nixon, *Slow Violence,* 2.

17. Berlant, *Cruel Optimism,* Kindle edition, loc. 586.

post-apocalyptic collapse of society.[18] If biolegitimacy is one of the rationalities by which a population is rendered governable, then one of the consequences of this mode of governmentality is an intense, resource-costly focus on the embodied self. Conveniently, a "properly" internalized gaze of self-care (paired with the time-consuming, salaried career and perhaps a heteronormative or homonormative family life) leaves little time or energy for resisting these bio-political mandates—or their necropolitical consequences.

CRITICAL HEALTH STUDIES, ACCUMULATED BODY PRIVILEGE, AND THE ZOERHETORICAL HIERARCHY

A healthy body of literature critiques vitality. Robert Crawford's coinage of the term *healthism* in 1980 crystallized an incipient critical health movement. Alarmed at the extent to which personal health had become a national preoc-cupation, Crawford denounced the elevation of health to a "super value" and metaphor for all that is good in life.[19] Similarly, philosopher Ivan Illich's lecture series in the eighties (provocatively titled "To Hell with Health") skewered health practices as leading toward a host of iatrogenic (doctor-caused) dis-eases while padding the pockets of the medical industries.[20] Subsequent schol-arship took positions ranging from mild critique to outrage against health practices, such as Petr Skrabanek's 1994 treatise that located a nascent totali-tarianism behind state coercions toward compulsory healthy lifestyles. Like Crawford, Skrabanek also objected to the preachy moralism accompanying health talk.

In the epigram that opens this chapter, Aristotle uses health, what he describes as "bodily excellence," as a self-evident example of a good thing. What is remarkable here is not just the health-loving spirit inherited from the Greeks but the ways in which this ancient embrace of health has morphed in late liberal times. The word *health* is mentioned twenty-three times through-out Aristotle's *On Rhetoric,* often as a *prima facie* part of the good life. Of course, Aristotle could never begin to predict the ways in which health itself would become its own status-laden attribution of virtue stitched through with classist and racist advantages.

As a scholar of rhetoric, I would be remiss to not mention the anti-health thread running through Kenneth Burke's corpus. During one of his

---

18. This latter example may seem far-fetched, but talk of survival after social collapse was surprisingly common in these fieldsites.

19. Crawford, "Healthism and the Medicalization of Everyday Life," 368.

20. Hoinacki and Mitcham, *The Challenges of Ivan Illich.*

lengthy word-association lists in *Counter-Statement*, he linked the following to a "healthy club-offer": efficiency, prosperity, increased consumption, higher standards of living, enthusiasm, faith.[21] As Debra Hawhee asserted, Burke was critical of the sterile, medical approach to health and believed that life "grows out of the rot."[22] Ellen Quandahl nicely summed Kenneth Burke's Janus-faced relationship to health with this sentence: "Burke is best known for his 'comic' attitude, but his work is deeply riven, divided between the smilingly hypochondriacal pursuit of health and wariness of the discursive regimes of order."[23] What is notable here is that Quandahl is essentially referencing Burke's twinned horror at and fascination with the Great Chain of Being and its relationship to well-being. While Burke was critical of the moralism attached to health practices, he was also drawn inexorably to their promises.

In an analysis with which Burke would certainly agree, Skrabanek asserted that "healthy" automatically equaled moral, patriotic, and pure, while "unhealthy" indexed the opposite poles: immoral, unpatriotic or foreign, and impure.[24] The most systematic collection of critical health studies to date, Jonathan Metzl and Anna Kirkland's edited book, *Against Health: How Health Became the New Morality*, followed this vein of health critique. Essays in this volume identified health discourses and practices as colonizing, stigmatizing, normalizing, medicalizing, and consumerist.[25] In daily conversations and media representations, health operates as a transparent, universal good employed to "make moral judgments, convey prejudice, sell products, or even to exclude whole groups of persons from health care."[26]

In a turn to the biopolitical, British sociologist Nikolas Rose asserted that healthism is the ideological linkage between "public objectives for the good ... with the desire of individuals for health and well being."[27] Later, in *The Politics of Life Itself*, Rose examined biomedicine's "molecularization," or the creation of a genomic body, and the concurrent shift from health as a practice of healing to a way of governing.[28] In an impressive body of work that at various times analyzed pregnancy, AIDS, food, fat, and fatherhood, Deborah Lupton identified *risk* as one of the pervasive health rhetorics that further encouraged the responsibilization of the individual and that brought forth a new health

---

21. I read "healthy club-offer" as a typographical error for "health club offer." Burke, *Counter-Statement*, 111.
22. Hawhee, *Moving Bodies*, 152.
23. Quandahl, "It's Essentially as Though This Were Killing Us," 20.
24. Skrabanek, *The Death of Humane Medicine and the Rise of Coercive Healthism*.
25. Metzl and Kirkland, *Against Health*.
26. Metzl, "Introduction: Why 'Against Health?,'" 2.
27. Rose, *Powers of Freedom*, 74.
28. Rose, *The Politics of Life Itself.*

consciousness in the polity.[29] Like Rose, Lupton formed the foundation for a scholarly dialogue that examined risk and other moral imperatives of health as modes of governance.

If health is a mode of governance, as these scholars claim, then rewards exist for those who successfully perform health, and punishments exist for those to fail to perform health. A series of social science investigations have used empirical measurements to capture the consequences of failing to successfully perform health. Body size is one dimension of health that has received attention. Research shows that fatter people are less likely to succeed at job interviews, to be acquitted by juries, or to be attributed positive qualities in general when compared with their thinner counterparts.[30] To a greater extent than men, women face penalties for deviating from the bodily ideal, a phenomena that has been documented in the areas of employment, education, and health.[31] Fat people are not only explicitly excluded from a range of careers because of their body size (such as those in the military, police force, or commercial aviation) but may also face higher charges for health care and health insurance. Even in mundane daily activities like moving through public space or using public transportation, larger bodies are persistently subject to what Nike Ayo called "gazes of repulsion."[32] Most of us have probably experienced that facial expression of disgust mixed with superiority and judgment— but the fattest among us experience these disgusted gazes more than others. Conversely, bodies that externally manifest the ideals of biolegitimacy receive gazes of approval. While it might be tempting to dismiss both disapproving and approving public gazes as minor events, we would be remiss to ignore the powerful effects of these micro-aggressions and micro-affirmations.[33] For these reasons, Sherri Irvin names body oppression a gendered and racialized social injustice.[34]

A successful biolegitimate performance of health, perhaps externally manifested as a slender body, operates as a visible status cue. Like race, gender, sexuality, or ability, body size/shape is one axis of an interlocking system of domination. As communication scholar Kathleen Lebesco observed, "If African Americans and Latinos are fatter than whites and Asians, and women are more likely than men to be fat, fatness haunts us as a reminder of deteriorating

29. Lupton, "Risk as Moral Danger."
30. Saguy, *What's Wrong with Fat?*
31. Donaghue and Clemitshaw, "I'm Totally Smart and a Feminist."
32. Ayo, "Understanding Health Promotion in a Neoliberal Climate," 104.
33. Irvin, "Resisting Body Oppression."
34. Irvin, "Resisting Body Oppression."

physical privilege in terms of race and sex."[35] This spate of research establishes body size/shape as another biopolitical fault line along which zoerhetorical status is re/distributed. The privileges of conforming to a bodily ideal reach far beyond the exigencies of vanity or self-advancement. The extent to which a body conforms to the slender ideal results in real, tangible, material payoffs—especially for women. Irvin writes,

> The issue, then, is not that attractive people are treated a bit more nicely than unattractive people. Instead, we have a picture whereby, from the moment of birth, attractive people (with a few exceptions) accrue positive social capital in families, schools, and workplaces, while unattractive people pay a very substantial penalty that may involve less positive parental attention, less support from teachers, less recognition for their qualifications, less help when they need it, more punishment, and so forth. Some are routinely teased, bullied, dehumanized, and ostracized.[36]

According to David Harvey, bodies accumulate the effects of the processes that "produce, support, sustain, and dissolve [them]."[37] Of course, a distinct unevenness persists as to how different bodies absorb capitalism's flows. According to Harvey, privileged bodies accumulate capitalism's rewards and less privileged bodies absorb capitalism's externalities, such as the consumption of nutritionally vacuous food or exposure to toxins. The vitality-performing biocitizen, then, is a figure whose body aggregates and stores the biopolitical privilege of embodied social capital. In turn, this figure is allowed to demonstrate this privilege daily with the performance of a physically fit, healthy, and even hyper-able body.

One further quality of the vitality-performing biocitizen is her durable association with virtue. A number of studies in the social sciences concur that we are more likely to make attributions of "goodness" and virtue to persons whose bodies conform to a thin, fit ideal.[38] If body size/shape is a biopolitical fault line along which consequential status is conferred or denied, then *virtue* is one of the primary discursive topoi for this particular zoerhetorical movement. Attributions of virtue here are deeply linked to another important zoerhetorical topos: biolegitimacy. Performances of virtue often draw on "life itself" to accrue the attributions of goodness and morality that render them virtuous. The occurrence of fat-shaming renders this concept in more

35. Lebesco, "Fat Panic and the New Morality," 74.
36. Irvin, "Resisting Body Oppression," 5.
37. Harvey, "Body as an Accumulation Strategy," 402.
38. Halse, "Bio-Citizenship"; Jutel, "Weighing Health."

concrete terms. While persons whose bodies do not conform to the ideal are shamed with gazes of repulsion, gazes of approval attribute virtue to bodies that mimic idealized forms. Although this equation of athleticism with virtue may seem like a new phenomenon, Debra Hawhee's *Bodily Arts* reminds us of the ancient Greek *aretē*, which she renders as *virtuosity* rather than *virtue* to emphasize the performative striving inherent in the concept.[39] Following Isocrates, Hawhee is attuned to the ways in which athletic training (taken together with oratorical training) "provides a program for shaping an entire self."[40] The links between embodied capacity and virtue and are thousands of years old.

HARDER, BETTER, FASTER, STRONGER: BECOMING VITAL BIOCITIZENS

If an ongoing rhetorical suturing continually binds health with virtue, this produces populations of citizens that have the opportunity to align themselves with the positive attributions of goodness that a healthy lifestyle offers. I refer to these persons as *vital biocitizens* and their series of practices of social belonging as they pertain to self-care as *vital biocitizenship*. For the term *biocitizenship*, I am indebted to a number of conversation partners. First, anthropologist Adriana Petryna coined the term in 2002 to describe the way in which Ukrainians affected by the Chernobyl disaster took radiation poisoning as a point of entry to demand redress from the state. For Petryna, biocitizenship referred to projects of health and well-being articulated in terms of relationship to the state.[41] As Petryna explained, biocitizenship is valuable insofar as it links "the matter of the living (biological, whether as an irradiated or infected body) and the meaning of politics (citizenship, in terms of social as well as civil rights . . .)."[42] Avoiding the portmanteau, Nikolas Rose and Carlos Novas offered the phrase *biological citizenship* in 2003 to encompass all "citizenship projects that have linked their conceptions of citizens to beliefs about the biological existence of human beings, as individuals, as families and lineages, as communities, as population and races, and as a species."[43] Petryna's and Rose and Novas's biocitizens make claims on the state from a place of bodily *dam-*

---

39. Hawhee, *Bodily Arts*, 17–18.
40. Hawhee, *Bodily Arts*, 6.
41. Petryna, *Life Exposed*.
42. Fassin, "Another Politics of Life," 51.
43. Rose and Novas, "Biological Citizenship," 2.

age. By contrast, Boulder's vital biocitizens pursue status recognition from a place of (purported) bodily *improvement*.

In the first multidisciplinary collected volume on biocitizenship, Kelly Happe, Jenell Johnson, and Marina Levina outline three broad meanings of biocitizenship in their critical genealogy: "as a redress for collective bodily injury by the state; as a mode of biopolitical governance; and as a form of health advocacy and activism."[44] The vital biocitizens that I discuss in this chapter belong in this last category, with one caveat. Rather than health *activism*, they are doing health *performance*. They are less invested in the importance of a biosociality or a collective by which to mobilize public claims for resources or to raise public awareness. Although vital biocitizens clump and cluster in friend groups and workout classes, *there is no attempt to speak as a political group*. For vital biocitizens, their relation to the state is submission. Beyond being mildly left-leaning, they do not enact a shared political identity among themselves.

In this way, my use of biocitizenship tracks well with that of Christine Halse, who described biocitizens as taking (self-)control of markers of health in order to live as good, ethical civic subjects.[45] In the contemporary figure of the biocitizen, Halse reads the birth of a new kind of human living among narratives of escalating urgency and crisis around the so-called obesity epidemic. Biocitizens can never be *too* industrious or *too* diligent when engaging in health practices. In a similar fashion, LeAnne Petherick described the production of biocitizens in high school physical education classes in Canada, especially as these young students used the culminating fitness test of the mile run as an opportunity to evaluate and manage their own fitness progress.[46] When Kathryn Henne described Olympic athletes as biocitizens, she described biocitizens as persons whose regimes of health and self-care intimately tied them to the state. As a result of their exceptional physical prowess, Olympic athletes both accrued transnational privilege (such as mobility) and garnered heightened surveillance (such as gender policing).[47] While most of the vital biocitizens at the gyms in Boulder neither approach this level of internationally elite athleticism nor garner the kind of surveillance of Olympian bodies, the concept of biocitizenship retains traction across this wide range of athletic performances. In some ways, the athletes at the gym demonstrate even more vital biocitizenship than Olympic athletes because they

---

44. Happe, Johnson, and Levina, *Biocitizenship: The Politics of Bodies, Governance, and Power*, 2.

45. Halse, "Bio-Citizenship."

46. Petherick, "Producing the Young Biocitizen."

47. Henne, "Tracing Olympic Bio-Citizenship."

maintain a level of conditioning at the elite amateur level while being committed to full-time, often high-status, white-collar careers. Architects, profes-
sors, lawyers, city council members, software developers, and start-up CEOs
exercise at both of the athletic clubs where I conducted research.

The vital biocitizen's quest for more bodily capacity sits uncomfortably
with critical disability studies as well as with Jasbir Puar's recent theorization
of debility. Underlying the goal of bodily improvement is the assumption that
more capacity (whether measured as strength, speed, flexibility, mobility, or
endurance) is *always better*. As Sunaura Taylor writes, "Disability studies and
activism call for recognizing new ways of valuing life that aren't limited by
specific physical or mental capabilities. Implicit in disability theory is the idea
that it is not specifically our intelligence, rationality, agility, physical indepen-
dence, or bipedal nature that give us dignity and value."[48] Juxtaposed with
critical disability studies, the vital biocitizen's perpetual striving for improvement unavoidably perpetuates ableism. Intended as an interruption to the
ability/disability binary, debility refers to the "slow wearing down of populations instead of the event of becoming disabled."[49] Debility extends slow death
by examining the economic collaboration between liberal frameworks of disability and debility. Slow life rides on the back of slow death.

The rhetoric of vital biocitizens could not be more clear in the preference
for some forms of human embodiment over others. While both the disabled
body and the hyper-abled body of the vital biocitizen are cast as unfinished
projects, their relations to vulnerability, fragility, and the medical gaze differ.[50]
This section's subtitle gets its name from a 2001 Daft Punk song played often
at both gyms, perhaps for its fitspo qualities. The lyrics are significant to ability and the body as an unfinished project, as the song's chorus repeats many
times: "Work it harder / Make it better / Do it faster / Makes us stronger." Like
the song, the gyms privilege bodies with able, or even hyper-able, capacities
regarding strength, endurance, mobility, and flexibility—these qualities are
just *better*.

I will amend my discussion of biocitizens with this reflexive disclosure.
Although I critique biocitizens, I also recognize that I am a vitality-aspirant
biocitizen. (And readers of this book likely are as well.) In fact, I feel comfortable condemning practices of vital biocitizenship precisely because they are
"my people." Of course, how my own body shows up in these spaces necessarily influenced the ways in which I experienced the gyms or how interview-
ers responded to me. If my body were bigger, for example, I think fewer vital

---

48. Taylor, *Beasts of Burden*, 57.
49. Puar, *The Right to Maim*, xii.
50. McLaughlin and Coleman-Fountain, "The Unfinished Body."

biocitizens I spoke with would have been so openly fat-shaming. Passing as a vital biocitizen brought me some access to their (our?) hidden scripts. At the same time, I never felt that I fully belonged. While my time in Boulder was probably a time when I was in the best shape of my life, I never felt that I fully passed as strong enough, slender enough, active enough. While my body was rarely subject to gazes of disgust (a privilege, I recognize), it seemed like so many other bodies were earning gazes of approval. Of course, this never-good-enough appraisal of one's body as an unfinished project is precisely the hinge on which the whole operation turns. Boulder's athletic clubs capitalize, in both senses of the term, on this affective attachment to the promise of improvement, so I turn my attention to them.

BIOCITIZENS AT BOULDER'S PREMIER ATHLETIC CLUBS

Smile, you're in Boulder!
—Sign in Whole Foods store parking lot

I made most of my observations while participating at two facilities, although this fieldwork quickly spilled over the boundaries of any physical site and infiltrated social time with friends, amateur race events in which I participated, and my general lifestyle living in downtown Boulder, Colorado. The first facility is an expensive athletic club with, according to its website, "a country club feel" tucked beneath one of the "nation's premier walking malls." In addition to other amenities, this gym offers a year-round saline outdoor pool and over one hundred fitness classes per week in spacious separate studios for spin cycling, bike training, Pilates, yoga, and group fitness. The second facility is a climbing gym in Boulder that boasts a world-class clientele, as many professional climbers reside or train in Boulder for its proximity to challenging climbing terrain, and yoga, cycling, and fitness classes.

Over the course of four years, from 2010 to 2014, I was a regular member of both facilities. At both sites, I collected field-note observations in dual modes, as both participant (climber, belayer, treadmill runner, fitness class attendee, hot-tub soaker) and observer (sitting in these spaces and taking notes). I spent roughly three to eight hours per week at the athletic club, where my membership did not lapse for four consecutive years. (My membership began on a "nanny pass"—the perk of a regular babysitting gig that I was using to stretch my graduate assistance funds. Therefore it is accurate to say that I began as an outsider.) My attendance at the climbing gym was less consistent; I purchased membership in three-month increments once or twice a year. Local outdoor climbing sites, like Boulder Canyon, Chautauqua, Eldorado Canyon, and Flagstaff Mountain also served as places where I encountered biocitizenly practices on real rock. The systematic data collection and interviews for this project began when I received IRB approval in late 2012. I interviewed a number of friends and acquaintances (and then their acquaintances) in a small snowball sample—in total there were four formal and about ten informal interviews. In many ways, I was immersed in Boulder's vital biocitizen subculture even at home, as my partner at the time was a rock climber, ice climber, and ultrarunner regularly in training. Because both facilities are reputed to exemplify the subculture of fitness and athleticism that defines Boulder, Colorado, I begin with a description of Boulder itself.

Biocitizenship in Boulder, Colorado

One summer, when my partner and I hosted a barbecue at a public park in Boulder, we realized that everyone gathered around the grill was currently or had at one point been a sponsored athlete in cyclocross, orienteering, or ultrarunning. A patch of triathletes chatted nearby. I have never lived in a place so inclined toward athletic endeavors; nor have I ever been invited to so many social gatherings that revolve around exercise in some way. Yet, as if by inertia, I began to regularly meet friends at cycling classes at the local gym in the evenings (for a few of them, it was the second workout of their day) and I completed my first sprint-distance triathlon in 2013. I trained in the climbing gym in the winter to "session my projects," as they say, in the summer, and I made regular use of the hiking trails, bike paths, and open green space for which Boulder is famous. Scores of professional cyclists, climbers, runners, and other athletes live in Boulder for access to these luxuries and to reap the hypoxic benefits of training at altitude.

Boulder is consistently ranked among the top cities for outdoor sports access and is reputed to be the most physically fit city in the most physically fit state in the nation. One GQ poll honored Boulder as the "worst dressed city that looks best naked," a reference to the shapely bodies underneath the athleisure wear.[51] Of course, not everyone in town is a well-conditioned athlete, nor does Boulder have the monopoly on status-oriented fitness practices. There is certainly some pushback against the "cult of the body" that feels compulsory here. It is telling that people will "out" themselves as "not Boulder enough"

51. The GQ rankings of worst-dressed cities can be found here: Zunger, "The 40 Worst-Dressed Cities in America." As the GQ poll notes, the city is obsessed with its high performance in fitness and lifestyle rankings.

if they do not pursue, at least somewhat competitively, a gamut of outdoor sports. Not surprisingly, as property values have inflated around Boulder, what was formerly celebrated as a progressive hippie town has become a place where persons performing consumption-oriented whiteness gather and gentrify. (Complaints abound about "Trustafarians," or wealthy white young adults who present themselves as countercultural hippies.) What Jessie Stewart and Greg Dickinson called the "Colorado lifestyle" is inextricably linked to consumption, as many of the nation's boutique fitness apparel stores, such as Mont Bell, Prana, Go Lite, or Skirt Sports locate their flagship stores on Boulder's Pearl Street mall.[52] For these reasons, the city of Boulder furnishes an excellent geographical location at which to build a theory around the embodied accumulation of privilege through practices of vitality.[53]

Boulder's identity as a fit city appears at the gyms, too, in personal interactions as well as promotional material. One perk for signing up for membership at the athletic club was three sessions with a personal fitness instructor. "Just don't start dieting and running three hours a day without telling me . . . believe me, it happens in Boulder," advised my personal fitness instructor, as she pinched a handful of fat from my abdomen to measure with calipers. Amid zero communication from me that I was unhappy with my current body weight, it was hard to not experience her advice as a subtle admonishment of my (failing) performance of vitality. Her subtext, as interpreted through my necessarily partial experience, was, "If you want to fit in here, you're going to have to change your current nutrition and exercise routine for a more demanding one." In a similar vein, the gym's website practically gushes:

> Even if you don't live or work in Boulder, you've likely heard how health and fitness is a major part of our lifestyle. Boulder consistently ranks among studies' and publications' fittest cities in America; walk into a grocery store and it seems like most of the shoppers just finished a trail run, a bike ride or a yoga class; internationally competitive athletes train in Boulder. Surrounded by so many positive influences, many of our Members don't need motivation to stay in shape; their focus is to simply work with talented, knowledgeable professionals.

---

52. Stewart and Dickinson, "Enunciating Locality in the Postmodern Suburb."

53. In focusing on upscale gyms, I do not mean to suggest that working-class communities of Boulder (and the nature of their fitness practices) are unimportant. I focus on the privileged groups precisely because I am interested in bodily accumulations of this privilege—especially the kind of accumulations that have consequential zoerhetorical effects.

Members do not need motivation to stay in shape, because they have fully and appropriately internalized regimes of vital self-care particularly salient in Boulder. The upscale local athletic club uses an affiliation with Boulder's vital biocitizen identity (while tapping the vague expertise of "studies and publications") to promote itself as a competent venue. In this paragraph we can also see the link between responsible fitness practices and responsible consumption ("walk into any grocery store"). In fact, the undertone of Boulder pride is best exemplified at a grocery store. The regional flagship Whole Foods market, just a few blocks from either gym, has signs in its parking lot that say "Smile, you're in Boulder!" After a morning group fitness class, club-goers descend on the juice bar and hot bar at the Whole Foods, perhaps in an attempt to consume "quality protein" calories within twenty minutes of strength training, as we are repeatedly advised by fitness instructors *cum* biopedagogues. This awareness of Boulder's physically fit and athletic reputation permeated both of my field sites.

Working Out at the Athletic Clubs

The glass triple-door entrance to the athletic club greets you with succulents and ferns. To advance into the main interior, you must show your membership card with photo ID to a person behind the counter, who welcomes you to the club and then says "Have a good workout!" The large indoor space opens as you pass a large stone fountain, wide-screen television, comfortable couches, and a snack bar called "Energy." Although I have visited the gym at every time of day, I liked it best during the late morning, past the prework rush. Many middle-aged women use the facility at that time, often dropping their kids off at the attached child-care center called "Blast," a kid's "active play" space, before their workout. One thing that makes Boulder different from other cities of its size is the number of people who are freelance consultants, work from home, or have flexible hours. As a result, there are people in the gyms at all times of the day, but both gyms still experience a post–5:00 p.m. rush.

That the women's locker room at the athletic club feels welcoming (warm, clean, even luxurious) is an achievement of the maintenance labor enacted there. The well-appointed locker rooms include shampoo, conditioner, body wash, hair dryers, body lotion, styling gel, Q-tips, tampons, shaving cream, razors, cotton balls, an iron and ironing board, and plastic combs bathing in Barbicide. The locker room's luxurious feel hinges on a custodial labor specifically designed to be invisible—so invisible that I first failed to recognize it as consequential for the zoerhetorical transvaluations that I sought to observe.

Sometimes after showering, it was hard to resist the saline hot tub, eucalyptus aromatherapy steam room, or sauna. With the half-closed eyes of reverie, I would sit in these spaces and be aware of the two or three Latinx women working in the locker room at any given time. Over and over again, these women wiped clumps of hair from shower drains, gathered soiled towels from the floor, restocked supplies, emptied waste bins, and cleaned toilets—in other words, they performed the repetitive, physically demanding, and poorly paid labor of maintenance.[54]

I initially overlooked the women cleaning the locker room, wrongly assuming that they were not significant to the zoerhetorics of vital biocitizenship. Consider, however, how their labor illustrates the material and relational movements of the zoerhetorical hierarchy. In order for the women at the club to experience the luxury of the locker room, other women must labor. These polar experiences of pampering and toiling are distributed predictably along racial and class divides. In an analogous vein, Elsa Barkley Brown insisted that the entrance of white middle-class American women into the workforce in the mid-twentieth century *was only possible* because women of color supported them at home, as cleaners, cooks, or child-care providers. She went on to claim that these relations are "grounded in the very deindustrialization and decentralization which has meant the export of capital to other parts of the world, where primarily people of color—many of them female—face overwhelming exploitation from multinational corporations."[55] Following Brown, the predominantly white and economically advantaged women experiencing the athletic club's locker room as welcoming and luxurious *is only possible* because of the undervalued labor of women of color and economically disadvantaged women who support them at home, care for their children, work in the factories that produce soap products or athletic apparel, or clean the locker room itself. A comparable claim about the men's locker room stands as well. The resources and labor that sustain existents targeted for life are extracted from existents designated with a lower status on the Great Chain. The continued privilege of vital biocitizens *requires* the appearance of bodies less deserving, so that the exploitation of these less deserving bodies can be rendered as the natural and obvious order of things. Locker room custodians are just one example of the undervalued labor that makes vital biocitizenship possible.

---

54. If I may share a vulnerable ethnographic note for the sake of transparency: I regret not interviewing these women during data collection for this project. In a testament to the invisibility of their labor, it did not even occur to me until a smart anonymous reviewer asked me to consider them.

55. Brown, "What Has Happened Here?," 299.

When I was washing or dressing in the locker room, I listened to the backstage conversations. The combination of the intimacy of nakedness, the close proximity between lockers, and the plush surroundings invited strangers to chat with one another. Mostly we chatted about what was in front of us: the content on one of the flat-screen televisions ("Are they always playing the Kardashians in here?"); the performance quality of different types of activewear ("Yeah, Gaiam's clothes are definitely for people who *move*"; "Under Armour's sports bras are the best because you can shop by cup size"); the aesthetic quality of different types of activewear ("That top is so cute—where did you get it?"); or the group fitness, cycling, or yoga class from which we recognize each other ("Oh my God, my butt is always so sore from Tracy's TRX class. Nothing makes you feel skinny when you put your jeans on more than sore glutes!"). I once heard a buff, tan, middle-aged woman asking another, "How do you work out when you're at your Aspen cabin?" The saddest line I ever overheard was one very thin middle-aged woman telling another, "I don't feel like myself until I exercise. That's when you know you have a problem, I guess."

Both gyms leveraged interior design choices and marketing discourse to exaggerate their level of environmental consciousness, a strategy known as greenwashing. According to the athletic club's website, their spacious square footage is "canvassed by earth-tone finishings, natural stone and energy efficient lighting." I am skeptical about this appeal to greenness. When you walk through the main fitness floor, tens of treadmills, elliptical machines, and Stairmasters each have a television in front of them that is usually on whether the machine is in use or not—what a waste of energy! When Greg Dickinson described a Starbucks, he linked the curved plant form, green colors, and wood paneling of the interior design with the intent to signal wide-open spaces, a minimal environmental footprint, the greenness of nature, and the greenness of money.[56] Like the corporate giant Starbucks, the climbing gym's attempt at a green image is also part of a careful marketing scheme. It features solar panels and a real-time display of the club's energy use in the lobby.

The climbing gym may not be as luxurious as the athletic club, but it dazzles. The main foyer opens into wide, carpeted stadium-style benches. Climbers are invited to watch people on the "gray wall," or the wall with the steepest terrain and most challenging set climbs. On any given evening, there are a handful of highly competent, even world-class, climbers working on one climb over and over again on the gray wall. This repeated work on one climb is called "sessioning a project" (or, for those in the know, "seshing a

---

56. Dickinson, "Joe's Rhetoric."

proj"). The gray wall arcs out over the seating area like a tidal wave about to crash, forming an amphitheater shape, and thereby underscoring the public nature of athletic performance at the gym. Because climbers use chalk on their palms and fingers for traction, the air in the climbing gym is often cloudy with fine white dust—a state that the building's designers tried to combat with an advanced ventilation system. Climbs are "set" (that is, designed and installed with removable plastic handholds and footholds), marked with colored tape, and then rated for difficulty (on a scale from 5.5 to 5.15). It was not uncommon to see a plastic, textured climbing hold with blood on it. No one seems to care. I have ripped open fingers and knees plenty of times on fake and real rock, and you don't always get the opportunity to clean the hold.

Both gyms entertain a relationship with spectatorship and display. Mirrors line the walls of the group fitness room, the cycling studio, the functional fitness floor, and the yoga studio of the athletic club. In fitness classes, we are entreated by instructors to use the side or front mirrors to check our alignment and make necessary self-adjustments. A handful of eager group fitness devotees arrive early to snag spots directly in front of the mirror (I confess to being one of these people). At the athletic club, the greater a particular fitness instructor's following, the earlier you have to arrive. At the climbing gym, by positioning the steepest wall in front of the stadium seating, the most skilled climbers cluster together for the viewer's pleasure. The treadmills and stationary bikes that ring the upper level of the gym also face the gray wall. The level of climbing is so advanced at the gym that it almost serves as an advertisement for the gym itself. Next to these talented athletes and feeling on display, it was difficult to not be self-conscious about my climbing skills in the arena-like viewing center.

A busy night at the climbing gym can turn into a who's who of the national or local climbing circuit. Acquaintances would whisper, "That's Jim Erickson, he had a ton of bad-ass first ascents in Eldo[rado Canyon]!" or "That's Brooke Raboutou, she's twelve, she's a prodigy. Her whole family climbs fourteens." The opportunity to climb right next to these "celebrities," and even cheer them on, can be inspiring but also enervating. For years I avoided climbing on the gray wall because it felt like I was not allowed in "their" space. The most elite crop of climbers at the gym were often sponsored by a popular brand of climbing shoes (such as 5.11 or Sportiva) or other outdoor apparel companies. Spotting Lynn Hill at the gym was not unusual but always a treat. She was the first person—not just the first woman—to free climb The Nose on El Capitan in Yosemite National Park. She is now a "Patagonia Ambassador," a fact that demonstrates the relationship between wearing the proper clothing, consumption, and the performance of vital biocitizenship.

Another feature of both gyms is the presence of skilled trainers roaming the facility. At the athletic club, these workers are available to spot you while you lift weights or answer questions about the use of a particular machine. At the climbing gym, these workers are more likely to be doing safety checks, to make sure people are belaying properly. One man I interviewed who worked at the climbing gym—a climber himself—had many stories to share about people taking life-threatening falls at the gym because of faulty equipment or incompetent belaying. For a few months, the climbing gym had a foot-shaped hole in the padded carpet beneath the highest point on the gray wall. (Climbing is dangerous. I had too many close calls, and I no longer do it.) Both facilities feature display walls with photographs and brief biographies of their certified trainers, and both facilities advertise and encourage paying for additional one-on-one sessions with their personal trainers.

As Dickinson noted of coffee-shop baristas, these trainers can be understood as "cultural workers," insofar as they interpret and "sell" the variety of goods available for the vital biocitizen's consumption.[57] These cultural workers are partially responsible for representing, and even branding, their respective gyms. During one revealing moment in a cycling class at the athletic club, I heard a fitness instructor say to a latecomer, "Oh, be careful, that bike is broken. Oh wait, I'm not supposed to say anything is broken. I am supposed to say that it 'requires maintenance.' Oops, I forgot!" She rolled her eyes, as if to suggest that that level of language policing was ridiculous. In that instant, her break from the top-down imposed script momentarily revealed the highly structured nature of interaction between the club's cultural workers and club-goers. An employee I interviewed at the climbing gym echoed this observation, by noting that he was provided a "huge, top-secret manual" that prescribed exactly what to say at the club in various situations.

Typically, bodies across both sites present as muscular, fit, and white. This is not to suggest that overweight bodies never frequent these places but rather to emphasize the homogeneity of Boulder's vital biocitizens, especially as they cluster and move at these athletic centers. This is embarrassing to relay, but one time while climbing with a friend, we saw a person of size at the gym. "Wow, he must be really brave," we said. "It must be really hard for him to be here." I recognize that kind of talk to be superior and patronizing, but I share it as a meaningful ethnographic datum that opens into some opportunity to reflexive engagement with how my own body influences my experience in these spaces. The list of various privileges that allows me to move comfortably through these gyms includes able-bodied-ness, whiteness, and a convention-

---

57. Dickinson, "Joe's Rhetoric," 18.

ally feminine presentation (especially influential regarding my experience in bathrooms and locker rooms).

Typically, there are a few more men than women at the climbing gym. At the athletic club, there are more women than men (reflective of national rates of health club memberships). However, gendered bodies cluster differently in the gym. What Shari Dworkin observed in her ethnography of a fitness club in 2003 was generally true of the fitness clubs in Boulder ten years later: more women tend to participate in group fitness classes and to use cardiovascular equipment, whereas more men tend to use weight-lifting equipment.[58]

The assumed level of fitness and mobility in group fitness classes at both sites serve as a good example of the homogeneity of bodies gathered there. Certified fitness instructors are typically trained to offer novice, intermediate, and advanced modifications for any one single exercise. For example, in Hot Yoga classes at the athletic club, I would often hear various modifications offered as options for a single *asana* (the Sanskrit word for "pose"). Through a series of visual observations, fitness instructors "read" the ability levels of the bodies present in order to determine the modifications they need to offer. As a result, especially at the climbing gym, the group fitness instruction assumes high fitness levels and ranges of mobility. Instructors often assumed, for example, that participants were willing and able to partake in activities such as jumping rope, unassisted pull-ups, or rapidly switching from supine to standing to inverted positions.

In addition to an assumed able-bodied-ness, there are a number of everyday social and capital privileges enjoyed by vital biocitizens. Here is a partial list of these privileges enjoyed by many of the biocitizens I have observed at these sites: a professional career or other mode of economic support (such as a trust fund) that allowed for the physical and psychological energy and time required for working out; the financial stability required to pay in excess of hundreds of dollars a month for sometimes multiple gym memberships, equipment, apparel, and race registration fees; access to the additional quality calories required to support a rigorous training regimen; social/familial networks who support or encourage time spent "training"; access to medical care in support of a training regimen (such as a sports massage therapy or physical therapy); residential proximity to athletic training facilities; and a self-conception that one's body is capable of improvement or even superior performance across a range of fitness indicators. Clearly the vitality-performing biocitizen reaps the benefits of her economic, social, and cultural capital.

58. Dworkin, "A Woman's Place Is in the . . . Cardiovascular Room?"

MAKING VITAL BIOCITIZENS: TRAINING AND WHITENESS

> Health today is not so much a biological imperative linked to survival as a social imperative linked to status.
>
> —Jean Baudrillard, *The Consumer Society*

When Baudrillard wrote *The Consumer Society,* in 1970, he had no idea of the proliferative ways in which performances of vitality would index social status in the ensuing fifty years. As they are performed across these two athletic clubs in Boulder, the biocitizen's self-promoting practices draw from rhetorics of *training* and *whiteness*. In the contemporary regime of living, these two rhetorics allow vitality-performing biocitizens to do what Burke would call "mount[ing] the hierarchy" in publicly sanctioned, socially approved ways.[59] Each of these overlapping rhetorics of training and whiteness illuminates characteristics of the slow, life-building, accretive practices of the vitality-performing biocitizen. Further, each of these zoerhetorics hews biocitizens *to* a range of positive qualities and *from* a range of negative qualities. In the ongoing and dynamic zoerhetorical movements in the contemporary US, the set of positive qualities associated with properly internalized regimes of self-care include goodness, virtue, discipline, self-control, responsibility, and autonomy. While adhering to zoerhetorically ascendant practices of health and fitness, the biocitizen, who cannot help but be materially and psychologically invested in the zoerhetorical hierarchy, reinscribes the hierarchy while reaping its rewards.

One of the key logics buttressing vitality-performing biocitizenship is an affective attachment to somatopeic body-making. Often this body-making takes the form of the assumption of nearly infinite body malleability. A plenum of rhetorics across both clubs forward the idea that the only thing standing between club-goers and the body of their dreams is hard work. There is no somatopeic body-making without a concomitant attribution of value that recommends an existent's place in something like the Great Chain of Being's hierarchy. Shaping one's body is rendered as the equivalent of shaping one's life.[60] The extension of this logic to its most brutal conclusion means that an imperfect body indicates an imperfect self.[61] The mythology of infinite body malleability suggests that the extent to which a body conforms to the ideal fit

---

59. The sexual implications of mounting are not lost on Kenneth Burke, of course. See Rueckert, *Encounters with Kenneth Burke*, 75.

60. Bordo, in her incredible book *Unbearable Weight*, excerpts an ad that says these words, 196.

61. The promise of cosmetic plastic surgeries serves this myth of infinite body malleability. For a further discussion of the rhetorical limits of body changeability, see Jordan, "The Rhetorical Limits of the 'Plastic Body.'"

athletic body acts as a reliable indicator of their social status. Again, persons whose bodies conform to the fit, able, athletic ideal are attributed a range of positive qualities in zoerhetorical ascendance; persons whose bodies fail to conform are attributed a range of negative qualities in zoerhetorical descendance. Vital biocitizens occupy the apex of humanhood.

The problem here is that bodies are not infinitely malleable, nor are they always consistently reliable indicators of privilege. They are recalcitrant and stubborn things. Some bodies will accumulate biocitizenly privileges quickly, displaying fitness and athleticism with little to no prompting, whereas some bodies will paunch and pull idealized lines despite ascetic self-management regimes. Bodies have a vital agency all their own, separate from the top-down executive function of willpower. They are mutable, but only to an extent. Like the mutability of fetal entities at memorials to the unborn, this mutability of bodies is both an opportunity and a threat for the gyms. That some bodies can and do change fuels a (perhaps Berlantian cruel) affective attachment to the myth of body malleability, but that some bodies remain stubbornly immune to training threatens membership numbers at the gyms. In the contemporary regime of living, aspirational body malleability keeps athletic clubs in business. At the same time, the fiction of body malleability also results in rhetorically descendent attributions to persons with imperfect bodies because we assume that they deserve these bodies due to unhealthy, indulgent practices.

Vital Biocitizens Train for Life

The discourse of training anchors the myth of body malleability to biolegitimacy. Various textual messages intended to inspire club-goers decorate the interior of the athletic club as well as its website. One poster reads, "Athletes *eat* and *train*—they don't *diet* and *exercise*."[62] Similarly, a personal trainer's tagline on the club website intones, "Train smart. Rest. Repeat." A preference for discourses and practices of *training* over those of *exercising* marks an important movement across both field sites. The scoffing of a white male ultrarunner with whom I am friendly first drew my attention to the biolegitimating narrative of *training*. He groused, "I don't understand fitness. It's pointless. You're not *doing* anything. Fitness for *what*?" In this particular case, he was mocking middle-aged women doing step aerobics, but the barb stung me, too. Chris went on to clarify, "When I work out, it's because I want to accomplish

---

62. Similarly, another quotable "fitspo" fragment that inspires identification with training is this one: "Joggers bounce up and down at red lights. Runners just stand there looking pissed."

or achieve something. I don't just work out to work out. I don't want to just spin my wheels." Chris wanted to make a distinction between mere exercise and a carefully planned and meticulously executed training regimen in pursuit of some goal. Although Chris might be an extreme case, even for Boulder, his preference for training over mere exercising aligns with many of the persons at the athletic clubs. In this subculture, palpable social approval is available for persons who *train* for a particular event. Although I was no serious athletic contender, I announced that I would compete in my first sprint triathlon to much high-fiving and pats-on-the-back. This announcement marked my zoerhetorically ascendant transition from mere exercise to training and the resulting social approval.

Club-goers I encountered were in various stages of training for (or recovering from) a dazzling range of athletic events: Nationally famous or local foot races of varying length across the country (including the Leadville 100-mile, the Boston marathon, or the 10K Bolder Boulder); the gamut of triathlon distances at race events across the country (from the Coeur d'Alene Ironman in Idaho to the women-only Outdoor Divas sprint triathlon in nearby Longmont); geo-specific climbing projects scattered around the world (whether traditional multi-pitch, sport climbing, or bouldering routes); Muddy Buddy–type races; hiking each of Colorado's 14,000-foot peaks; upcoming local aerial yoga, aerial dance, or partner yoga performances or demonstrations; and local cyclocross and orienteering events. This impressive list is just from a sampling of people within the relatively small social community of amateur athletes with whom I am acquainted.

The range of events, across dispersed geographic locales, demonstrates a few things about vitality-performing biocitizens. Perhaps most obviously, biocitizens who train have access to the financial resources required not only to complete the training itself but also to purchase a round-trip commercial airline flight, a hotel stay, and race registration fees. (For longer races like the Ironman, registration fees can reach over one thousand dollars.) Second, competing at these events often entails the consumption of a tourist experience, especially as many of the events take place in desirable locations. According to ironman.com, the Coeur d'Alene Ironman vies for the "most breathtaking scenery" on the Ironman circuit, because it takes place "in the pristine heart of one of Idaho's prettiest areas." Here we see the conflation of *life itself* with *lifestyle,* as the burgeoning race event management industry tailors to vitality-performing biocitizens.

More importantly, training for any of these events infuses the biocitizen's performances of vitality with purpose and direction. Like the good neoliberal citizen, the vital biocitizen is goal-directed and future-oriented. The biocitizen on a treadmill is not a hamster on a wheel; she does not exercise for the sake of exercise. She does not nonchalantly determine the timing, duration, or vigor of her exercise as it suits her mood. Rather, she is engaged in an organized, charted, and planned self-disciplinary regime, which may include multiple workouts per day and planned meals. Even activities that seem relaxing, such as "gentle" or "restorative" yoga classes (offered at both gyms), are justified through discourses of training. Biocitizens are encouraged to partake in these restorative activities because they offer muscle recovery processes crucial to athletic training and performance. (A sign next to the chair massage area at the athletic club says "You have a training plan. But do you have a recovery plan?") In this community, the proactive management of "life itself" requires diligence and forethought.

Rhetorics of training further serve the vital biocitizen in terms of bio/ legitimizing the demanding and time-consuming practices of vitality. Many of the biocitizens with whom I interact at the gym expend large amounts of time, financial resources, and physical effort in these practices. At times, these resource expenditures run counter to common sense. For example, people who do not enjoy financial stability spend their limited monetary resources on multiple gym memberships, fancy road bikes and other equipment, or Whole Foods fare that they cannot afford. I would count my graduate-student self among these vitality-aspirant fiscal fools. Many vital biocitizens sustain chronic, debilitating injuries. Climbers wrap injured hands and fingers in white medical tape in order to keep climbing, and stuff their feet into tiny, downturned, excruciating rubber-soled climbing shoes. Because climbing performance is so integrally tied to body weight, even amateur athletes will drop weight to tackle a project for which they have been training. Stress fractures, blisters, dehydration, fatigue, and sprained or torn muscles are just a few of the common maladies suffered as a result of these intense training regimes.

One man I interviewed, Joe, successfully completed the famous Leadville 100, a 100-mile run at altitude with punishing vertical terrain. Joe's pride in this accomplishment overshadowed his resulting debilitating ankle injury. When I asked Joe whether his training and competition resulted in a net gain for his overall health, he admitted that it probably did not. In fact—and I am fascinated by this disclosure—he conjectured that there was probably more harm than good done to his body as a result of his exertions. (Joe's qualifications as a physical therapist lend his assessment of his overall health some additional credibility.) At the same time, he insisted that the glory of the completed achievement was "absolutely worth it." From these sustained bodily injuries, we can infer that sometimes the pressures of competition and achievement exceed the imperative of health.

If Joe or others like him were "merely" exercising, their multihour-per-day workout habits might raise eyebrows or fuel suspicions of pathological relationships with exercise. But the rhetorically (bio)legitimate rhetoric of training sanctions all sorts of behaviors that would otherwise be deemed compulsive, shallow, appearance-obsessed, or disordered. The statement "I've got to keep up with my training schedule" will continue to carry more rhetorical force than "I've got to keep up with my exercise routine." When the vital biocitizen is in training, we are invited to admire her fortitude and drive. Training functions as a rationalization of the intense resources, including time, energy, and money, spent on the self.

A commitment to "life itself" appears in other rhetorics of training. For two years I regularly attended a group fitness class at the club called Bosu Explosion.[63] The class combined agility drills, weight lifting, and balance training on the unstable inflated surface of a Bosu Ball. During one Saturday-morning class, I was moved by the instructor's impassioned oratory during a "max effort" agility drill. I paraphrase Walter here:

> Why are you doing this? Why are you here today? I can bring the energy, but you have to bring the effort. If you want what you've never had before, be willing to work like you never have before. This is *your* workout. What do you want from your life? Do you want to be around for the people you love? Do you want to be around a few more years for your kids? Then you have to *work* for it. You have to earn it, right here, right now.

In this exhortation, the instructor introduced a causal link between prolonged *life* (as mere existence, "be[ing] around") and the effort exercised in the agility drill. To motivate participants, he invoked a biolegitimate rhetoric of life itself as the ultimate goal toward which we work. In his role as group fitness *instructor*, Walter operates as both cultural worker and biopedagogue, guiding participants toward performances of proper biocitizenship. In this example, biocitizenship requires vigorous physical effort in order to attain *life* itself. In response to Walter's invitation, a little voice in me cried, "I want to be around for my children!" I knifed my knees up to my chest to the loud beats of the music with vociferous effort. That I did not have children at the time was immaterial. For a brief moment I was affectively suspended in the endorphin-supplemented joy of working toward my future life.

---

63. When I first began working out at the gym, the class was called Bosu Blast. The name change reflected a club-wide decision to engage more male-identified persons in group fitness classes, which also included expanding the number of group fitness classes led by men.

The rhetorics of training orient in different ways to a concept of earning. The first way is by a labor metaphor—results are earned through hard work. Training is the vehicle by which aspiring athletes *earn* the speed, strength, endurance, or agility required to perform in their goal event, or required to earn the good life. The second is a metaphor of earning calories from food. After a long run, ride, or hike, biocitizens like to discuss how they have *earned* the food or drink they consume afterwards. I have frequently heard vitality-performing biocitizens say something like "The best part of training is earning calories. I work out this hard so I can eat whatever I want." Similarly, members of this community often express that food tastes better when it has been "earned" through physical effort. I heard a female Ironman say once, "I am in training, so all calories taste amazing right now." It is not just club-goers who espouse these rhetorics of earning calories—the instructors at both gyms do as well. One woman instructing a cycling class at the climbing gym announced, "I am going to visit family in South Carolina next week—I better train hard today to earn my biscuits and gravy tomorrow!" Marathon runners often talk about how incredible beer tastes after running twenty-six miles.

Because I belong to the group of vital biocitizens under study, I feel entitled to judgments that I would normally suspend in qualitative research. I will name one of those judgments here: arrogance. An entitled arrogance often lurks beneath these rhetorics of earned calories. Earning calories implies that persons who fail to train have not properly earned, and therefore do not rightly deserve, indulgent foods. It assumes that persons not engaged in regular, vigorous exercise have not *earned* the energy from food that they need to survive. In this way it is indirectly accusatory toward fat people, who (we are forced to infer) must be consuming *unearned* calories, calories that they do not deserve. There is a remarkable parallel of deservingness discourses between fat people failing to earn calories and poor people failing to earn social welfare. In both cases, sustenance (whether by food or financial resources) is undeserved for those who fail to conform to the neoliberal ideal of what a working body should be and do. What's more, in the very moment when vital biocitizens feel superior for having "earned" their eggs benedict or truffle fries or craft IPAs, their bodies are demanding more calories (and therefore more of the globe's resources like coal, fresh water, and topsoil intimately tied to global food production) than they otherwise would consume. Like many people who experience social privilege, vital biocitizens overlook larger social structures and recast their privileges as that which they have earned by dint of their own hard work.

Consuming food is not the only way that Boulder's vital biocitizens participate in regimes of contemporary capitalism. Although they were discussing the growing trend of extreme obstacle course races like the Tough Mudder,

Matthew Lamb and Cory Hillman showed that contemporary fitness practices allow participants to gain "rhetorical proof of their fitness" in order to succeed "within the milieu of corporate capitalism."[64] Given that these races are often marketed to white-collar professionals, Lamb and Hillman argue that these demanding physical challenges function as sites for proving masculinity, which they correlate with corporate culture's celebration of fearlessness and risk-taking. It is crucial to note, as Lamb and Hillman do, that this status of masculinity is available to both men and women.

As a rhetorical resource, *training* allows vitality-performing biocitizens to do a number of things. First, rhetorics of training infuse performances of vitality with purpose and direction, aligning biocitizens with the positive qualities of disciplined neoliberal citizens. Second, training provides a justification for biocitizens to exercise more often, at high intensities, and with more negative consequences (such as chronic injury) than would otherwise be socially sanctioned. Third, rhetorics of training insist on the ascendant zoerhetorics of *earned* privilege, thereby demoting the status of existents who have not earned calories or fitness in one specific way. As a result, it is all too easy for biocitizens to overlook the myriad set of privileges required to even begin a training regimen, such as access to time, financial resources, energy, nutritious food, and sports-specific knowledge.

Thus, any accumulated privilege that results in a higher status on the zoerhetorical hierarchy—such as a leaner, more muscular physique or more adept and able-bodied physical movements in a public place—is couched as the result of something that the biocitizen has earned through hard work at the gym. In practice, this may or may not be true, but the emphasis on training, work, and effort forecloses the possibility for an accessible, popular, public narrative where we can identify vitality-performing biocitizens as likely members of a privileged population. Even as Jacqui Alexander maintains that there is no innocence in the empire, it is almost easier to come to the biocitizen's defense than it is to indict her. After all, it required a lot of *work* for her body to accumulate that much privilege in the form of a strong, flexible, mobile, hyper-able athleticism.

Vital Biocitizens Perform Whiteness

A joke in circulation around the gyms hints at the vital biocitizen's complicated relationship with whiteness. Question: why are triathlons so popular in Boulder? Answer: because Kenyans can't afford $15,000 road bikes. This joke

---

64. Lamb and Hillman, "Tough Mudder," 83.

tells us a lot about Boulder's vital biocitizens. Like the implied audience of this joke, for example, vital biocitizens are white. (I am pretty sure that if I were not white, this joke would not be told in my presence.) Whiteness operates as both a mode of social belonging and an unmarked universal norm across spaces of vital biocitizenship. The social and financial capital of vital biocitizens marks them as appropriate neoliberal consumers that being "Kenyan" (that is, being racially and economically othered, in this case) precludes. To further indict this line of joking, it is precisely Kenya's violent colonial history that results in this racial and economic othering. I first heard this joke in the climbing gym at Boulder, where it takes on additional meaning among the very white, masculine, muscular, slender bodies that assemble there. For the white people who circulate the joke, part of its appeal is the magnanimous acknowledgment of Kenyan athletic prowess, which invokes (or attempts to invoke) the charm of self-deprecation. In this section, I explore the intersection of whiteness and vital biocitizenship as enacted across the field sites.

What Joseph Pugliese called "infrastructural whiteness" identifies the ways in which whiteness both structures everyday life and paradoxically remains invisible.[65] While there is no true "essence" to race, phenotypically or otherwise, race is constantly restaged as an ontological truth written on the body, usually in the form of skin color.[66] Performances of whiteness as a strategy of social belonging are not limited to persons with white skin. Whiteness deeply structures the practices and experiences of vital biocitizens at the gym. For example, as scholars have shown, the curve-free, slender female idealized body (toward which we may imagine the female vital biocitizen labors) is an implicitly white body.[67] Furthermore, white bodies are already culturally linked to the temperance, restraint, and good judgment that performances of biolegitimacy require.[68] It is no accident that the now defunct blog "Stuff White People Like" included entries related to performances of vital biocitizenship, such as "Yoga," "Marathons," and "Outdoor Performance Clothes."[69]

In June of 2014, the implicit whiteness of the Boulder vital biocitizen was underscored and made momentarily visible. In a letter to the editor of the

65. Pugliese, "Biometrics, Infrastructural Whiteness, and the Racialized Zero Degree of Nonrepresentation."

66. Ehlers, "Hidden in Plain Sight."

67. Duncan and Robinson, "Obesity and Body Ideals in the Media."

68. Shugart, "Ruling Class."

69. See http://stuffwhitepeoplelike.com. Of white people and marathons, the (white) author wrote: "If you find yourself in a situation where a white person is talking about a marathon, you must be impressed or you will lose favor with them immediately. Running for a certain length of time on a specific day is a very important thing to a white person and should not be demeaned." "#27 Marathons."

local Boulder newspaper the *Daily Camera,* Shannon Burgert aired her concerns regarding a large, fence-high banner that rings the pool of one of the upscale athletic clubs in town. (This club is owned by the same company that owns the one at which I participant-observed.) Her complaint? All fifty of the "larger than life . . . fun in the sun" people on the banner were white.[70] Burgert argued that the banner was not representative of the diverse community in which we live. Activating her identity as a schoolteacher, Burgert challenged the athletic club to help "establish environments that make diversity natural for our kids." We can read this letter as a moment of critical, vernacular pushback against the implicit whiteness of the vital biocitizen. However, the implicit whiteness of Boulder's vital biocitizens is not always so visible or so publicly critiqued.

There is a choreographed dance exercise class on regular offer at the athletic club called Zumba. Again, usually whiteness as an unmarked norm stays right below the surface, but in one particular moment of rupture, it made itself present in a crowded Zumba class. Through its format, Zumba provides a tourist experience without one having to leave Boulder. Each song hails from a different country, and the choreographed dance that accompanies it mimics the native style of dancing (or, more accurately, the stereotype of the "native" style of dancing) for that particular country or ethnic group. Randy Martin described a similar racial appropriation in this ethnographic work taking hip-hop aerobic classes in California.[71] While Zumba, as a brand, has more of a focus on weight loss (its tagline is "Shake, Shake, Shrink") than is usually the norm for the athletic club, it is still a popular class, especially for middle-aged women.

In an uncomfortable moment in Zumba class, the instructor shouted, "Let's see those African arms, ladies!" In a song coded as "tribal," we were invited to perform a dance coded as "African." In an analogous moment, during a song coded as "Latin," we were invited to shimmy, or to move our shoulders back and forth quickly. The fitness instructor, whose shimmy was admittedly agile, said, "Some people ask me if I am Latina because I can shimmy and shake so well! Nope, not a single drop!" In this group fitness class, the instructor promotes a commitment to ethnicity as an ontological essence while also providing (mostly) white women an opportunity to consume racial and ethnic otherness as exotic and fun. The group fitness instructor's shimmy is operating in a way analogous to Helene Shugart's description of Jennifer Lopez's bot-

---

70. Burgert, "Banner Is Not Representative of Our Diversity," letter to the editor, *Daily Camera,* June 14, 2014.

71. Martin, "The Composite Body."

tom. The "Latina butt," like the Latina shimmy, authorizes seemingly authentic proof of cultural diversity while shoring up a white norm.[72]

In a similar way, the "Total Body Bootcamp" group fitness classes also offer a touristic glimpse into (again, a stereotype of the) working-class military lifestyle. Club-goers are invited to consume this experience of class otherness—without, of course, any of the high stakes or danger of actually going through military boot camp. What practices of Zumba in white, upper middle-class spaces do across race, Total Body Bootcamp does across socioeconomic status. Fitness instructors blow whistles, shout, and use the US military parlance of "side straddle hops" in place of the more familiar "jumping jacks." Depending on the proclivities of the instructor, participants may be asked to "military crawl" under imaginary barbed wire and to swing heavy ropes. As we are invited to identify with soldiers, Diane Keeling would argue that we are also invited to identify with masculinist ideals of strength and bodily invulnerability.[73] Total Body Bootcamp offers another lifestyle experience at the athletic club available for consumption by the implicitly white vital biocitizen. There is an interesting irony operating when upper-middle-class club-goers mimic the exercises of soldiers. Recall Foucault's docile bodies, ready to accept control and submission from the state. Vitality-performing biocitizens, at their most warriorlike, strengthened, stretched, cardiovascularly efficient, hydrated, and protein-fueled, are simultaneously at their most submissive in terms of obedience to the neoliberal ideal. As demonstrated by the rhetoric of Total Body Bootcamp, whiteness is an implicitly well-resourced subject position.

Whiteness also operates as a mode through which vital biocitizens can align themselves with American-identified social belonging. In any instantiation of the concept, biocitizenship is always about *citizenship*—about relating the materiality of the body, broadly construed, to projects of social belonging and recognition. In a landmark essay, Thomas Nakayama and Robert Krizek identified whiteness as an everyday rhetoric of belonging. In one of the strategic rhetorics of whiteness they described, whiteness was conflated with nationality—a move that they suggest territorializes the assemblage of the nation by sharpening the national borders.[74] The body-improvement projects of implicitly white vital biocitizens often inflect national identification. As Kathleen Lebesco has observed, questioning the scheme of vitality-building in the US is "downright unpatriotic, which explains our former Surgeon General

---

72. Shugart, "Crossing Over."

73. Keeling, "His/tory of (Future) Progress."

74. Nakayama and Krizek, "Whiteness: A Strategic Rhetoric."

Richard Carmona's equation of obesity with the September 11 terror attacks."[75] Vitality-performing biocitizens are enfolded into American-identified social belonging through the prism of whiteness. Importantly, Kathryn Henne linked citizenship, whiteness, and social belonging to distributions of privilege:

> While citizenship can take on a myriad of configurations including imagined, global, sexual, biological and even genetic dimensions, there is a common tenet: citizenship entails a form of boundary work that delineates insiders—those who enjoy a particular status and benefits—and outsiders—those who may desire such privileges but are denied.[76]

The biocitizenly boundary work that Henne referenced here is necessarily zoerhetorical, as it partakes in status re/distributions.

In sum, whiteness as an infrastructural, strategic, and occasionally invisible mode of social belonging operates across performances of vital biocitizenship. While biocitizenly club-goers rarely (except in moments of bawdy humor like the joke that opened this section) reference their race, whiteness structures the experiences of the vital biocitizen in a way that reflects the dominance of whiteness in the zoerhetorical hierarchy. The slender, fit ideal for which biocitizens labor is essentially white. Furthermore, an implicitly white vital biocitizen consumes racial (and class) otherness in a variety of experiences offered at the athletic club, such as Zumba and Total Body Bootcamp. Finally, whiteness is a mode of social and national belonging. In the strategic rhetoric of whiteness, the *citizen* part of biocitizen becomes important. Levy-Navarro asserted, "The fat body . . . obstruct[s] what should be our manifest destiny—to progress as a nation or civilization."[77] We can also assume the opposite: the slender, athletic, white body manifests our exceptional destiny as a (white) nation.

CONCLUSION: TOWARD A CRITIQUE OF LIFE-BUILDING

I opened this chapter with this question from feminist studies scholar Jacqui Alexander: "What do lives of privilege look like in the midst of war and

---

75. Lebesco, "Fat Panic," 77. There are further links between fitness and combat training. President Eisenhower first mandated physical fitness in schools because the US would need fit bodies to come to its defense (against foreign Others). For more, see Petherick, "Young Biocitizen."

76. Henne, "Olympic Bio-Citizenship," 83.

77. Levy-Navarro, *The Culture of Obesity*, 5.

the inevitable violence that accompanies the building of an empire?"[78] I have generated a critique of vitality-aspiring performances of health and physical fitness as they circulate at two athletic facilities in Boulder, Colorado. The zoerhetorics of training and whiteness combine to encourage and legitimate these unequal distributions of social status.

What does this add to zoerhetorical theory? Populations can be nourished toward vitality, neglected toward attenuation, or targeted for death. A particular subset of populations nourished toward vitality—the fit, vital biocitizens on whom I have focused—engage a range of biolegitimate rhetorics to justify their accumulation of privilege. Returning to Didier Fassin's claim that biolegitimacy *produces inequalities,* Fassin identified the ways in which "technologies of government produce inequalities of life but simultaneously erase their traces."[79] Although in that moment Fassin was referring to the inability of population statistics practices in South Africa under apartheid to identify wide gaps of inequality, his insight is useful for broader zoerhetorical theory concerns. We can read the practices of the vital biocitizen as a means by which these inequalities are produced just as the traces of these inequalities are erased in rhetorics of training and whiteness. In the oscillation between the blurred modes of accruing and enjoying privilege that occur at these athletic clubs, vital biocitizens are consistently invited to understand their privileges as earned (rather than as an accident of geospatial location, birth family, race, etc.). Through training and through proper consumption, these bodies congeal the performances of both biocitizenship and whiteness.

The working poor, the chronically ill, the illegally detained, the moderately to severely disabled, and the fat constitute populations whose performances of vitality cannot possibly aspire to match those of the inimitable vital biocitizen, who "exercises" his or her hegemonic capacity for a full range of "functional" physical movement and labor. As aspirant vital-biocitizens, we (I use the inclusive pronoun shamefully now) do not tell each other that we are going to raise our social status, or that we are going to accumulate embodied privilege, or that we are on the lucky side of capitalism's mean flows. Rather, we tell ourselves that we are working toward our health, our future, our life. But even as we work toward life, we still require an/other to bound or delineate this social belonging. Practices of vitality might accrue attributions of virtue, but as these practices are obsessively internalized in the gyms at which I made observations, these attributions of virtue have nothing to do with the ethical obligations of social justice.

---

78. Alexander, *Pedagogies of Crossing,* 1–2.
79. Fassin, "Another Politics of Life," 55.

When I think back on the multiday alpine climbs I completed, or the thirty-mile bike rides up razor-steep mountains, or the hundreds of spin classes I sweated through—I think, what was it for? Surely the push-ups and planks purchased me something, besides just a short feeling of well-being? A brief cessation of the continual, compulsory urge to do more, to be harder, better, faster, stronger? In addition to these congealed privileges, working out purchased a momentary respite from the haunting compulsion of a national culture that says go, go, go with a local inflection that says more, more, more.

The rhetoric of training funnels attention toward biocitizenly privilege as *earned* rather than *unearned*. In doing so, it strengthens a system that attributes rhetorical agency to existents higher on the zoerhetorical hierarchy and robs the agency of existents lower on the hierarchy. In other words, as vitality-performing biocitizens are attributed agentic qualities of self-control, discipline, autonomy, and strength, their high position on the hierarchy is legitimated and sedimented. They are granted more rhetorical agency, in the traditional sense. That is, people are more likely to listen when they speak; establishing *ethos* is less difficult for persons whose privilege-accumulating bodies conform to a normative ideal.[80] The rhetoric of whiteness acts as a strategy of social belonging—and therefore exclusion—for biocitizens. Through performances of whiteness, club-goers shore up zoerhetorically ascendant attributions of national belonging.

I opened this chapter with a vignette about Blaine and his friends watching *The Biggest Loser* while racing each other on their stationary bike trainers. Their story allows me to remark on another feature of the zoerhetorical hierarchy as it operates across my field sites. Existents not only aspire toward "mounting" the hierarchy; they also fear sliding down the hierarchy. In racial terms, scholars have identified not just an aspiration toward whiteness but also repulsion by "anti-blackness."[81] Within the world of the vignette, Blaine and his buddies were both aspiring toward vitality and literally *racing away* from something (or some Other) low on the zoerhetorical hierarchy: fatness. Yet note that the socially sanctioned, publicly visible zoerhetorical trajectory was the upward one: the pure becoming. Privileged persons near the top of the hierarchy have material and discursive investments in maintaining the hierarchy. From this tenet we can infer that attempts at zoerhetorical ascendance are as much about rhetorically grafting to higher entities/qualities on the hierarchy as they are about rhetorically separating from lower entities/qualities. The

---

80. We concede this truth when we instruct our public-speaking students to attain credibility by dressing and speaking "professionally." The performance of public professionalism indexes hegemonic race, gender, and class mandates.

81. Sexton and Lee, "Figuring the Prison."

word *hew* is useful here, with its two contradictory meanings of both "to split from" and "to adhere to." Zoerhetorical movements *hew*, in both senses of the word, as all splittings are graftings somewhere else.

Finally, one take-home message of this chapter is a caution against the valorization of health that we see across a range of social sciences, including my home discipline of communication studies. In these studies, health automatically equals goodness. We should especially be skeptical of the social approval we grant to privileged bodies in the process of accumulating more privilege in the form of vitality and well-being. A host of zoerhetorics work to distribute social status to this particular entity of the vital biocitizen in ways that structurally exclude and other large groups of persons. To expand the scope of my claims in this chapter, I critique more than just a handful of vital biocitizens in one town in Colorado. Vital biocitizens all over the US, clustering together as white elites do in liberal, urban, and suburban communities, enact slow violence in their life-building labors.

CONCLUSION

Humanhood's Ambit

I OPENED this book with an example of a zoerhetoric circulating during President Obama's open-secret weaponized drone program. Rendered intelligible within the logics of empire and violent racial assemblages, *collateral damage* is a common phrase whose demotional effects are easy to apprehend. I bookend my discussion by returning to drone warfare to highlight two zoerhetorics with demotional effects that are perhaps more slippery. The first is biolegitimacy, or the virtue associated with appeals to life itself. The second will bring us squarely into the Trump presidency, where instead of zoerhetorical appeals to biolegitimacy regarding drones, we get silence.

At the vital center of Obama administration drone rhetorics were the terms *life, lives,* or *life-saving.* Drone-related messaging from President Obama's administration demonstrated the ways in which *life itself*—usually rendered as saving lives—justified the use of particular weaponry in the ongoing war on terror.[1] The message, coordinated across a number of speeches and public statements, was simple: drones save lives. Drones, we were repeatedly told, save the lives of servicepersons, the lives of civilians abroad, and the lives of ordinary, innocent Americans at home. These appeals were best summarized in this plain-dealing, candid assertion from President Obama:

---

1. Rowland, "Life-Saving Weapons."

"Simply put, these strikes have saved lives."[2] In February 2013 Press Secretary Jay Carney briefed the press in one of the Obama administration's first public mentions of the drone campaign. In this speech, the invocation of *life* rose to thrice-repeated chorus:

> We have acknowledged, the United States, that sometimes we use remotely piloted aircraft to conduct targeted strikes against specific al Qaeda terrorists in order to prevent attacks on the United States and to *save American lives*. We conduct those strikes because they are necessary to mitigate ongoing actual threats, to stop plots, prevent future attacks, and, *again, save American lives*. . . . The U.S. government takes great care in deciding to pursue an al Qaeda terrorist, to ensure precision and *to avoid loss of innocent life*.[3]

The straightforward frankness of these appeals reaffirms life as the object of primary concern—but whose life? Carney's first two mentions of saving lives referred to American lives, while the last referred to innocent civilian lives abroad. When the Obama administration was not touting the life-saving benefits of drones for Americans, it was establishing the US as the nation with unprecedented vested interest in saving lives—that is, the nation with the most biolegitimacy. Representatives of the Obama White House would have us believe that the Predator and Reaper drones that soared and struck over undeclared theaters of war were on par with necessary life-giving medical therapies.

Drone strikes were often compared to the cleanliness, sterility, and precision of surgery. Aligning drone warfare with medicine was no mistake; it was one of the Obama White House's most successful zoerhetorical strategies for justifying drone policies. In April 2012, when John Brennan was senior counterterrorism advisor, he said in a speech on national security, "It's this surgical precision—the ability, with laser-like focus, to eliminate the cancerous tumor called an al Qa'ida terrorist while limiting damage to the tissue around it—that makes this counterterrorism tool so essential."[4] One effect of comparing drone warfare with surgery is the characterization of the enemy as cancerous tissue that requires excision. If terrorist groups are cancer, a disease where body cells divide uncontrollably to form tumors, then American-identified people must constitute the otherwise healthy body tissue, well-behaved and

---

2. Obama, "Remarks by the President at the National Defense University."
3. Carney, "Press Briefing"; my emphasis.
4. Brennan, "Brennan's Speech on Counterterrorism."

in control. Therefore, while comparisons to medicine shore up drone warfare with the credibility and virtue of the medical establishment, they also invite a winnowing operation. The enemies (cancer) are cleaved from an American-identified in-group (healthy tissue), furthering a conceptual distance between them. As the logic of the Chain dictates, the greater the distance between two groups of existents, the greater the difference in status.

Like a troll under a bridge, beneath these claims to biolegitimacy dwells one ugly assumption: American-identified lives are intrinsically better (or more important, or more virtuous, or more valuable) than the lives of people living in Pakistan (or Yemen, or Somalia). The Obama-era White House rhetoric of drone warfare, then, is a powerful example of a zoerhetoric for many reasons. First, it illustrates that life-building and life-promoting rhetorics are often, and rather counterintuitively, the most dangerously effective zoerhetorical demotions. The rhetorical strategy of biolegitimacy, and its discursive monopoly on virtue on the global stage, is partially from where these zoerhetorical demotions gather their persuasive force and credibility. Second, it underscores the ways in which ongoing violent racial assemblages condition the zoerhetorical hierarchy. In other words, American-identified people already inhabit and participate in discursive formations where people of color are routinely devalued, and these devaluations and their consequences are presented as a matter of nature running its course or common sense. Equating people living in Pakistan with a cancerous tumor is an *intelligible, comfortable,* and ultimately *effective* zoerhetorical strategy for the many US Americans to whom it was addressed.[5]

Fast-forward about five years to the head-spinning presidency of Donald J. Trump. Drone strikes intended for al Qaeda (or, now, ISIS or Syrian) targets still occur, but they offer an entirely different set of lessons for zoerhetorical theory. The spectacularly saturated national political landscape is dominated by provocative presidential tweets, scandals, and personnel changes. (Last week's ado was about whether Robert Mueller will be fired; today's is Stormy Daniels's *60 Minutes* interview with Anderson Cooper; tomorrow Trump's lawyer, Michael Cohen, will have his office raided.)

Amid this fracas, American-issued drone strikes have not resurfaced as part of a national conversation. Compare this with the early 2010s, when President Obama's drone campaign produced expressions of public outrage across a swath of media outlets, including investigative pieces in both the *New York*

---

5. This is to say nothing of the fraught distinction between militant and civilian. As of this writing, the Bureau of Investigative Journalism estimates between 737 and 1,551 civilians were killed by American drone strikes between 2004 and 2017.

Times and the *Washington Post*. The New America Foundation even named 2011 the "year of the drone."[6] Yet not only does President Trump continue the practice of drone strikes in unofficial theaters of war, his administration has rolled back important drone policies. As reported by the *New York Times*, Trump's White House has recently discarded Obama-era regulations that limited strikes to high-level operatives.[7] What's more, President Trump's first year in office saw triple the number of strikes in Somalia and Yemen.[8] Trump has not only embraced the drone program; he has ramped up its activity while decreasing oversight and transparency. And no one is talking about it.

The agenda-setting function of the news media is notable here for its unintentional zoerhetorical consequences. At this moment, instead of a rhetorical strategy of biolegitimacy justifying drone strikes, we have near total silence regarding drone strikes from the Trump administration.[9] An absence of public discourse, in this case, demotes the people whose bodies bear the violence of these strikes. For all of the much-deserved critique Trump garners, his control of the national conversation, mostly via tweet, is shrewdly canny. Amid the turbid morass of Trump's administration, very few people are demanding explanations about US drone strikes in international territories.

Across Obama's and Trump's drone policies, different zoerhetorics intersect with violent racial assemblages to condition livability unevenly across the globe. In the Obama era, a zoerhetoric of biolegitimacy shapes drone politics. In the Trump era, we are so distracted by holding Trump to account for such a range of notorious actions that the minor news stories discussing an elevated drone campaign barely bubble to the surface of a national conversation. In this case, a zoerhetoric of omission shapes drone politics. For those of us exploring President Trump's drone policies, it does not feel like there is room to elbow into the mosh pit.

A few paragraphs ago, I compared the zoerhetorical valuations underlying relations of empire as hidden and pernicious, a proverbial troll under the bridge. A lurking monster is not exactly the right metaphor. The metaphor requires an addition to fully capture the way that necropolitical exploitation buttresses the Great Chain's persistent hierarchy. The troll is not just hiding under the bridge; the troll is structurally integral to the bridge.

---

6. Bergen and Tiedemann, "Year of the Drone."
7. Savage and Schmitt, "Trump Poised to Drop Some Limits on Drone Strikes."
8. Purkiss, "Trump's First Year in Numbers."
9. There are a few exceptions, of course, such as the *New York Times* article cited earlier. A handful of organizations such as Amnesty International and the ACLU have asked the Trump administration to clarify their drone policies. Still, I maintain that drone strikes are not part of the US national conversation in the way that they were in 2010–13.

TOWARD ZOERHETORICAL THEORY

My brief conclusory foray into drone warfare by no means exhausts the issue, but it does support my contention that the zoerhetorical hierarchy remains remarkably similar to the days of the lauded Great Chain of Being. While zoerhetorical appeals change often in magnitude, public saturation, range of circulation, and rhetorical strategy, the zoerhetorical hierarchy itself maintains a stalwart consistency over time. The hierarchy continues to structure distributions of livability, authority, agency, virtue, and intellectual capacity. At the same time, it requires constant conditioning and upkeep, in the form of circulating and percolating zoerhetorics. Zoerhetorics are where the obdurate yet ductile hierarchies of living existents meet language.

Zoerhetorical theory offers pathways to understanding the discursive formations that support necropolitical hierarchies. This is a fancy way of saying that zoerhetorics are the ways in which we come to believe that some lives matter, or matter more or less than other lives. If biopolitical and necropolitical regimes function as machines for producing bodies nourished toward life, neglected for deterioration, and targeted for death, then zoerhetorics are the means by which these inequalities are *publicly* justified and legitimated. My intention in *Zoetropes and the Politics of Humanhood* was to make a case for zoerhetorical literacy by propping open, however briefly, the black box of necropolitics to reveal the inner workings of the incessant differentiation of living existents. In these closing remarks, I make a series of observations across the three case studies, in the effort to sketch some propositions for a zoerhetorical theory. I offer a series of topoi, horoi, and patterns of zoerhetorics as they circulate in the contemporary US.

Each case study offered a zoerhetorical reading of a group of existents with unique status vis-à-vis humanhood: the microbial-human superorganism, the human fetus, and the vital biocitizen. Taken together, the zoerhetorical patterns and trajectories of these three existents provided a broad-ranging overview of how zoerhetorics operate in the US today. The case studies traversed realms of privilege, markers of humanhood, and attributions of vice and virtue. Across case studies, we saw the durability of privileges like whiteness, citizenship, social belonging, and innocence. Zoerhetorics produce, legitimate, and maintain radical cleavages in livability.

Zoerhetorical Topos: Biolegitimacy

For each of his three branches of epideictic, deliberative, and forensic rhetoric, Aristotle offered accompanying special topoi for invention, or templates for discovering new arguments. For deliberative oratory, by way of example, Aristotle offered four topoi: the good and the unworthy, the advantageous and the disadvantageous. Like classical deliberative rhetoric, zoerhetorics also draw on the good and the unworthy as topics by which to invent arguments. The worthy/unworthy topics of invention often manifest zoerhetorically as biolegitimacy and bio-illegitimacy, as we saw in Obama-era drone rhetorics. Singular in its lethality, biolegitimacy operates as one of the most common and persuasive zoerhetorical resources.

Biolegitimacy names the power of life itself, and it remains one of the most productive topics of invention for zoerhetorics. I extend French medical anthropologist Didier Fassin's original concept of biolegitimacy by understanding it as a rhetorical strategy. Biolegitimacy emerged in the nineties as a "crucial issue in the moral economies of contemporary societies."[10] In a 2009 essay, Didier Fassin defined biolegitimacy as the legitimacy attached to life, or recognition of the "sacredness of life as such."[11] Three years later, he expanded this definition of biolegitimacy as "this recognition of life as the highest of all values—life that must be understood in the sense of being alive."[12] My intervention is to cast biolegitimacy as a rhetorical strategy and therefore public achievement rather than an essential ontological status. Instead of describing the underlying essence of a nation or an existent, a consistent biolegitimate designation in the global public sphere bears little relation to the lethality of a given regime. Importantly, biolegitimacy refers not to the number of people that an institution or nation-state kills but to the extent to which they are able to persuade dominant publics that they kill in the name of and in defense of life itself. Individuals, institutions, or nation-states can achieve a biolegitimate status through iterative, successful performances of acknowledging the sanctity of life itself. A successful rhetorical performance of biolegitimacy purchases credibility among publics nominally invested in life-loving biopolitical regimes.[13]

In the publics particular to each of the three case studies presented in this book, biolegitimacy circulates as a status marker and winnowing device—albeit with differing emphases and effects. In the world of the American Gut Project, biolegitimacy is distributed via species, where eukaryotic existents

---

10. Fassin, "Another Politics of Life," 50.

11. Fassin, "Another Politics of Life," 50.

12. Fassin, *Humanitarian Reason*, Kindle edition, loc. 5241. Note that Fassin's concept of "life in the sense of being alive" bears similarities to Giorgio Agamben's concepts of bare life and *zoe*, mere biological existence. Both scholars draw from Hannah Arendt to refigure Foucauldian biopolitics.

13. Rowland, "Life-Saving Weapons."

(humans) and prokaryotic existents (gut microbes) metonymically stand in for white colonizers in paternalistic relation to people of color. What becomes virtuous in the name of *life itself* is to attend to the (bio)diversity of one's internal cultivated garden, to expand the conditions of its flourishing.

While biolegitimacy is a tertiary topos to the popular science publics affiliated with the American Gut Project, it takes center stage in pro-life rhetorics and training at the gym. In the world of the National Memorial for the Unborn, biolegitimacy topoi take the permutation of innocence/guilt. In the world of Boulder's vital biocitizens, biolegitimacy topoi take the permutation of fitness/fatness. Notably, each of these dichotomies, where one pole of a binary deserves life and the other pole does not, is false. We can tentatively observe that transvaluations upward tend to draw from biolegitimacy as a topic of invention whereas transvaluations downward tend to drawn from bio-illegitimacy as a topic of invention. As a powerful topos of zoerhetorics, biolegitimacy, inflected as it is in the contemporary US with Judeo-Christian and liberal moralism, provides a stock of familiar and compelling material. In a delightful little volume called *Joyful Militancy*, Carla Bergman and Nick Montgomery describe liberal morality and state violence as close kin:

> Liberal morality seeps into movements [of liberation] in the form of incessant regulation and pacification of struggles. It replaces the transformative power of dignity with moral indignation and its tendencies of shame and self-righteousness. . . . It is the morality of the cop who tells you to calm down with one hand on his gun.[14]

The productivity and effectiveness of biolegitimacy as a zoerhetorical strategy proffers an important lesson for us: beware the voice of moral virtue in these late liberal times. More specifically, as the metaphor of the police officer with his hand on his gun intends to remind us, we should beware the admonishing tone of existents attributed more zoerhetorical value on the dominant hierarchy. In this quotation, Bergman and Montgomery were inspired by Erich Fromm. In his critique of moral indignation, Fromm links the sentiment directly to hierarchy, declaring:

> There is perhaps no phenomenon which contains so much destructive feelings as "moral indignation," which permits envy or hate to be acted out under the guise of virtue. The "indignant" person has for once the satisfac-

---

14. Montgomery and Bergman, *Joyful Militancy*, 205–6.

tion of despising and treating a creature as "inferior," coupled with the feeling of his own superiority and rightness."[15]

Perhaps the hierarchy implied by moral indignation is the most evident at a place like the National Memorial for the Unborn, which benefits from both Judeo-Christian moral stances and the solemnity of declaring a thing sacred. But we would be remiss to ignore that the same moral indignation vitalizes biocitizens at the Colorado gyms (and likely, gyms for white elites in other places). We see this at the American Gut Project, insofar as the ethic of paternal care cannot shake the traces of a subordinating colonialism. I would tentatively suggest that there is a strain of moral indignation idiosyncratic to zoerhetorical appeals in the US—a certain all-too-easy attribution of credibility to moralizing voices. Moral indignation must not always accompany biolegitimacy, but it often serves as biolegitimacy's crotchety handmaiden.

The Horoi of the Zoerhetorical Hierarchy

In ancient Greece, stone markers called horoi delimited the geographic boundaries of the Athenian agora. A horos marked the place where a territory began and ended, often in the first person. "I am the horos of the agora," declared a slab stele recovered by archeologists in Athens.[16] This book takes special interest in the horoi that mark humanhood's ambit.

Topoi, as places, are defined by the horoi that mark their edges. Although the horoi of ancient Greece were very literally border rhetorics—that is, rhetorics declaring a border—they can be employed metaphorically as well. Like horoi, the boundary between the human and nonhuman is re/inscribed in acts of re/territorialization. Attending to horoi moves attention from the commonplace of topoi to the boundaries.

In similar ways, the zoerhetorical hierarchy is sectioned off with boundary markers or thresholds. To be transvalued across one of these boundary markers produces consequential results for livability. Humanhood is one of the most salient of these horoi—and as a result, one of the most zoerhetorically contested of these boundary markers. In addition to species, the other biopolitically entrenched markers of difference that operate as zoerhetorical horoi include citizenship, race, gender, sexuality, body size, and ability. So structurally integral are these boundary markers that we can claim that zoerhetorics

---

15. Fromm, *Man for Himself,* 235.
16. Ober, "Greek Horoi."

are only consequential when they traverse a horos. In other words, zoerhetorics influence livability in the very moment that an existent's status changes across one of these horoi. By definition, *rhetorics* become *zoerhetorics* when two related conditions are fulfilled: first, they traverse a horos; and second, this traverse bears consequential effects for livability.

We can think of these horoi as the thresholds or bottlenecks of the zoerhetorical hierarchy. The *Oxford English Dictionary* provides a definition of *threshold* as the "magnitude or intensity that must be exceeded for a certain reaction or phenomenon to occur."[17] A rhetorical force must reach a certain magnitude or intensity in a given public—whether by energetic emphasis, magnitude, or public saturation—in order to pass through a zoerhetorical threshold. It generally requires more rhetorical force to jump (trope) or slide (metonymically shift) an entity across one of these boundaries, just as it takes more force to push matter through an actual bottleneck.

Although each case study is animated by the horos of humanhood—a consequential zoerhetorical threshold—different horoi become salient across different publics. At the American Gut Project and its affiliated popular science publics, racial assemblages condition public understandings of microbial life.[18] A racial hierarchy is inscribed onto the microbial life of our innards as popular science publics struggle to accommodate the transformative possibilities of microbiome research. The "place" they end up finding is an old, even predictable wilderness ripe for paternalistic cultivation. Through naming, en-voicing, en-facing, and embodying, the National Memorial for the Unborn rhetorics energetically troped the unborn upwards through the bottlenecked horoi of humanhood. Of course, they did not stop there. As I showed, the NMU understood the unborn not only as people but also as hegemonically gendered people with American-identified embodied habits. At the Colorado gym, the threshold of import was whiteness—often conflated with health and the good life. For Boulder's vital biocitizens, whiteness became an important horos in the slow accumulation of embodied privilege. Judith Butler may as well have been referencing horoi when she remarked that "the inhuman, the beyond the human, the less than human, is the border that secures the human in its ostensible reality."[19] There is a simple test to determine the important horoi for a given hierarchy. If an entity's transvaluation across a certain threshold results in differences in livability, we can think of this threshold as a horos of the zoerhetorical hierarchy.

---

17. *Oxford English Dictionary,* s.v. "threshold."
18. On racial assemblages, see Weheliye, *Habeas Viscus.*
19. Butler, *Undoing Gender,* 30.

Zoetropes: How Zoerhetorics Meet Language

Through this book, I have identified a number of means by which zoerhetorics "meet" language or get uttered, practiced, or performed into being. There are a handful of common zoerhetorical forms or patterns that I have explored in the case studies, all of which depend on the Great Chain of Being for their intelligibility: sticky sliding together (metonymy), naming (antonomasia), envoicing (apostrophe), en-facing (prosopopeia), and em-bodying (somatopeia). Following an intellectual lineage from Friedrich Nietzsche, Paul de Man, and Diane Davis, tropes are moments when language turns from its "straight" usage. Zoetropes are instances where such departures promote or demote the status of a life or lives. As Paul Ricoeur observed, in the moment of their turning, tropes *deviate* from their prescribed meanings.[20] According to Christian Lundberg, reading Jacques Lacan, "The economy of tropes and investments constitute the subject and its discourses."[21] We are all rhetorically made in these movements of deviation from straight discourse. We all have a crooked, queer birth.

Following Sara Ahmed's work in *The Cultural Politics of Emotion*, which suggests that Others get stuck together on a kind of metonymic slide, I identified a lumping/splitting of living existents along a hierarchy indexed by god and devil terms.[22] The associational and dissociational hewing and cleaving movements of existents were made possible by the pliant, gradient nature of the zoerhetorical hierarchy—qualities inherited from ancient Greek hierarchies and the early Christian Great Chain of Being, along with modern regimes of patriarchy, racism, heterosexism, and ableism. Mel Chen's notion of animacy hierarchies, what Chen called the transubstantiations and transmatterings of existents, was also key in bringing forward the way bodies become regulated in language regimes.[23]

Across three case studies, I have repurposed classic tropes to understand their zoerhetorical effects. At the AGP, the metonymical stickiness of bodies to nations produced a host of effects, including multiple, subtle equations of our inner microbial life with people of color. I described these zoetropes as somatopeic, and identified the ways in which the American Gut Project drew from a postcolonial rhetoric of cultivation and care for (bio)diversity. At the National Memorial for the Unborn, we saw a series of zoetropes in full effect. In order to territorialize their particular construction of the fetal entity as a

20. Ricoeur, *The Rule of Metaphor.*
21. Lundberg, *Lacan in Public*, 73.
22. Ahmed, *The Cultural Politics of Emotion.*
23. Chen, *Animacies.*

sacred human, the NMU relied on a series of strategic, iterative zoetropes. In the third chapter, I analyzed these zoetropes as they occurred at the NMU: antonomasia (naming), apostrophe (en-voicement), prosopopeia (en-face-ment), and somatopeia (em-bodiment). These rhetorical devices were the means by which the slow, iterable accumulation of humanhood was achieved for the unborn. At the same time, I acknowledge that not all human-identified existents share the feature of the fetus that makes it so malleably "available" for zoetroping; namely, silence. Finally, at the Colorado gym, the somatopeic equation of body-building with nation-building appeared again. My hope has been that the series of zoetropological movements that I have identified across the case studies can be used to understand the rhetorical making of humanhood more broadly. All human-identified existents are embedded within the accumulated effects of zoetropological gestures. Of course, not all tropes are zoetropes. That is, not all rhetorical devices participate in a zoe-rhetorical hierarchy. However, tropes mark moments where zoerhetorics are uniquely persuasive, and therefore zoetropes have important effects on distributions of livability.

Five Propositions of Zoerhetorical Theory

1. Zoerhetorics co/present.

Trajectories of promotion and demotion present together in zoerhetorics. In this way, zoerhetorics are dynamic and interdependent. All promotions probably involve demotions elsewhere. When tropes "turn" to promote one group of existents they likely "turn away" from another group of existents. Attempts at zoerhetorical ascendance are as much about conceptually grafting an entity to higher entities/qualities on the hierarchy as they are about conceptually separating an entity from lower entities/qualities on the hierarchy. As I have identified earlier, the word *hew* is useful here, with its twin antonymic meanings of "to split from" and "to adhere to." All zoerhetorical transvaluations *hew*, in both senses of the word, splitting entities off from some group and grafting them on to another. Lumpings necessarily split and splittings necessarily lump. While complex public discourses could never cleanly transfer to Newtonian principles, the law of conservation of momentum metaphor obtains a richness for understanding zoerhetorical movement. Every action has an equal and opposite reaction. Repurposed for our considerations, a good rule of thumb is to look for the shadow behind every promotional zoerhetoric.

Each case study exhibited simultaneous vectors of both promotion and demotion. At the American Gut Project, the lowly microbe rose, only to be met with the concomitant rising transvaluation of the superorganism who cultivates the microbe—effectively maintaining the microbe's original position vis-à-vis the existent bearing humanhood. At the National Memorial for the Unborn, we witnessed the multipronged promotion of fetal existents across discourses and practices. At the same time, people whose reproductive practices do not conform to those sanctioned by the NMU—that is, people who want abortions, get abortions, or fight for abortion access—were demoted. In the world of Boulder's vital biocitizen, as gym-goers accrued and "exercised" privilege, persons with absent or unsuccessful performances of vital biocitizenship, especially along lines of body size or ability, were demoted.

Kenneth Burke ends a likely original snippet of poetry in *The Rhetoric of Religion* with "What God or Devil makes men climb / no end?"[24] The God or Devil part is important here, because it is not just ascendance that moves us, not just the aspiration toward God or perfection or goodness or other things on top of the hierarchy (as he implied at the end of *A Rhetoric of Motives*). Rather, we are also moved by the Devil, which, logologically speaking, stands in for a host of repulsions. In a much-quoted line on hierarchy in *A Rhetoric of Motives*, Burke implies a desire for ascendant aspiration but not repulsion from below: "each kind striving towards the perfection of its kind, and so towards the kind next above it, while the strivings of the entire series head in God as the beloved cynosure and sinecure, the end of all desire."[25] I would keep Burke's attunement to hierarchy but amend its unidirectionality. Existents are not interested solely in pure, ascendant, upward movement. They are also motivated by repulsion from what is at the bottom of the hierarchy. Some scholars have called this repulsion anti-blackness to describe the ways that racial assemblages register not just a preference for whiteness, but also a deeply ingrained cultural disregard for blackness.[26] Hierarchical impulses are affectively fueled from both directions, by both desire and disgust, by longing and aversion.

I opened the fourth chapter with a story where Blaine and his friends were racing each other for mileage on stationary bikes while watching *The Biggest Loser*. This vignette is helpful for understanding the double affective movement of repulsion/aspiration. Within the world of the anecdote, Blaine and his buddies were aspiring toward vitality but also literally *racing away* from something (or some Other) low on the zoerhetorical hierarchy. In this

---

24. Burke, *The Rhetoric of Religion*, 42.
25. Burke, *A Rhetoric of Motives*, 333.
26. Sexton and Lee, "Figuring the Prison."

case, we may consider how an anti-blackness intersects with fatphobia.[27] The socially sanctioned, publicly visible zoerhetorical trajectory was the upward one: the pure becoming. In fact, Blaine's vignette is reproachable exactly to the extent that we identify the bikers as recognizing themselves as superior to the *Biggest Loser* contestants.

2. Zoerhetorics are in/visible.

A scopic politics structures zoerhetorical claims; zoerhetorics are both visible and invisible. One of the patterns emerging from these case studies is that ascendant zoerhetorics are typically visible, even hypervisible, whereas descendent zoerhetorics are often concealed, denied, invisible, or euphemistic. I am speaking here of the dominant American-identified public. Raising existents is usually more socially sanctioned than lowering existents. Campaigns to raise a group of existents are exactly that—*campaigns,* an activity designed explicitly to circulate publicly, *visibly,* with a clear set of goals. My understanding of the visual is influenced by Wendy Hesford, who, rather than setting the visual against the textual, sought to integrate the two, reminding us that "images acquire social value and symbolic overtones from larger frames of reference."[28] Black Lives Matter. Sex workers' rights are human rights. The Wall of Names at the National Memorial for the Unborn. All of these discourses are expressly designed for public circulation. By contrast, descendent zoerhetorics usually require some sort of excavation, some digging, some reading for subtext. They may be buried in Byzantine policies, obscure legal maneuvers, or euphemism. The *collateral damage* of drone warfare exemplifies a euphemistic zoerhetoric that obscures (to only partial success) its demotional transvaluations.

Perhaps this pattern of zoerhetorical in/visibility manifests most clearly at the American Gut Project, where the violent racial formations of colonialism are immanent to the chipper optimism of "microbiomania." We also see concomitant in/visibility at memorials to the unborn across the nation. Of the myriad possible responses to abortion, only grief, regret, and their kin have a stage at fetal memorials. As fetal memorials promote the fetus, they demote anyone expressing other responses to abortion. At the gym, the practices around the "cult of the body" are just about the most virtue-laden, generally

---

27. For more on the intersection between anti-blackness and fatphobia, see Mollow, "Unvictimizable"; for a discussion of thinness as American exceptionalism, see Strings, *Fearing the Black Body.*

28. Hesford, *Spectacular Rhetorics,* 8. See Hesford for a critique of visibility as a dominant trope of human rights discourse.

approved, unequivocal *good* operating in the contemporary US. It should be no surprise that one of the most hypervisible and socially sanctioned ascendant zoerhetorical narratives—the will to health—would drag the largest Jungian shadow. The descendent vector includes persons who do not perform vital bio-citizenship—or perform vital biocitizenship in a way that shows visible results.

In a kindred vein to in/visibility, zoerhetorics are both expressed and suppressed. Sometimes silence serves a zoerhetorical function—as when, for example, the *New York Times* spends minimal above-the-fold inches on the deaths of civilians in the Federally Administered Tribal Areas of Pakistan but the deaths of American citizens get pages and pages. Zoerhetorics need not always speak loudly, circulate widely, or decree explicitly to bear effects. We can think of suppressed zoerhetorics as a kind of *paralipsis*—a moment where, in the very gesture of saying little, what is omitted is emphasized. In the case of a suppressed or concealed zoerhetoric, *paralipsis* furnishes the opportunity to insinuate a transvaluation, without having to assert it outright.

There are some disruptions to this general pattern of zoerhetorical visibility. One might, for example, argue that Trump's campaign rhetoric, and the blistering and inflammatory front-stage racism at his rallies, prove that descendent zoerhetorics *can* be socially sanctioned and hypervisible in the contemporary moment. However, as Eduardo Bonilla-Silva argues, Trump is still circumscribed within the colorblind politics of the day. He must still offer the pretense of being, as Bonilla-Silva quotes him as saying, "the least racist." What's more, Trump still bends to the pressure of appearing nonracist by organizing symbolic meetings with black and Latinx celebrities and politicians.[29] Of course, as Bonilla-Silva notes, Trump then quickly ignores the advice these groups give him. What is remarkable here, though, is the fact that even President Trump responds to pressure to *appear* nonracist. A scopic regime structures zoerhetorical movements.

3. Zoerhetorics are grounded in counter/publics.

Zoerhetorics circulate in already racialized (and gendered and sexualized) discursive formations. They simultaneously reanimate existing hierarchies and inclusions/exclusions. People don't become brown out of the blue. Robin Jensen employs the apt metaphor of percolation for the ways in which rhetorics accrue and interact. Inspired by the philosopher Michael Serres, she writes:

---

29. Bonilla-Silva, *Racism without Racists*, 222.

As part of this process, consistent attention must be directed both toward the rhetorical circulation of ideas and toward historical topoi and their percolation in contemporary times. This requires, first, detailed analysis of the flow and circulation of such topoi within chronologically related moments. . . . [this project] speaks to the diverse ways that arguments, appeals, and narratives come to be, circulating and percolating, flowing and repeating . . . Given that rhetoric is a transdisciplinary discursive practice—less a static product than a moving, boundless process—situating its study within the context of circulating, dynamic rhetorical ecologies, as well as historically percolating topoi, ensures that movement plays a central role in its scholarly representation.[30]

Extending her own metaphor, she continues, one page later, to ground percolation in soil: "The synergy among these different layers of rhetoric (and their conflicting echoes of historical topoi) functioned to complicate and diversify the medicalization process [of infertility], just as different layers of soil pile on top of one another and then develop as interactive, inimitable, evolving systems."[31] Helpful about Jensen's metaphor are the multiple vectors of interaction for discourses over time.

Unlike Jensen's project, the focus of this book's inquiry is contemporary rather than historical. At the same time, any (zoe)rhetorical analysis would do well to model Jensen's ecological attunement. The Great Chain of Being has percolated through various channels and moments in the flow of time. Sometimes the relationship between existents shifts, and sometimes the hierarchy is upended or disturbed in various eddies and backchannels (that is, counterpublics, flowing against the river's current), yet the hierarchy remains remarkably consistent. A zoerhetoric becomes consequential insofar as its magnitude of circulation suffices to form a public, in Michael Warner's sense of a public formed in relation to the circulation of texts.[32] This is an important rejoinder to similar theories, such as Mel Chen's animacy hierarchy, which pays little attention to publics.

Drone warfare bears another crucial lesson for zoerhetorical theory. A group of existents can be considered fully human among the members of one public and subhuman among the members of another public. I have called this phenomenon *zoerhetorical sweep,* or the range of attributions of status for a given existent across multiple publics. Human fetuses are attributed an enormous range of zoerhetorical sweep. Importantly, there is no one correct,

30. Jensen, *Infertility,* 167–68.
31. Jensen, *Infertility,* 169.
32. Warner, "Publics and Counterpublics."

accurate, or true zoerhetorical status for any given existent. This is a crucial counter to theories of humanity (like David Livingstone Smith's) where the status of the human existent is taken for granted as self-evident.

In the case of fetal memorialization at the National Memorial for the Unborn, volunteers and visitors spoke for unborn babies, with identifiable promotional zoerhetorical effects. In this project I have chiefly explored how the status of a group of existents can be mediated through other-directed zoerhetorics, while spending less time exploring how existents can and do zoerhetorically modulate their own statuses (the unborn, conceivably, among these entities).

Vital biocitizens were the exception to this pattern. In the rhetorics of fitness practices at the athletic club, participants speak for themselves with, again, identifiable zoerhetorical effects for both selves and others. In their zoerhetorical exertions, vital biocitizens attempted to inflate their own status. Perhaps because of this "auto-zoerhetorical" movement (that is, zoerhetorics acted on the self), vitality-aspirant biocitizens at the gym had to do some interesting maneuvering to justify their intensely self-obsessed gazes. The rhetorics of training, "earning" accumulated body privilege, "earning" calories, the mythology of infinite body malleability, the virtue of health practices—all these things served to rationalize an "economy of attention" where "self" is the chief agent, substrate, and workstation.[33] There is a more general manifestation of attributions of credibility as a function of privilege here. Self-directed, upward-troping zoerhetorics are more likely to "stick" to high-status existents, who then potentially gain another dimension of rhetorical agency in their self- and life-affirming performances. The Great Chain's distributions of credibility and agency, in turn, ensure its self-preserving intractability.

4. Zoerhetorics are extra/ordinary.

The zoerhetorical hierarchy is built and rebuilt in spectacular, headline-making moments as well as in everyday habits and practices such as going to the gym. Drone strikes are marked, striking, spectacular events. When I planned the case studies for this book, I intended the everyday mundanity of working out at the gym as a counter to the spectacle, or at least the strangeness, of fetal memorials. Lauren Berlant offered a theoretical foothold for making sense of this with her theory of "slow death." This book project has been largely inspired by Achille Mbembe's vision of necropolitical deathworlds, where populations targeted for death are crucial to (and not merely a sad accident of) biopolitical regimes of living. Pivotal to Berlant's slow death is an everyday

33. Lanham, *Economics of Attention*.

ordinariness for which Mbembe's extraordinary crises failed to account. Arguably, consequential shifting of an existent's status occurs in small, everyday, iterable movements.

Berlant was interested in tracking the livability of life for people who were not spectacularly murdered but rather just neglected for a slow deterioration. The working-class obese represented this population for her. In my chapter on the vital biocitizen, I extended Berlant's concept of "slow death" with a concept of "slow life." Vital biocitizens were engaged in daily, repeated, zoerhetorically consequential habits of life-building. Drone-strike rhetorics cover both poles of the ordinary and extraordinary. The actual missile strike itself can be read as a spectacular zoerhetorical event. Yet the American-identified zoerhetorics justifying drone strikes accumulate force in slow, daily iterations. Memorials to the unborn are also extra/ordinary. Most people are shocked to hear that they exist—they depart from the ordinary, in that sense. At the same time, they are also ordinary in that visitors and volunteers participate in slow, daily practices of fetal life-building. An interesting question for future research is whether ordinary zoerhetorics take different forms, or perform different operations, from extraordinary ones.

Along the lines of expanding zoerhetorical theory, it would also be productive to track zoerhetorics longitudinally for a given group of existents. Because zoerhetorics are slow accumulations or slow depletions of status, an inquiry engaged with the diachronic dimensions of status for a particular group would be useful. One zoerhetoric does not a human make. Zoerhetorical transvaluations occur over a long sweeping period of time. In her work on companion species, Donna Haraway gestured in this direction.[34] The relatively high status of companion animals like dogs is remarkably different today from what it was hundreds of years ago. Similarly, Nathan Stormer's corpus of work identifies various discourses and strategies of fetal ascendance over a range of historical periods in the US. While neither of these projects is attuned to zoerhetorics per se, both make observations about the valuation of a group of existents over time. In an analogous vein, I prescribe more sustained and rigorous inquiry regarding the Great Chain of Being. As the hierarchy that continues to structure contemporary zoerhetorics, the Great Chain almost appears to assert its own agentic self-preserving force.

5. Zoerhetorics de/stabilize.

Within a particular public, zoerhetorics can work toward the stability of the dominant hierarchy (I call this a *maintenance zoerhetoric*) or trouble the dom-

34. Haraway, *The Companion Species Manifesto*; Haraway, *When Species Meet*.

inant order, a rupturing or destabilizing zoerhetoric. If the zoerhetorical hierarchy is a muscle, maintenance zoerhetorics tone and strengthen the muscle whereas destabilizing zoerhetorics strain and sprain it. Importantly, the same artifact or utterance can be stabilizing for one public and destabilizing for another. There are no qualities or properties intrinsic to zoerhetorics that lean them toward sustaining the Great Chain of Being; rather, this is a function of the rhetorical ecological milieu in which the zoerhetoric is introduced. Consider the vast momentum of the Great Chain of Being. While there can be disruptions and upsets to that Chain, the Chain seems to assert a frightening level of resilience and intractability over time. The most ingrained and habitual economic relations, discursive resources, daily practices, and habits of mind support the Great Chain. For this reason, as a general rule, maintenance zoerhetorics are received with less friction in a given public than destabilizing zoerhetorics.

By the same token, it stands to reason that the most deeply destabilizing zoerhetorics would experience an intelligibility problem. Given the extent to which the Great Chain influences the formation of concepts of self and other, a zoerhetoric promoting a mode of being far different from the Chain's hierarchy may trouble any one person's concepts of self and other to the extent that it is rejected immediately. If a discourse or practice stands to shake up, rupture, or topple the dominant hierarchy, even if it is ideologically congruent with the identifications of many people, it still may be difficult to apprehend. The Occupy Wall Street (OWS) movement furnishes an important case to consider in this light. As Kelly Happe theorizes it, OWS was difficult to make sense of—there was no list of demands, it was digitally organized but profoundly corporeal, and there were clear tactics but no strategy.[35] Yet inherent in the daily, embodied process of occupying was a zoerhetorical appeal to equality, to a leveling of the hierarchy. This is what Happe and others described as the *opening* quality of OWS. While a group of existents may not be attuned to destabilizing zoerhetorical gestures, appeals, and rhythms, that does not mean that destabilizing zoerhetorics do not circulate.

Toward Zoerhetorical Attunement

This book names a material-discursive phenomenon that everyone participates in and knows about. What's more, this phenomenon has consequential

---

35. Happe, "*Parrhēsia*, Biopolitics, and Occupy."

effects for all our lives, and the lives of all earthly dwellers. My primary goal in this book was to provide a way to talk about publicly circulating transvaluations bound tightly to hierarchy. Admittedly, my secret fantasy is that a journalist or citizen could identify a snippet of, say, US presidential rhetoric as *zoerhetorical* and, in so doing, leverage enough shared conceptual traction to mobilize a response. An inability to name the implicit functions of hierarchy mitigates zoerhetorical attunement—and therefore mitigates our ability to intervene. Conversely, as we learned regarding fetuses, the capacity to name has a powerful condensation and bounding effect on the thing named. In the language of assemblage theory, naming territorializes; it sharpens boundaries. One could argue that a scholarly treatise needs to do more than merely name, and this is true. This is why I have offered a range of case studies that ultimately cohere into a set of zoerhetorical propositions. Any utility wrung from zoerhetorical theory in the future pivots on the affordance of *naming* a set of discursive practices as zoerhetorics.

Zoerhetorics matter. Across the case studies I have enumerated the way in which zoerhetorics produce consequential distributions of livability for gut microbes, fetal entities, and vital biocitizens. I have also tried to discuss the ways in which the zoerhetorics around microbe-human superorganisms, fetuses, and vital biocitizens affect the groups against which they push for boundedness: people of color, people who abort, and working-class fat Americans. Zoerhetorics matter not just for these people but also for all living existents. The case studies presented in this book were bound to the narrow geographical and historical limits of contemporary US America, yet at the risk of sounding dramatic, I would still claim that zoerhetorics are a matter of life and death, of lives livable and unlivable, across this damaged planet we share. (Of course, even as I make that very humanist claim, I draw on the very topos of biolegitimacy that zoerhetors turn to again and again.) I conclude this book with an invitation to zoerhetorical attunement. The existents for whom zoerhetorics matter traverse humanhood and other horoi.

In addition to its geographical and historical remit, I have also limited the scope of this book by focusing only on zoerhetorics crafted by and addressed to existents attributed humanhood. If we take seriously the refreshing and compelling subfield of rhetorical theory that defines rhetoric beyond what *homo rhetoricus* declares significant, then certainly we should consider that a range of existents—whether attributed humanhood or not—participate in the conditioning of zoerhetorical living arrangements. Multispecies ethnography, speculative fiction (channeling Donna Haraway here), rhetorical ecologies— all these methods gestate with promise for apprehending modes of living-together that are not always already grafted to the Great Chain of Being. The publics and counterpublics that come into existence by means of discursive artifacts circulating and percolating within and between them are populated with existents of all sorts. Even if existents like jellyfish, fungi, and forests are not themselves harnessed to a language regime predicated on a zoerhetorical hierarchy, their tentacles and toadstools and trees bear marks of the Great Chain.

BIBLIOGRAPHY

Abbott, Don Paul. *Rhetoric in the New World: Rhetorical Theory and Practice in Colonial Spanish America.* Columbia: University of South Carolina Press, 1996.

———. "Diego Valadés and the Origins of Humanistic Rhetoric in the Americas." In *Rhetoric & Pedagogy: Its History, Philosophy, and Practice,* edited by Winifred Bryan Horner and Michael Leff, 227–42. New York: Routledge, 2013.

Agamben, Giorgio. *Homo Sacer: Sovereign Power and Bare Life.* Translated by Daniel Heller-Roazen. Stanford, CA: Stanford University Press, 1998.

Ahmed, Sara. *The Cultural Politics of Emotion.* New York: Routledge, 2013.

Ahuja, Neel. *Bioinsecurities: Disease Interventions, Empire, and the Government of Species.* Durham, NC: Duke University Press, 2016.

Alexander, M. Jacqui. *Pedagogies of Crossing: Meditations on Feminism, Sexual Politics, Memory, and the Sacred.* Durham, NC: Duke University Press, 2005.

Allinson, Jamie. "The Necropolitics of Drones." *International Political Sociology* 9, no. 2 (2015): 113–27.

Archibald, J. David. *Aristotle's Ladder, Darwin's Tree: The Evolution of Visual Metaphors for Biological Order.* New York: Columbia University Press, 2014.

Aristotle. *On Rhetoric.* Translated by George Kennedy. Oxford: Oxford University Press, 1991.

Augustine. *On Christian Doctrine.* Oxford: Oxford University Press, 2008.

Ayo, Nike. "Understanding Health Promotion in a Neoliberal Climate and the Making of Health Conscious Citizens." *Critical Public Health* 22, no. 1 (2012): 99–105.

Balsamo, Anne. "Public Pregnancies and Cultural Narratives of Surveillance." In *Revisioning Women, Health and Healing: Feminist, Cultural, and Technoscience Perspectives,* edited by Adele Clark and Virginia Olesen, 231–53. New York: Routledge, 1999.

Baudrillard, Jean. *The Consumer Society: Myths and Structures.* Thousand Oaks, CA: Sage, 1998.

Benjamin, Ruha. *People's Science: Bodies and Rights on the Stem Cell Frontier.* Stanford, CA: Stanford University Press, 2013.

Bennett, Jane. *Vibrant Matter: A Political Ecology of Things.* Durham, NC: Duke University Press, 2009.

Bergen, Peter, and Katherine Tiedemann, "Year of the Drone: An Analysis of U.S. Drone Strikes in Pakistan, 2004–2010." *New America Foundation,* 2010. http://vcnv.org/files/NAF_YearOfTheDrone.pdf.

Berlant, Lauren. *Cruel Optimism.* Durham, NC: Duke University Press, 2011.

Bitar, Adrienne Rose. *Diet and the Disease of Civilization.* New Brunswick, NJ: Rutgers University Press, 2017.

Black, Jason Edward. "Extending the Rights of Personhood, Voice, and Life to Sensate Others: A Homology of Right to Life and Animal Rights Rhetoric." *Communication Quarterly* 51, no. 3 (2003): 312–31.

Blair, Carole, Marsha Jeppeson, and Enrico Pucci Jr. "Public Memorializing in Postmodernity: The Vietnam Veterans Memorial as Prototype." *Quarterly Journal of Speech* 77, no. 3 (1991): 263–88.

Blake, Cecil. *The African Origins of Rhetoric.* New York: Routledge, 2010.

Boni, Federico. "Framing Media Masculinities: Men's Lifestyle Magazines and the Biopolitics of the Male Body." *European Journal of Communication* 17, no. 4 (2002): 465–78.

Bonilla-Silva, Eduardo. *Racism without Racists: Color-Blind Racism and the Persistence of Racial Inequality in America,* 5th ed. Lanham, MD: Rowman & Littlefield, 2017.

Bordo, Susan. *Unbearable Weight: Feminism, Western Culture, and the Body.* Oakland: University of California Press, 2003.

Bourdieu, Pierre. "The Forms of Capital." In *Handbook of Theory and Research for the Sociology of Education,* edited by John Richardson, 15–29. New York: Greenwood, 1986.

Braidotti, Rosi. "The Ethics of Becoming Imperceptible." In *Deleuze and Philosophy,* edited by Constantin V. Boundas, 133–59. Edinburgh, Scotland: University of Edinburgh Press, 2006.

———. *Transpositions: On Nomadic Ethics.* Cambridge: Polity Press, 2006.

Brennan, John. "Brennan's Speech on Counterterrorism: The Ethics and Efficacy of the President's Counterterrorism Strategy." April 2012. https://obamawhitehouse.archives.gov/blog/2012/04/30/watch-live-john-brennan-president-s-counterterrorism-strategy.

Brown, Elsa Barkley. "'What Has Happened Here': The Politics of Difference in Women's History and Feminist Politics." *Feminist Studies* 18, no. 2 (1992): 295–312.

Bureau of Investigative Journalism. "Drone Warfare: Current Statistics." https://www.thebureauinvestigates.com/projects/drone-war.

Burgert, Shannon. "Banner Is Not Representative of Our Diversity." Letter to the editor. *Daily Camera,* June 14, 2014. http://www.dailycamera.com/Opinion/ci_25956842/Shannon-Burgert:-Banner-is-not-representative.

Burke, Kenneth. *Counter-Statement.* Berkeley: University of California Press, 1968.

———. "Four Master Tropes." *The Kenyon Review* 3, no. 4 (1941): 421–38.

———. *A Grammar of Motives.* Berkeley: University of California Press, 1969.

———. *Language as Symbolic Action: Essays on Life, Literature, and Method.* Berkeley: University of California Press, 1966.

——. *On Symbols and Society*. Chicago: University of Chicago Press, 1989.

——. *A Rhetoric of Motives*. Berkeley: University of California Press, 1969.

——. *The Rhetoric of Religion: Studies in Logology*. Berkeley: University of California Press, 1970.

Butler, Judith. *Bodies That Matter: On the Discursive Limits of "Sex."* New York: Routledge, 1993.

——. *Frames of War: When Is Life Grievable?* London: Verso, 2009.

——. *Gender Trouble*. 10th anniversary ed. New York: Routledge, 1999.

——. *Precarious Life: The Powers of Mourning and Violence*. London: Verso, 2004.

——. "Torture and the Ethics of Photography." *Environment and Planning D: Society and Space* 25, no. 6 (2007): 951–66.

——. *Undoing Gender*. New York: Routledge, 2004.

Carney, Jay. "Press Briefing." February 5, 2013. https://obamawhitehouse.archives.gov/the-press -office/2013/02/05/press-briefing-press-secretary-jay-carney-2513. Accessed October 20, 2019.

Casper, Monica. *The Making of the Unborn Patient: A Social Anatomy of Fetal Surgery*. New Brunswick, NJ: Rutgers University Press, 1998.

Castañeda, Claudia. *Figurations: Child, Bodies, Worlds*. Durham, NC: Duke University Press, 2002.

Charland, Maurice. "Constitutive Rhetoric: The Case of the *Peuple Quebecois*." *Quarterly Journal of Speech* 73, no. 2 (1987): 133–50.

Chase, Cynthia. *Decomposing Figures: Rhetorical Readings in the Romantic Tradition*. Baltimore, MD: Johns Hopkins University Press, 1986.

Chen, Mel. *Animacies: Biopolitics, Racial Mattering, and Queer Affect*. Durham, NC: Duke University Press, 2012.

[Cicero.] *Rhetorica ad Herennium*. Translated by Harry Caplan. Loeb Classic Library 403. Cambridge, MA: Harvard University Press, 1954.

Cisneros, J. David. "Rhetorics of Citizenship: Pitfalls and Possibilities." *Quarterly Journal of Speech* 100, no. 3 (2014): 375–88.

City of Boulder Colorado. "Best of Boulder—Community Honors." Accessed August 21, 2013. https://bouldercolorado.gov/communications/best-of-boulder-community-honors.

Cohen, Ed. *A Body Worth Defending: Immunity, Biopolitics, and the Apotheosis of the Modern Body*. Durham, NC: Duke University Press, 2009.

——. "Self, Not-Self, Not Not-Self But Not Self, or The Knotty Paradoxes of 'Autoimmunity': A Genealogical Rumination." *Parallax* 23, no. 1 (2017): 28–45.

Condit, Celeste. *Decoding Abortion Rhetoric: Communicating Social Change*. Champaign: University of Illinois Press, 1994.

Cooren, François. *Action and Agency in Dialogue: Passion, Incarnation and Ventriloquism*. Philadelphia: John Benjamins, 2010.

Councilor, K. C. "Feeding the Body Politic: Metaphors of Digestion in Progressive Era US Immigration Discourse." *Communication and Critical/Cultural Studies* 14, no. 2 (2017): 139–57.

Crawford, Robert. "Healthism and the Medicalization of Everyday Life." *International Journal of Health Services* 10, no. 3 (1980): 365–88.

Dadlez, Eva M., and William L. Andrews. "Post-Abortion Syndrome: Creating an Affliction." *Bioethics* 24, no. 9 (2010): 445–52.

Davis, Angela. "Racism, Birth Control and Reproductive Rights." In *Feminist Postcolonial Theory: A Reader,* edited by Reina Lewis and Sara Mills, 353–67. New York: Routledge, 2003.

Davis, Diane. "Autozoography: Notes toward a Rhetoricity of the Living." *Philosophy & Rhetoric* 47, no. 4 (2014): 533–53.

———. *Inessential Solidarity.* Pittsburgh, PA: University of Pittsburgh Press, 2010.

De Man, Paul. *The Resistance to Theory.* Minneapolis: University of Minnesota Press, 1986.

———. *The Rhetoric of Romanticism.* New York: Columbia University Press, 2013.

Decoteau, Claire. *Ancestors and Antiretrovirals: The Biopolitics of HIV/AIDS in Post-Apartheid South Africa.* Chicago: University of Chicago Press, 2013.

Deutscher, Penelope. "Reproductive Politics, Biopolitics and Auto-immunity: From Foucault to Esposito." *Journal of Bioethical Inquiry* 7, no. 2 (2010): 217–26.

Derrida, Jacques. *The Animal That Therefore I Am.* Translated by David Wills. Fordham, NY: Fordham University Press, 2008.

———. "'Signature, Event, Context.'" In *Limited, Inc.,* edited by Gerald Graff. Translated by Jeffrey Mehlman and Samuel Weber, 1–23. Evanston, IL: Northwestern University Press, 1988.

Dickinson, Greg. "Joe's Rhetoric: Finding Authenticity at Starbucks." *Rhetoric Society Quarterly* 32, no. 4 (2002): 5–27.

Dillon, Stephen. "Possessed by Death: The Neoliberal-Carceral State, Black Feminism, and the Afterlife of Slavery." *Radical History Review* 112 (2012): 113–25.

Dinan, Timothy G., and John F. Cryan. "Gut–Brain Axis in 2016: Brain–Gut–Microbiota Axis—Mood, Metabolism and Behaviour." *Nature Reviews Gastroenterology & Hepatology* 14, no. 2 (2017): 69–70.

Ding, Huiling. *Rhetoric of a Global Epidemic: Transcultural Communication about SARS.* Carbondale: Southern Illinois University Press, 2014.

Donaghue, Ngaire, and Anne Clemitshaw. "'I'm totally smart and a feminist . . . and yet I want to be a waif': Exploring Ambivalence towards the Thin Ideal within the Fat Acceptance Movement." *Women's Studies International Forum* 35, no. 6 (2012): 415–25.

DuBois, Page. *Centaurs and Amazons: Women and the Pre-History of the Great Chain of Being.* Ann Arbor: University of Michigan Press, 1991.

Dubreuil, Laurent, and Clarissa Eagle. "Leaving Politics: Bios, Zoe, Life." *diacritics* 36, no. 2 (2006): 83–98.

Duncan, Margaret, and T. Tavita Robinson. "Obesity and Body Ideals in the Media: Health and Fitness Practices of Young African-American Women." *Quest* 56, no. 1 (2004): 77–104.

Dunn, Rob. "FAQs." American Gut Project. http://americangut.org/faqs-2/.

———. *The Wild Life of Our Bodies: Predators, Parasites, and Partners That Shape Who We Are Today.* New York: HarperCollins, 2011.

Dworkin, Shari. "A Woman's Place Is in the . . . Cardiovascular Room? Gender Relations, the Body, and the Gym." In *Athletic Intruders: Ethnographic Research on Women, Culture, and Exercise,* edited by Anne Bolin and Jane Granskig, 131–58. Albany: SUNY Press, 2003.

Eagleton, Terri. *Walter Benjamin, or, Towards a Revolutionary Criticism.* London: Verso, 1981.

Ehlers, Nadine. "Hidden in Plain Sight: Defying Juridical Racialization in *Rhinelander v. Rhinelander.*" *Communication and Critical/Cultural Studies* 1, no. 4 (2004): 313–34.

Esposito, Roberto. *Bíos: Biopolitics and Philosophy*. Translated and with an introduction by Timothy Campbell. Posthumanities 4. Minneapolis: University of Minnesota Press, 2008.

Evans, Kasey. "Prosopopoeia and Maternity in Edmund Spenser and Thomas Lodge." *ELH* 85, no. 2 (2018): 393–413.

Fahnestock, Jeanne. *Rhetorical Figures in Science*. Oxford: Oxford University Press, 2002.

———. *Rhetorical Style: The Uses of Language in Persuasion*. Oxford: Oxford University Press, 2011.

Fassin, Didier. "Another Politics of Life Is Possible." *Theory, Culture & Society* 26, no. 5 (2009): 44–60.

———. *Humanitarian Reason: A Moral History of the Present*. Berkeley: University of California Press, 2012.

Finnegan, Cara A., and Lisa Keränen. "Review Essay: Addressing the Epidemic of Epidemics: Germs, Security, and a Call for Biocriticism." *Quarterly Journal of Speech* (2011): 224–44.

Fixmer-Oraiz, Natalie. *Homeland Maternity: US Security Culture and the New Reproductive Regime*. Champaign: University of Illinois Press, 2019.

Foley, Megan. "Voicing Terri Schiavo: Prosopopeic Citizenship in the Democratic Aporia between Sovereignty and Biopower." *Communication and Critical/Cultural Studies* 7, no. 4 (2010): 381–400.

Ford, Norman. *When Did I Begin: Conception of the Human Individual in Philosophy and Science*. Cambridge: Cambridge University Press, 1991.

Foucault, Michel. *The History of Sexuality*. Vol. 1, *An Introduction*. Translated by Robert Hurley. New York: Vintage Books, 1990.

———. *The History of Sexuality*. Vol. 3, *The Care of the Self*. Translated by Robert Hurley. New York: Pantheon, 1986.

———. *Society Must Be Defended: Lectures at the Collège de France, 1975–1976*. Translated by David Macey. New York: Picador, 2003.

Freud, Sigmund. "A Difficulty in the Path of Psychoanalysis." 1917. In vol. 17 of *The Standard Edition of the Complete Psychological Works of Sigmund Freud*, 137–44. Translated by James Strachey. London: Hogarth, 1957–74.

Fromm, Erich. *Man for Himself: An Inquiry into the Psychology of Ethics*. New York: Rhinehart, 1947.

Gibson, Katie L. "The Rhetoric of *Roe v. Wade*: When the (Male) Doctor Knows Best." *Southern Communication Journal* 73, no. 4 (2008): 312–31.

Gordon, Linda. *The Moral Property of Women: A History of Birth Control Politics in America*. Champaign: University of Illinois Press, 2002.

Green, Jessica, and Karen Guillemin. "You Are Your Microbes." TED-Ed Video. https://ed.ted.com/lessons/you-are-your-microbes-jessica-green-and-karen-guillemin.

Greenwald, Glenn. "The Tragic Consulate Killings in Libya and America's Hierarchy of Life." *The Guardian*, September 12, 2012. http://www.theguardian.com/commentisfree/2012/sep/12/tragic-consulate-killings-libya.

Gronnvoll, Marita, and Jamie Landau. "From Viruses to Russian Roulette to Dance: A Rhetorical Critique and Creation of Genetic Metaphors." *Rhetoric Society Quarterly* 40, no. 1 (2010): 46–70.

Gunn, Joshua. "ShitText: Toward a New Coprophilic Style." *Text and Performance Quarterly* 26, no. 1 (2006): 79–97.

Guttmacher Institute. "Fact Sheet: Induced Abortion in the United States." January 2017. https://www.guttmacher.org/fact-sheet/induced-abortion-united-states.

Halse, Christine. "Bio-Citizenship: Virtue Discourses and the Birth of the Bio-Citizen." In *Biopolitics and the "Obesity Epidemic": Governing Bodies,* edited by Jan Wright and Valerie Harwood, 45–59. New York: Routledge, 2009.

Happe, Kelly. *The Material Gene: Gender, Race, and Heredity after the Human Genome Project.* New York: NYU Press, 2013.

———. "*Parrhēsia,* Biopolitics, and Occupy." *Philosophy & Rhetoric* 48, no. 2 (2015): 211–23.

Happe, Kelly, Jenell Johnson, and Marina Levina, eds. *Biocitizenship: The Politics of Bodies, Governance, and Power.* New York: NYU Press, 2018.

Haraway, Donna. "The Biopolitics of Postmodern Bodies: Determinations of Self in Immune System Discourse." *Differences: A Journal of Feminist Cultural Studies* 1 (1989) 3–44.

———. *The Companion Species Manifesto: Dogs, People, and Significant Otherness.* Chicago: Prickly Paradigm, 2003.

———. *Modest–Witness@Second–Millennium. FemaleMan Meets OncoMouse: Feminism and Technoscience.* New York: Psychology Press, 1997.

———. *When Species Meet.* Minneapolis: University of Minnesota Press, 2008.

Hariman, Robert. "Status, Marginality, and Rhetorical Theory." *Quarterly Journal of Speech* 72, no. 1 (1986): 38-54.

Harkinson, Josh. "The Exorcists: Pro-Life Activists Take Over an Abortion Clinic and Cast Out the Demons Within." *Pittsburgh Post-Gazette,* June 10, 2007. Accessed July 29, 2016. https://www.newspapers.com/newspage/96656857/.

Hartelius, Johanna. "Face-ing Immigration: Prosopopeia and the 'Muslim-Arab-Middle Eastern' Other." *Rhetoric Society Quarterly* 43, no. 4 (2013): 311–34.

Harvey, David. "The Body as an Accumulation Strategy." *Environment and Planning D* 16, no. 4 (1998): 401–22.

Hauser, Gerard A. *Prisoners of Conscience: Moral Vernaculars of Political Agency.* Columbia: University of South Carolina Press, 2012.

Hawhee, Debra. "Agonism and Aretê." *Philosophy & Rhetoric* 35, no. 3 (2002): 185–207.

———. *Bodily Arts: Rhetoric and Athletics in Ancient Greece.* Austin: University of Texas Press, 2004.

———. *Moving Bodies: Kenneth Burke at the Edges of Language.* Columbia: University of South Carolina Press, 2009.

———. *Rhetoric in Tooth and Claw: Animals, Language, Sensation.* Chicago: University of Chicago Press, 2016.

Hayden, Sara. "Revitalizing the Debate between <Life> and <Choice>: The 2004 March for Women's Lives." *Communication and Critical/Cultural Studies* 6, no. 2 (2009): 111–31.

Helmreich, Stefan. "*Homo Microbis* and the Figure of the Literal." *Cultural Anthropology Online* 17 (2011): 24.

Henne, Kathryn. "Tracing Olympic Bio-Citizenship: The Implications of Testing for Ineligibility." In *Problems, Possibilities, Promising Practices: Critical Dialogues on the Olympic and Paralympic Games,* edited by Janice Forsyth and Michael K. Heine, 83–87. Ontario, Canada: International Centre for Olympic Studies, 2012.

Hesford, Wendy. *Spectacular Rhetorics: Human Rights Visions, Recognitions, Feminisms.* Durham, NC: Duke University Press, 2011.

Hird, Myra. *The Origins of Sociable Life: Evolution After Science Studies.* New York: Springer, 2009.

Hoinacki, Lee, and Carl Mitcham, eds. *The Challenges of Ivan Illich: A Collective Reflection.* Albany: SUNY Press, 2002.

Houf, Jessica R. "The Microbial Mother Meets the Independent Organ: Cultural Discourses of Reproductive Microbiomes." *Journal of Medical Humanities* (2017): 1–17.

Howard, Gregory T. *Dictionary of Rhetorical Terms.* Bloomington, IN: Xlibris, 2010.

Irvin, Sherri. "Resisting Body Oppression: An Aesthetic Approach." *Feminist Philosophy Quarterly* 3, no. 4 (2017): 1–25.

Jensen, Robin E. *Infertility: Tracing the History of a Transformative Term.* RSA Series in Transdisciplinary Rhetoric 3. University Park: Pennsylvania State University Press, 2016.

Johnson, Barbara. "Apostrophe, Animation, and Abortion." *diacritics* 16, no. 1 (1986): 29–47.

Johnson, Jenell. "Disability, Animals, and the Rhetorical Boundaries of Personhood." *JAC* (2012): 372–82.

Jordan, John. "The Rhetorical Limits of the 'Plastic Body.'" *Quarterly Journal of Speech* 90, no. 3 (2004): 327–58.

Jutel, Annemarie. "Weighing Health: The Moral Burden of Obesity." *Social Semiotics* 15, no. 2 (2005): 113–25.

Kaposy, Chris. "Proof and Persuasion in the Philosophical Debate about Abortion." *Philosophy and Rhetoric* 43, no. 2 (2010): 139–62.

Keach, Benjamin. *Preaching from the Types and Metaphors of the Bible.* 12th ed. Grand Rapids, MI: Kregel, 1972.

Keane, Helen. "Foetal Personhood and Representations of the Absent Child in Pregnancy Loss Memorialization." *Feminist Theory* 10, no. 2 (2009): 153–71.

Keeling, Diane. "His/tory of (Future) Progress: Hyper-Masculine Transhumanist Virtuality." *Critical Studies in Media Communication* 29, no. 2 (2012): 132–48.

Kelly, David. "Church Plans to Bury the Ashes of Fetuses from Abortion Clinic." *Los Angeles Times,* January 22, 2005. Accessed July 28, 2016. http://articles.latimes.com/2005/jan/22/nation/na-fetus22.

Kelly, Kimberly. "The Spread of 'Post-Abortion Syndrome' as Social Diagnosis." *Social Science & Medicine* 102 (2014): 18–25.

Kennedy, David. *The Dark Sides of Virtue: Reassessing International Humanitarianism.* Princeton, NJ: Princeton University Press, 2005.

King, Claire Sisco. "Hitching Wagons to Stars: Celebrity, Metonymy, Hegemony, and the Case of Will Smith." *Communication and Critical/Cultural Studies* 14, no. 1 (2017): 83–102.

Kuswa, Kevin, Paul Achter, and Elizabeth Lauzon. "The Slave, the Fetus, the Body: Articulating Biopower and the Pregnant Woman." *Contemporary Argumentation and Debate* 29 (2008): 166–85.

Lamb, Matthew D., and Cory Hillman. "Whiners Go Home: Tough Mudder, Conspicuous Consumption, and the Rhetorical Proof of 'Fitness.'" *Communication & Sport* 3, no. 1 (2015): 81–99.

Landau, Jamie. "Feeling Rhetorical Critics: Another Affective-Emotional Field Methods for Rhetorical Studies." In *Text + Field: Innovations in Rhetorical Method,* edited by Sara McKinnon, Robert Asen, Karma R. Chávez, and Robert Glenn Howard, 72–85. University Park: Pennsylvania State University Press, 2016.

Landecker, Hannah. "Antibiotic Resistance and the Biology of History." *Body & Society* 22, no. 4 (2016): 19–52.

Lanham, Richard. *The Economics of Attention: Style and Substance in the Age of Information.* Chicago: University of Chicago Press, 2006.

———. *A Handlist of Rhetorical Terms.* Berkeley: University of California Press, 1991.

Lakoff, Andrew, and Stephen J. Collier. "Ethics and the Anthropology of Modern Reason." *Anthropological Theory* 4, no. 4 (2004): 419–34.

Lakoff, George, and Mark Turner. *More Than Cool Reason: A Field Guide to Poetic Metaphor.* Chicago: University of Chicago Press, 1989.

Layne, Linda. *Motherhood Lost: A Feminist Account of Pregnancy Loss in America.* New York: Routledge, 2003.

Leach, Jeff. "Going Feral: My One-Year Journey to Acquire the Healthiest Gut Microbiome in the World (You Heard Me!)." *The Human Food Project* (blog), January 19, 2014. http://human-foodproject.com/going-feral-one-year-journey-acquire-healthiest-gut-microbiome-world-heard/.

———. "Microbial Diversity: Sometimes You Have It, Sometimes You Don't." *The Human Food Project* (blog), October 29, 2014. http://humanfoodproject.com/microbial-diversity-sometimes-sometimes-dont/.

———. "(Re)Becoming Human." *The Human Food Project* (blog), September 30, 2014. http://humanfoodproject.com/rebecoming-human-happened-day-replaced-99-genes-body-hunter-gatherer/.

———. "Slumdog Microbiome More Diverse." *The Human Food Project* (blog), February 20, 2013. http://humanfoodproject.com/slumdog-microbiome-more-diverse/.

Lebesco, Kathleen. "Fat Panic and the New Morality." In *Against Health: How Health Became the New Morality,* edited by Jonathan Metzl and Anna Kirkland, 72–82. New York: NYU Press, 2010.

Levy-Navarro, Elena. *The Culture of Obesity in Early and Late Modernity: Body Image in Shakespeare, Jonson, Middleton, and Skelton.* New York: Palgrave Macmillan, 2008.

Lorimer, Jamie. "Gut Buddies: Multispecies Studies and the Microbiome." *Environmental Humanities* 8, no. 1 (2016): 57–76.

Lovejoy, Arthur. *The Great Chain of Being: A Study of the History of an Idea.* Piscataway, NJ: Transaction, 2009.

Lundberg, Christian. "Enjoying God's Death: *The Passion of the Christ* and the Practices of an Evangelical Public." *Quarterly Journal of Speech* 95, no. 4 (2009): 387–411.

———. *Lacan in Public: Psychoanalysis and the Science of Rhetoric.* Tuscaloosa: University of Alabama Press, 2012.

Lupton, Deborah. "'Precious Cargo': Foetal Subjects, Risk and Reproductive Citizenship." *Critical Public Health* 22, no. 3 (2012): 329–40.

———. "Risk As Moral Danger: The Social and Political Functions of Risk Discourse In Public Health." *International Journal of Health Services* 23, no. 3 (1993): 425–35.

Lynch, John. "Stem Cells and the Embryo: Biorhetoric and Scientism in Congressional Debate." *Public Understanding of Science* 18, no. 3 (2009): 309–24.

———. *What Are Stem Cells? Definitions at the Intersection of Science and Politics.* Tuscaloosa: University of Alabama Press, 2011.

Lyne, John. "Bio-rhetorics: Moralizing the Life Sciences." In *The Rhetorical Turn: Invention and Persuasion in the Conduct of Inquiry,* edited by Herbert W. Simons, 35–57. Chicago: University of Chicago Press, 1990.

Manne, Kate. *Down Girl: The Logic of Misogyny.* Oxford: Oxford University Press, 2017.

Martin, Emily. "The End of the Body?" *American Ethnologist* 19, no. 1 (1992): 121–40.

———. "Toward an Anthropology of Immunology: The Body as Nation State." *Medical Anthropology Quarterly* 4, no. 4 (1990): 410–26.

Martin, Randy. "The Composite Body: Hip-hop Aerobics and the Multicultural Nation." *Journal of Sport & Social Issues* 21, no. 2 (1997): 120–33.

Mbembe, Achille. "Necropolitics." Translated by Libby Meintjes. *Public Culture* 15, no. 1 (2003): 11–40.

McKerrow, Raymie E. "Critical Rhetoric: Theory and Praxis." *Communication Monographs* 56, no. 2 (1989): 91–111.

McKinnon, Sara L., Robert Asen, Karma R. Chávez, and Robert Glenn Howard, eds. *Text + Field: Innovations in Rhetorical Method.* University Park: Pennsylvania State University Press, 2016.

McKittrick, Katherine, ed. *Sylvia Wynter: On Being Human as Praxis.* Durham, NC: Duke University Press, 2015.

McLaughlin, Janice, and Edmund Coleman-Fountain. "The Unfinished Body: The Medical and Social Reshaping of Disabled Young Bodies." *Social Science & Medicine* 120 (2014): 76–84.

Melonçon, Lisa, and J. Blake Scott, eds. *Methodologies for the Rhetoric of Health & Medicine.* New York: Routledge, 2018.

Mertus, Julie. "Fake Abortion Clinics: The Threat to Reproductive Self-Determination." *Women & Health* 16, no. 1 (1990): 95–113.

Metzl, Jonathan. "Introduction: Why 'Against Health?'" In *Against Health: How Health Became the New Morality,* edited by Jonathan Metzl and Anna Kirkland, 1–14. New York: NYU Press, 2010.

Metzl, Jonathan, and Anna Kirkland, eds. *Against Health: How Health Became the New Morality.* New York: NYU Press, 2010.

Middleton, Michael K., Samantha Senda-Cook, and Danielle Endres. "Articulating Rhetorical Field Methods: Challenges and Tensions." *Western Journal of Communication* 75, no. 4 (2011): 386–406.

Mignolo, Walter. *The Darker Side of the Renaissance: Literacy, Territoriality, and Colonization.* Ann Arbor: University of Michigan Press, 2003.

———. *The Darker Side of Western Modernity: Global Futures, Decolonial Options.* Durham, NC: Duke University Press, 2011.

Mignolo, Walter, and Catherine Walsh. *On Decoloniality: Concepts, Analytics, Praxis.* Durham, NC: Duke University Press, 2018.

Miller, Carolyn. "Genre Innovation: Evolution, Emergence, or Something Else?" *The Journal of Media Innovations* 3, no. 2 (2016): 4–19.

Mitchell, Lisa. *Baby's First Picture: Ultrasound and the Politics of Fetal Subjects.* Toronto, Canada: University of Toronto Press, 2001.

Mitchell, Robert. "Humans, Nonhumans, and Personhood." In *The Great Ape Project: Equality Beyond Humanity,* edited by Paola Cavalieri and Peter Singer, 237–47. London: Fourth Estate, 1993.

Mollow, Anna. "Unvictimizable: Toward a Fat Black Disability Studies." *African American Review* 50, no. 2 (2017): 105–21.

Montgomery, Nick, and Carla Bergman. *Joyful Militancy: Building Thriving Resistance in Toxic Times.* Chico, CA: AK Press, 2017.

Musial, Jennifer. "Fetal Citizenship in the Borderlands: Arizona's House Bill 2443 and State Logics of Racism and Orientalism." *Social Identities* 20 no. 4–5 (2014): 262–78.

Nakayama, Thomas, and Robert Krizek. "Whiteness: A Strategic Rhetoric." *Quarterly Journal of Speech* 81, no. 3 (1995): 291–309.

Nash, Roderick. *Wilderness and the American Mind.* New Haven, CT: Yale University Press, 2014.

National Memorial for the Unborn. "Homepage." Accessed March 23, 2014. http://www.memorialfortheunborn.org/.

———. "Testimonials." Accessed March 23, 2014. http://www.memorialfortheunborn.org/about-us/testimonials.

Nealon, Jeffrey T. *Plant Theory: Biopower and Vegetable Life.* Stanford, CA: Stanford University Press, 2015.

Nixon, Rob. *Slow Violence and the Environmentalism of the Poor.* Cambridge, MA: Harvard University Press, 2011.

Obama, Barack. "Remarks by the President at the National Defense University," May 23, 2013. https://obamawhitehouse.archives.gov/the-press-office/2013/05/23/remarks-president-national-defense-university.

Ober, Josiah. "Greek Horoi: Artifactual Texts and the Contingency of Meaning." In *Methods in the Mediterranean: Historical and Archeological Views on Texts and Archeology,* edited by Davis Small, 91–123. Boston, MA: Brill, 1995.

Parekh, Bhikhu. *Rethinking Multiculturalism: Cultural Diversity and Political Theory.* Cambridge, MA: Harvard University Press, 2002.

Paxson, Heather. *The Life of Cheese: Crafting Food and Value in America.* Berkeley: University of California Press, 2012.

Paxson, Heather, and Stefan Helmreich. "The Perils and Promises of Microbial Abundance: Novel Natures and Model Ecosystems, from Artisanal Cheese to Alien Seas." *Social Studies of Science* 44, no. 2 (2014): 165–93.

Peacham, Henry. *The Garden of Eloquence Conteyning the Figures of Grammar and Rhetorick Set Foorth in Englishe* [Facsimile Reproduction]. 1577.

Pear, Robert, and Thomas Kaplan. "Abortion Adds Obstacle as Republicans Plan to Unveil Health Bill." *New York Times,* June 21, 2017. Accessed June 22, 2017. https://www.nytimes.com/2017/06/21/us/politics/abortion-republicans-health-bill.html?smid=pl-share.

Petchesky, Rosalind P. "Fetal Images: The Power of Visual Culture in the Politics of Reproduction." *Feminist Studies* 13, no. 2 (1987): 263–92.

Peters, John Durham. *Speaking into the Air: A History of the Idea of Communication.* Chicago: University of Chicago Press, 2012.

Peterson, Christopher. *Bestial Traces: Race, Sexuality, Animality.* Fordham, NY: Fordham University Press, 2013.

Petherick, LeAnne. "Producing the Young Biocitizen: Secondary School Students' Negotiation of Learning in Physical Education." *Sport, Education and Society* 18, no. 6 (2013): 711–30.

Petryna, Adriana. *Life Exposed: Biological Citizens after Chernobyl*. Princeton, NJ: Princeton University Press, 2013.

Planned Parenthood Federation of America. "Types of State Attacks on Abortion." Accessed December 23, 2015. https://www.plannedparenthoodaction.org/issues/abortion/types -attacks.

Pollan, Michael. "Some of My Best Friends Are Germs." *New York Times*, May 15, 2013. https:// www.nytimes.com/2013/05/19/magazine/say-hello-to-the-100-trillion-bacteria-that-make -up-your-microbiome.html.

Povinelli, Elizabeth A. *Geontologies: A Requiem to Late Liberalism*. Durham, NC: Duke University Press, 2016.

Puar, Jasbir. *The Right to Maim: Debility, Capacity, Disability*. Durham, NC: Duke University Press, 2017.

———. *Terrorist Assemblages: Homonationalism in Queer Times*. Durham, NC: Duke University Press, 2007.

Pugliese, Joseph. "Biometrics, Infrastructural Whiteness, and the Racialized Zero Degree of Nonrepresentation." *boundary 2* 34, no. 2 (2007): 105–33.

Puhvel, Jann. "The Origins of Greek *Kosmos* and Latin *Mundus*." *The American Journal of Philology* 97, no. 2 (1976): 154–67.

Purkiss, Jessica. "Trump's First Year in Numbers: Strikes Triple in Somalia and Yemen." *Bureau of Investigative Journalism*, January 19, 2018. https://www.thebureauinvestigates.com/stories/ 2018-01-19/strikes-in-somalia-and-yemen-triple-in-trumps-first-year-in-office.

Quandahl, Ellen. "'It's Essentially as Though This Were Killing Us': Kenneth Burke on Mortification and Pedagogy." *Rhetoric Society Quarterly* 27, no. 1 (1997): 5–22.

Reardon, Jenny, and Kim TallBear. "'Your DNA Is Our History': Genomics, Anthropology, and the Construction of Whiteness as Property." *Current Anthropology* 53, no. S5 (2012): S233–45.

Rhodes, Jacqueline. "Counterpoint: Calling Out Publics." *Rhetoric Society Quarterly* 47, no. 1 (2017): 74–80.

Ricoeur, Paul. *The Rule of Metaphor: The Creation of Meaning in Language*. New York: Routledge, 2003.

Riffaterre, Michael. "Prosopopeia." *Yale French Studies* 69 (1985): 107–23.

Roberts, Dorothy. *Killing the Black Body: Race, Reproduction, and the Meaning of Liberty*. New York: Pantheon, 1997.

Romano, Susan. "Rhetoric in Latin America." In *The Handbook of Communication History*, edited by Peter Simonson, Janice Peck, and Robert T. Craig, 397–411. New York: Routledge, 2013.

Rose, Nikolas. *The Politics of Life Itself: Biomedicine, Power, and Subjectivity in the Twenty-First Century*. Princeton, NJ: Princeton University Press, 2006.

———. *Powers of Freedom: Reframing Political Thought*. Cambridge: Cambridge University Press, 1999.

Rose, Nikolas, and Carlos Novas. "Biological Citizenship." In *Global Assemblages: Technology, Politics, and Ethics as Anthropological Problems*, edited by Aihwa Ong and Stephen Collier, 1–40. Malden, MA: Blackwell, 2003.

Rosen, James. "Obama Aides Defend Claim of Low Civilian Drone Casualties after Drone 'Kill List' Report." *Fox News*, May 30, 2012. Accessed June 3, 2014. http://www.foxnews.com/poli-

tics/2012/05/30/obama-aides-defend-claim-low-civilian-drone-casualties-after-kill-list
-report.html.

Rowland, Allison L. "Life-Saving Weapons: The Biolegitimacy of Drone Warfare." *Rhetoric & Public Affairs* 19, no. 4 (2016): 601–27.

———. "Zoetropes: Turning Fetuses into Humans at the National Memorial for the Unborn." *Rhetoric Society Quarterly* 47, no. 1 (2017): 26–48.

Rueckert, William. *Encounters with Kenneth Burke.* Champaign: University of Illinois Press, 1994.

Sacred Heart of Mary. "Memorial Wall." Accessed August 5, 2012. http://www.sacredheartofmary.org/memorial-wall.

Sadler, Thomas W. *Langman's Medical Embryology.* Baltimore, MD: Lippincott Williams & Wilkins, 2011.

Saguy, Abigail. *What's Wrong with Fat?* Oxford: Oxford University Press, 2013.

Savage, Charlie, and Eric Schmitt. "Trump Poised to Drop Some Limits on Drone Strikes and Commando Raids." *New York Times,* September 21, 2017. https://www.nytimes.com/2017/09/21/us/politics/trump-drone-strikes-commando-raids-rules.html.

Schiappa, Edward. "Analyzing Argumentative Discourse from a Rhetorical Perspective: Defining 'Person' and 'Human Life' in Constitutional Disputes over Abortion." *Argumentation* 14, no. 3 (2000): 315–32.

Scott, J. Blake. "Afterword: Elaborating Health and Medicine's Publics." *Journal of Medical Humanities* 35, no. 2 (2013): 229–35.

Seigel, Marika. *The Rhetoric of Pregnancy.* Chicago: University of Chicago Press, 2013.

Senapathy, Kavin. "Keep Calm and Avoid Microbiome Mayhem." *Forbes,* May 7, 2017. https://www.forbes.com/sites/kavinsenapathy/2016/03/07/keep-calm-and-avoid-microbiome-mayhem.

Serle, Jack, and Jessica Purkiss. "Drone Wars: The Full Data." *Bureau of Investigative Journalism,* January 1, 2017. https://www.thebureauinvestigates.com/stories/2017-01-01/drone-wars-the-full-data.

Sexton, Jared. "People-of-color-blindness: Notes on the Afterlife of Slavery." *Social Text* 103 28, no. 2 (2010): 31–56.

Sexton, Jared, and Elizabeth Lee. "Figuring the Prison: Prerequisites of Torture at Abu Ghraib." *Antipode* 38, no. 5 (2006): 1005–22.

Shugart, Helene. "Crossing Over: Hybridity and Hegemony in the Popular Media." *Communication and Critical/Cultural Studies* 4, no. 2 (2007): 115–41.

———. "Ruling Class: Disciplining Class, Race, and Ethnicity in Television Reality Court Shows." *The Howard Journal of Communications* 17, no. 2 (2006): 79–100.

Singh, J. P. *Sweet Talk: Paternalism and Collective Action in North-South Trade Relations.* Stanford, CA: Stanford University Press, 2017.

Skrabanek, Petr. *The Death of Humane Medicine and the Rise of Coercive Healthism.* London: Social Affairs Unit, 1994.

Smith, David Livingstone. *Less Than Human: Why We Demean, Enslave, and Exterminate Others.* New York: St. Martin's, 2011.

Sontag, Susan. *Illness as Metaphor and AIDS and Its Metaphors.* New York: Picador, 1977.

Squier, Susan. "Fetal Subjects and Maternal Objects: Reproductive Technology and the New Fetal/Maternal Relation." *Journal of Medicine and Philosophy* 21, no. 5 (1996): 515–35.

St. John Taylor, Jeannie. *101 Stories of Answered Prayers*. Chattanooga, TN: Living Ink Books, 2002.

Stabile, Carol A. "Shooting the Mother: Fetal Photography and the Politics of Disappearance." *Camera Obscura* 10, no. 1 (1992): 178–205.

Stewart, Jessie, and Greg Dickinson. "Enunciating Locality in the Postmodern Suburb: FlatIron Crossing and the Colorado Lifestyle." *Western Journal of Communication* 72, no. 3 (2008): 280–307.

Stoler, Laura Ann. *Duress: Imperial Durabilities in Our Time*. Durham, NC: Duke University Press, 2016.

Stuff White People Like. "#27 Marathons." January 26, 2008. http://stuffwhitepeoplelike.com/2008/01/26/27-marathons/.

Stone, Sandy. "The Empire Strikes Back: A Posttranssexual Manifesto." *The Transgender Studies Reader*, edited by Susan Stryker and Stephen Whittle, 221–35. New York: Routledge, 2006.

Stormer, Nathan. *Articulating Life's Memory: U.S. Medical Rhetoric about Abortion in the Nineteenth Century*. Lanham, MD: Lexington Books, 2002.

———. "Looking in Wonder: Prenatal Sublimity and the Commonplace 'Life.'" *Signs: Journal of Women in Culture and Society* 33, no. 3 (2008): 647–73.

———. "Mediating Biopower and the Case of Prenatal Space." *Critical Studies in Media Communication* 27, no. 1 (2010): 8–23.

———. "Prenatal Space." *Signs: Journal of Women in Culture and Society* 26, no. 1 (2000): 109–44.

Strings, Sabrina. *Fearing the Black Body: The Racial Origins of Fat Phobia*. New York: NYU Press, 2019.

Sutton, Jane, and Mari Lee Mifsud. "Figuring Rhetoric: From Antistrophe to Apostrophe through Catastrophe." *Rhetoric Society Quarterly* 32, no. 4 (2002): 29–49.

Taylor, Janelle. "The Public Fetus and the Family Car: From Abortion Politics to a Volvo Advertisement." *Public Culture* 4, no. 2 (1992): 67–80.

Taylor, Sunaura. *Beasts of Burden: Animal and Disability Liberation*. New York: The New Press, 2017.

Tirrell, Lynne. "Genocidal Language Games." In *Speech & Harm: Controversies Over Free Speech*, edited by Ishana Maitra and Mary Kate McGowan, 174-221. Oxford: Oxford University Press, 2012.

United States Senate Select Committee on Intelligence. "Open Hearing on the Nomination of John O. Brennan to be Director of the Central Intelligence Agency." U.S. Senate Select Committee on Intelligence Reports, February 7, 2013. Accessed February 10, 2017. https://www.intelligence.senate.gov/sites/default/files/hearings/transcript.pdf.

Veracini, Lorenzo. *The Settler Colonial Present*. New York: Springer, 2015.

Vicaro, Michael Paul. "Deconstitutive Rhetoric: The Destruction of Legal Personhood in the Global War on Terrorism." *Quarterly Journal of Speech* 102, no. 4 (2016): 333–52.

Virno, Paolo. *A Grammar of the Multitude: For an Analysis of Contemporary Forms of Life*. Los Angeles; New York: Semiotext(e), 2004.

Wald, Priscilla. *Contagious: Cultures, Carriers, and the Outbreak Narrative*. Durham, NC: Duke University Press, 2007.

Waldby, Catherine. *AIDS and the Body Politic: Biomedicine and Sexual Difference*. New York: Routledge, 2003.

Warner, Michael. "Publics and Counterpublics." *Public Culture* 14, no. 1 (2002): 49-90.

Weheliye, Alexander G. *Habeas Viscus: Racializing Assemblages, Biopolitics, and Black Feminist Theories of the Human.* Durham, NC: Duke University Press, 2014.

White, Hayden. *Tropics of Discourse: Essays in Cultural Criticism.* Baltimore, MD: Johns Hopkins University Press, 1978.

Whittle, Stephen. "Foreword." In *The Transgender Studies Reader,* edited by Susan Stryker and Stephen Whittle, xi–xiv. New York: Routledge, 2006.

Williams, Wendy, and Ann Caldwell. *Empty Arms: More Than 60 Life-Giving Stories of Hope from the Devastation of Abortion.* Chattanooga, TN: Living Ink Books, 2005.

Wynn, James. *Citizen Science in the Digital Age: Rhetoric, Science, and Public Engagement.* Tuscaloosa: University of Alabama Press, 2017.

Yong, Ed. *I Contain Multitudes: The Microbes Within Us and a Grander View of Life.* New York: Random House, 2016.

Zarranz, Libe Garcia, and Evelyne Ledoux-Beaugrand. "Affective Assemblages: Entanglements & Ruptures—An Interview with Lauren Berlant." *Atlantis: Critical Studies in Gender, Culture & Social Justice* 38, no. 2 (2017): 12–17.

Zunger, Nurit. "The 40 Worst-Dressed Cities in America." *Gentleman's Quarterly,* July 15, 2011. http://www.gq.com/style/fashion/201107/worst-dressed-cities-america#slide=1.

INDEX

10% Human (Collen), 42

101 Stories of Answered Prayers (St. John Taylor), 82

aborted baby. *See* fetus (human)

abortion: and biopower, 77; clinic, 82, 82n42; and the culture wars, 71; and grief, 72, 83; and health care debates, 71; and Post-Abortion Syndrome, 83–84; pro-choice rhetorics of, 76; pro-life books about, 82; pro-life narrative of healing from, 89; US statistics on, 71–72

affect: and attachment to bodily improvement, 116, 125–26; and attachment to imperial state, 2, 48, 63–64; as contagion, 88–89; as cruel attachment, 126; and fecal matter, 53; at the gym, 114–15, 129; and hierarchy, 150; and interviews, 88–89, 116, 126; and joy, 129; and Lauren Berlant, 126; and longing/repulsion, 45n6, 65–66, 89, 96, 111, 137, 150; and microbes, 48; at the National Memorial for the Unborn, 88–89; and rhetorical field methods, 13–14, 14n39; as unconscious, 14n39

Against Health (Metzl and Kirkland), 110

Agamben, Giorgio, 2–3, 3n3, 21–26, 144n12. See also *Homo Sacer*

agenda-setting (function of news media), 142

Ahmed, Sara, 33, 148

Ahuja, Neel, 24, 48, 50, 63

Alexander, M. Jacqui, 105–6, 135

American Gut Project (AGP): as citizen science, 14, 42; 51–60; cost of participation in, 52; and fecal matter, 53, 66; and Jeff Leach, 53, 61–67; and Michael Pollan, 51, 53; and paternalism, 60–61; and popular science, 53–54; and race, 61–69; and somatopeia, 57–67; and zoerhetorical theory, 67–69; and zoetropes, 57–69

Ancestors and Antiretrovirals (Decoteau), 23, 26

Animacies (Chen), 79, 90, 148

animacy hierarchy, 17, 27, 78, 148, 153

antonomasia, 73, 89, 91–93

apostrophe: Barbara Johnson on, 95; definition of, 6, 93; as en-voicing, 15, 73, 89, 93–101; and the Great Chain of Being, 36, 148; and hierarchy, 36, 101, 148; Johanna Hartelius on, 93, 96–97; Lauren Berlant on, 95–96; Nathan Stormer on, 6; at the

Ricoeur, Paul, xi, 148

Riffaterre, Michael, 96

Roberts, Dorothy, 76

Roe v. Wade, 76, 86

Rose, Nikolas, 110–11, 113

Sacred Heart of Mary Church, 81

Sacred Heart Memorial Wall, 81

Senapathy, Kavin, 53

sexuality, 8, 10, 11, 16, 22, 66, 111, 146

Skrabanek, Petr, 109–10, 110n24

slow death, 108, 115, 154–55

slow life, 108, 115, 155

slow violence, 108, 138

socioanagogic criticism, 36–38. *See also* Kenneth Burke

somatopeia: and biopolitics, xi; definition of, x–xi, 16; as em-bodying, x–xi, 7, 55–56, 66–67, 98–101; empire and, 44; etymology of, xi; example of, xi; and fetal existents, 15, 98–101, 149; and human microbiome discourse, 14, 44, 55–58, 62, 148; and humanhood, 44; and necropolitics, ix, 7, 13, 55–56, 67; and prosopopeia, xi, 98–101; repetition of, 99–100; spelling of, xn4; and vital biocitizens, 56, 125–26, 149; and zoerhetorical theory, x–xii, 101, 148. *See also* tropes

Sontag, Susan, 46–47. See also *Illness as Metaphor*

Stormer, Nathan, 75, 77–78. *See also* prenatal space

subhuman, 7, 11, 13, 28. *See also* not-quite-human

super subject, 76

superorganism, 14, 41, 51, 56, 69, 143, 150, 157

Taylor, Janelle, 76

Taylor, Sunaura, 115. *See also* disability

textual analysis, 13

thanatopolitics, 22–23, 23n12

thing power, 74

training (rhetoric of): and biolegitimacy, 129, 145; and earning, 130–31, 154; and hierarchy, 136; oratorical, 113; and somatopeia, 125–26; and vital biocitizenship, 15, 106, 126–31, 136

transvaluation (zoerhetorical): xii, 13, 22, 27, 29, 33, 39, 150; and biolegitimacy, 145; and constitutive rhetoric, 8; as determining distributions of livability, 73, 147; diachronic dimension of, 155; as hewing, 149; and humanhood, 11, 16; and low-wage labor, 119; and paralipsis, 152

tropes: Christian Lundberg on, 5; Cicero on, 5; classic definition of, xi, 5; Cynthia Chase on, 7; Diane Davis on, 7; Donna Haraway on, 5; as epistemological, 5; four master, 5, 91; Friedrich Nietzsche on, 6–7, 148; as generative, 5, 73; and the Great Chain of Being, 20, 36; Greek terms for, 89; and intelligibility, 7; Johanna Hartelius on, 93, 96–97; Kenneth Burke on, 5, 91; Lauren Berlant on, 95–96, 106; and methodology, 13; Nathan Stormer on, 6–7; Paul de Man on, 6–7, 91; Paul Ricoeur on, xi, 148; repetition of, 99–100; as turns, xi, 5, 80, 148; and vitality, 5–7, 89, 95. *See also* antonomasia; apostrophe; metonymy; prosopopeia; somatopeia

tropos (Greek), 5. *See also* trope

Trump, Donald, 2, 56, 66n65, 68, 139, 142, 152

Turner, Mark, 30–31, 30n37, 36

unborn baby. *See* fetus (human)

Valadés, Diego: 34–36

Vietnam Veterans Memorial, 90

violence: Achille Mbembe on, 26; and drone strikes, 4, 142; Kate Manne on, 12; misogynistic, 12; and necropolitics, 27, 56; preconditions for, 12; privilege in the midst of, 105, 135–36; of racial assemblages, 4, 59; rationalizations for, 12; slow, 108, 138; state, 145; and zoerhetorical demotion, 8, 12

Virno, Paolo, 22

virtue: and *arete*, 113; and Aristotle, 109; of medicine, 141; and moral indignation, 145; as privilege of humanhood, 13, 143; and vital biocitizenship, 105, 112–13, 125, 136, 139, 151. *See also* biolegitimacy

vital biocitizens: and biocitizenship, 113–14; and biological citizenship, 113; in Boulder, Colorado, 117–18; definition of, 106, 112; and disability, 115, 150; Christine Halse on, 114; as implicitly white, 132–35;

NEW DIRECTIONS IN RHETORIC AND MATERIALITY

BARBARA A. BIESECKER, WENDY S. HESFORD, AND CHRISTA TESTON,
SERIES EDITORS

Current conversations about rhetoric signal a new attentiveness to and critical appraisal of material-discursive phenomena. New Directions in Rhetoric and Materiality provides a forum for responding to and extending such conversations. The series publishes monographs that pair rhetorical theory with an analysis of material conditions and the social-symbolic labor circulating therein. Books in the series offer a "new direction" for exploring the everyday, material, lived conditions of human, nonhuman, and extra-human life—advancing theories around rhetoric's relationship to materiality.

Zoetropes and the Politics of Humanhood
ALLISON L. ROWLAND

Ecologies of Harm: Rhetorics of Violence in the United States
MEGAN EATMAN

Raveling the Brain: Toward a Transdisciplinary Neurorhetoric
JORDYNN JACK

Post-Digital Rhetoric and the New Aesthetic
JUSTIN HODGSON

Not One More! Feminicidio on the Border
NINA MARIA LOZANO

Visualizing Posthuman Conservation in the Age of the Anthropocene
AMY D. PROPEN

Precarious Rhetorics
EDITED BY WENDY S. HESFORD, ADELA C. LICONA, AND CHRISTA TESTON

www.ingramcontent.com/pod-product-compliance
Lightning Source LLC
Chambersburg PA
CBHW020354270326
41926CB00007B/424